OSPEL PR

— FEATURING —

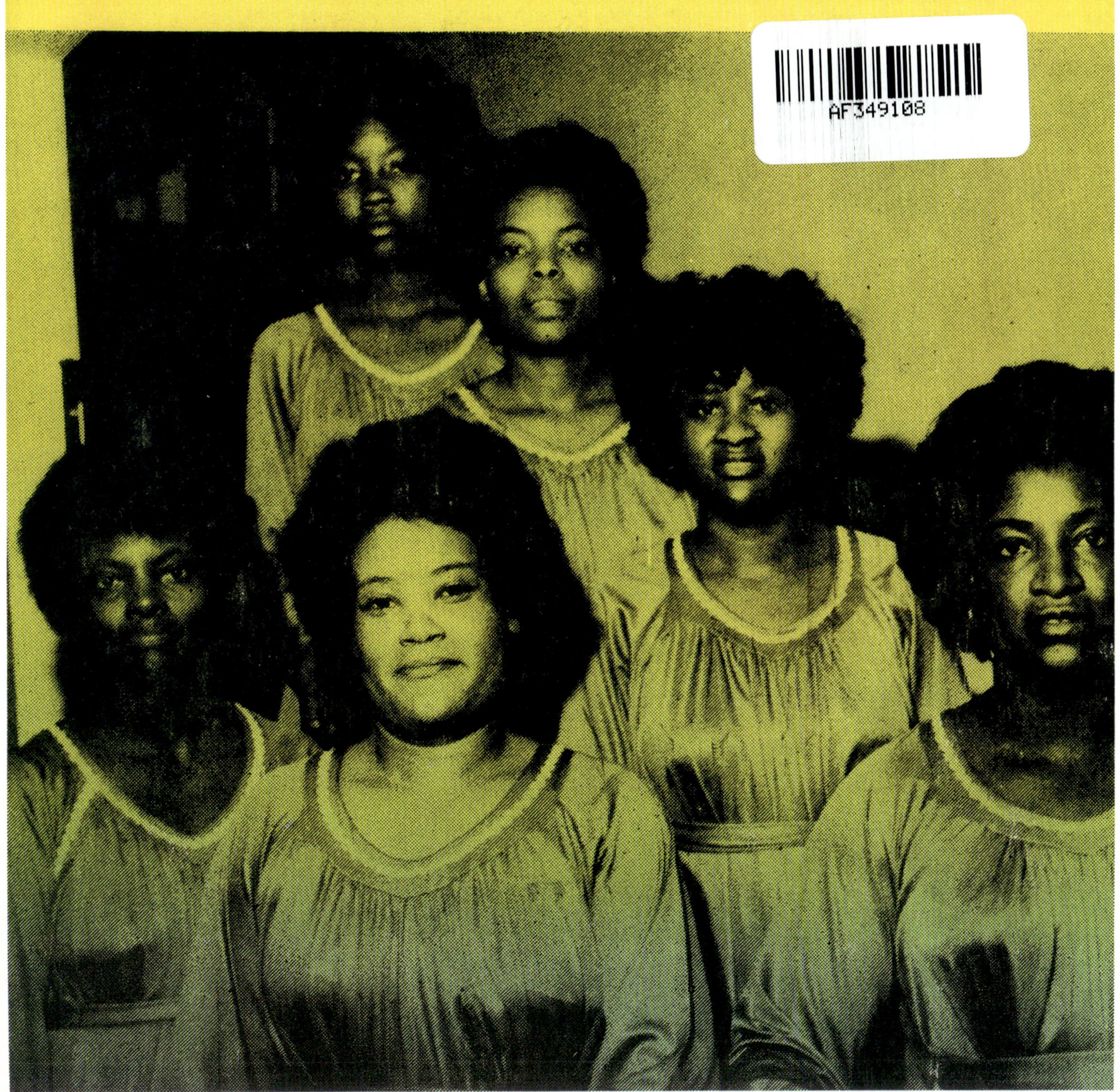

ALLEN RUPPERSBERG
COLLECTORS PARADISE
2012

NO TIME LEFT TO START AGAIN
The B (birth) and D (death) of R'n'R

By Allen Ruppersberg

Levon Helm (1940–2012) The Band
Captain Beefheart (1941–2010)
Clarence Clemons (1942–2011) The E Street Band
George Harrison (1943–2001) The Beatles
John Entwistle (1944–2002) The Who
Arthur Lee (1945–2006) Love
Dickie Peterson (1946–2009) Blue Cheer
Syd Barrett (1946–2006) Pink Floyd
Warren Zevon (1947–2003)

WHAT TIME IS IT?

If there is NO TIME LEFT TO START AGAIN then what time is it anyway? I have asked
myself this question before.

In some cases, if you live long enough you begin to see the endings of the things
in which you saw the beginnings. It seems as if worlds disappear before your eyes
and ears have a chance to take them in. Just as you can't invent over again what
came to be known as rock and roll, it's hard now to even remember how it first
appeared in your life. I was eight in 1952 when the Moondog Coronation Ball was
held in the Cleveland Arena, a dance promoted by Alan Freed with mostly black R&B
stars, which he featured on his radio show, *The Moondog Rock 'n' Roll House Party*,
broadcast on Cleveland station WJW. Said to be the first rock and roll show and Freed
the coiner of the term as well, it caused a minor riot in downtown Cleveland as I was
quietly growing up in a nearby suburb. It was another seven years before I could go
there myself. Alan Freed had moved on to the Paramount Theatre in New York some
years before but at the Record Rendezvous, again in downtown Cleveland, the music
stayed on the air and I bought my first LP there around 1960. It was *Have Guitar, Will
Travel* by Bo Diddley and when I got it home my aunt called it "race music" and asked
what was I doing with that. So much for what time it was then.

EVERYTHING IS COLLECTED BUT NOTHING IS SAVED

Now I will begin talking about leftovers and the work titled NO TIME LEFT TO START
AGAIN, of which this book, *Collector's Paradise*, is a part. As with many things, it all
seemed to start with a record. A few years ago, on a trip back to Cleveland, I went
to the Rock and Roll Hall of Fame for the first time. I found it fun enough, lots of
memorabilia, film clips, old records, of course, and the now familiar story of R'n'R,
told again in the basically familiar way. On a subsequent trip I was looking around
an antique store in mid-Ohio and saw, lying in a back room, a 78rpm Little Richard
record that I not only had had a 45rpm of when it came out, but had also just seen in
a vitrine at the Hall of Fame. I bought it for a dollar. Afterwards I wondered what other
great artifacts from this familiar history, now over fifty years long, clearly as old as I
was and seemingly as distant as Atlantis, could be lying around. What I found was
more than I could have imagined.

Over a period of about three years of searching in flea markets, junk stores and antique malls for these leftover materials from the era, in an effort to try and construct a random history for myself of what R'n'R was, how it came to be and what became of it, I amassed over 4,000 records, mostly 78rpms, with a sampling of 45s. Some of the early 78s dated back to just after the turn of the century and to the popularization of recorded sound. I collected approximately 500 pieces of sheet music going back to minstrel days along with hundreds of musical songbooks and other ephemera related to the history of American popular song, some material dating to just after the Civil War. When Harry Smith began his search in the late 1940s for the artists who would wind up in his *Anthology of American Folk Music* he had only to look twenty or so years before his time. By the early 1960s, a folk and blues revival of music more than thirty years in the past had sparked a major interest in the collecting of this material and influenced generations in the process. In 2012, The *Anthology of American Folk Music* will celebrate its fiftieth anniversary. Finding records that appeared on this famous anthology, recorded now roughly eighty years ago on fragile, shellac discs, would seem to be impossible. It was not. I have some of them in this collection.

While putting together this collection of music, I also searched out a history of vernacular photography in order to give a parallel dimension to the popular sounds spreading out across the country via the new technologies of radio and the phonograph. Listen to the songs and take a picture, simple as that. The availability of the new and inexpensive personal camera added billions of snapshots to this growing archive of the commercial past still floating around on the edges of the world. Now, of course, I realize again that I am not the only one who is doing the collecting as the common past is being scooped up by every sort of collector, archivist, and entrepreneur running around the country. It's a gathering storm, to see who can snatch up first and most completely all that is left of an original American culture. And this has been going on for some time.

With the advent of sites like eBay and with enough time and money, anyone can conceivably construct a collection and a history on just about any subject. You may not be able to get all of it, or the extremely rare or the very rare, but it would seem you could come pretty close. What I was interested in, however, was closer to the idea of an archeological dig, where the removing of layers of whatever kind of sediment slowly reveals an unfolding story, artifact by artifact, of a history and a culture that was not visible before. And by roaming the miles of aisles in antique malls, flea markets, etc., looking for something quite specific, the unseen has more of a chance to appear and the story can begin to tell itself in a more personal way. The way a collection can be arranged so as to make a history visible is a subject I love and have explored in other works. To some my random methods of collecting might not seem so different from eBay shopping but I believe it is. Once, while driving around farm country in central Ohio with my sister, we took a wrong turn and ended up on a much smaller road heading in another direction. Passing through a virtual flyspeck of a town there was an antique store that happened to be open. It was watched over by a Vietnam vet who must have been there for a long time, as he seemed to know what belonged to whom, even if the prices were sometimes unknown. Upstairs was an old, broken, crank record player from the 1930s, not much good to anyone. But as I looked inside the case there was a pocket where the records were meant to be stored. They were still in there. Out came six or seven Black Label Columbias in very fine condition, still shiny and black and probably not played for at least fifty years. How much for the records I asked? I'll have to call up and see was the answer. After a few minutes and some chatting from the other end, I gave him about 15 bucks, 25 if I wanted the record player also. Listening to these records, the history that seemed so familiar in the Rock and Roll Hall of Fame became again unfamiliar and a much richer and more original understanding was made possible.

THE BOOK

This book is part of the larger work NO TIME LEFT TO START AGAIN, a work inspired by and composed of the collection of material found in the search described above. THE BOOK is called *Collector's Paradise* and it takes the form of a collectors' catalogue or magazine. The selection and listing by year of the top 1,500 records, down from the original 4,000, represents not only my personal choices as to which are the best records in and of themselves but which can also stand as a history of American recorded music. The list is presented in chronological order from *The Darkies' Awakening* by Vess L. Ossman recorded in 1906 to Al Green's 1975 *Could I Be the One?* As I mentioned before, I collected mostly 78s and some 45s. Most of the history I was interested in is contained on 78 recordings. The earliest recordings, from around the turn of the century, were on wax cylinders but this was relatively short-lived and now belongs to the world of the specialist. But the 78rpm record lasted for over forty years and lived on into at least the mid-50s. Even after the invention of the 33 and 45rpm recording processes in 1948 and 1949, processes which soon became the more popular forms of recording, 78s were continuing to be produced. This explains why I had the more common and inexpensive Little Richard 45 when it was first released and not the 78 until finding it in the antique store in 2009. I chose to stop the collection in the period of the early 1970s, as it seems to me, as it does to many others, that at about that time rock and roll was becoming something other than its original self. The spark of invention that was once so new and exciting had begun to change into something we now call rock. Some would date the demise to the death of Elvis Presley. I just stopped a little earlier. It was reinvented in the late 1970s with the birth of punk but that's someone else's story.

A complete description of the work NO TIME LEFT TO START AGAIN, of which *Collector's Paradise* is one of many elements, is included at the back of this book. When installed, NO TIME LEFT TO START AGAIN becomes a sort of giant, deluxe walk-in boxed set of one possible history of rock and roll. But it could also be the museum exhibition of a passionate collector or some kind of expanded archival display in a small town museum or many other possibilities, including a work of art. At the very least, it is one re assembling of the history of rock and roll and an examination of collected leftovers from two favorite vernacular cultures, popular records and personal, snapshot photographs. Both were once common, everyday objects in the world, but are now soon to disappear forever.

It seemed to me at the beginning of this project that this was the last possible moment to be able to gather any of this material in the manner I did and I am even more convinced now that I was right.

Chuck Berry (1926–
Jerry Lee Lewis (1935–
Fats Domino (1928–
Little Richard (1932–

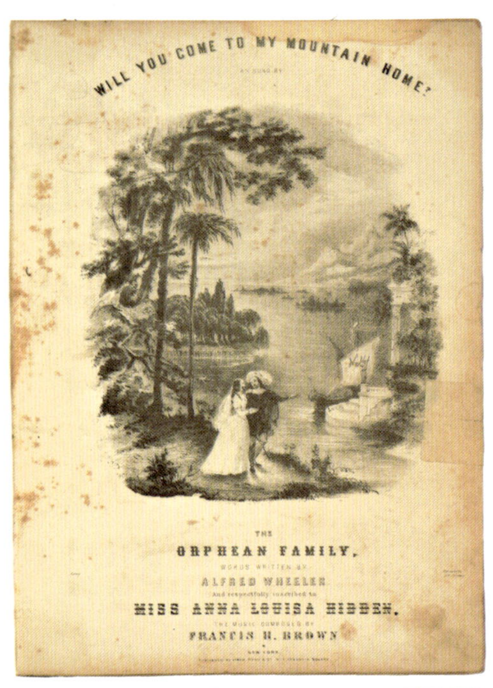

WILL YOU COME TO MY MOUNTAIN HOME?
THE ORPHEAN FAMILY.
ALFRED WHEELER
MISS ANNA LOUISA HIDDEN
FRANCIS H. BROWN

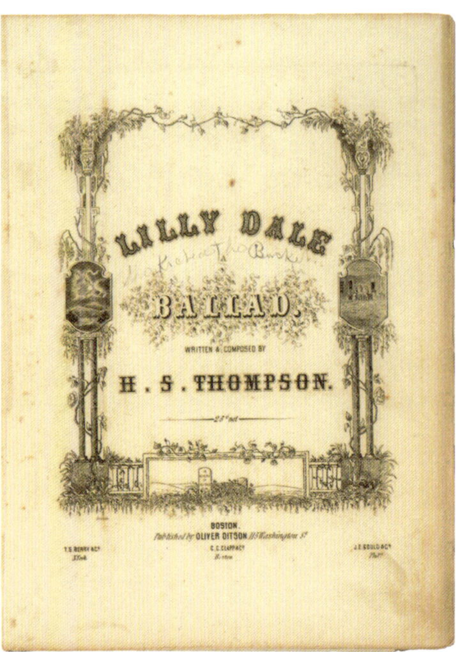

LILLY DALE
BALLAD
WRITTEN & COMPOSED BY
H. S. THOMPSON.
BOSTON
Published by OLIVER DITSON

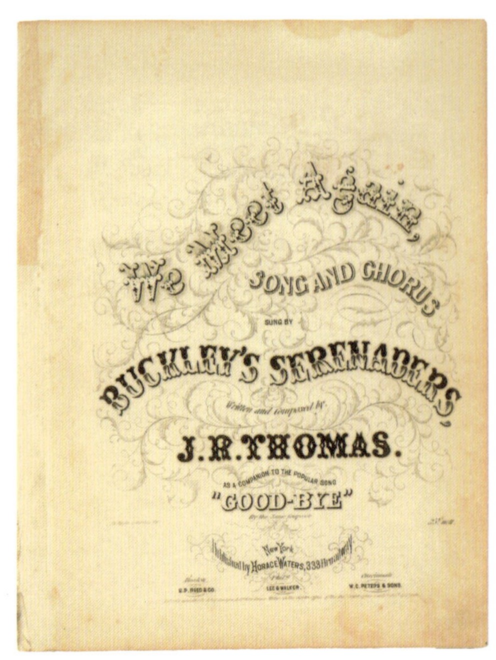

WE'D MEET AGAIN
SONG AND CHORUS
SUNG BY
BUCKLEY'S SERENADERS
J. R. THOMAS.
"GOOD-BYE"
New York
Published by HORACE WATERS

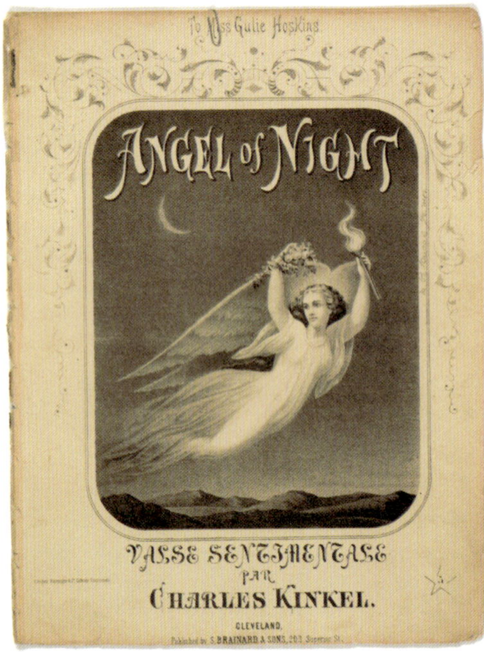

ANGEL of NIGHT
VALSE SENTIMENTALE
PAR
CHARLES KINKEL.
CLEVELAND.

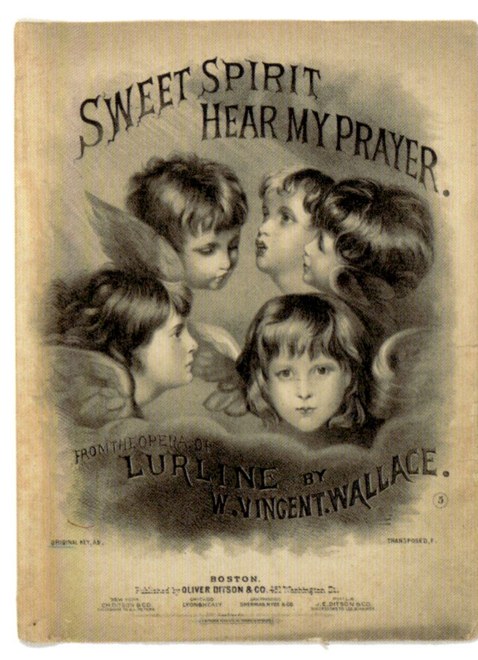

SWEET SPIRIT
HEAR MY PRAYER.
FROM THE OPERA OF
LURLINE BY
W. VINCENT WALLACE.
Published by OLIVER DITSON & CO.

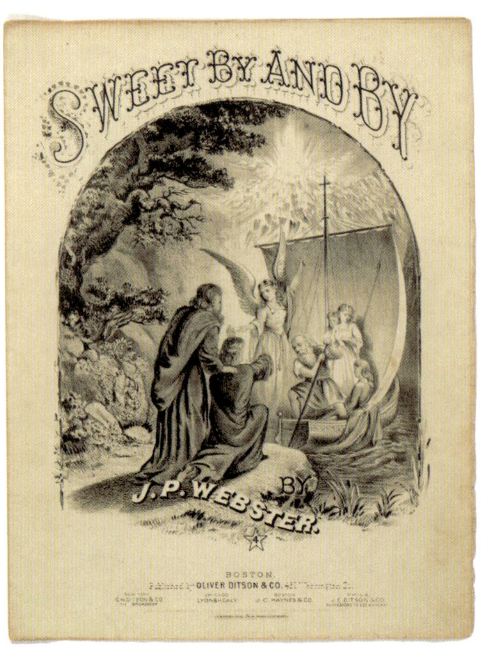

SWEET BY AND BY
BY
J. P. WEBSTER.
BOSTON.
Published by OLIVER DITSON & CO.

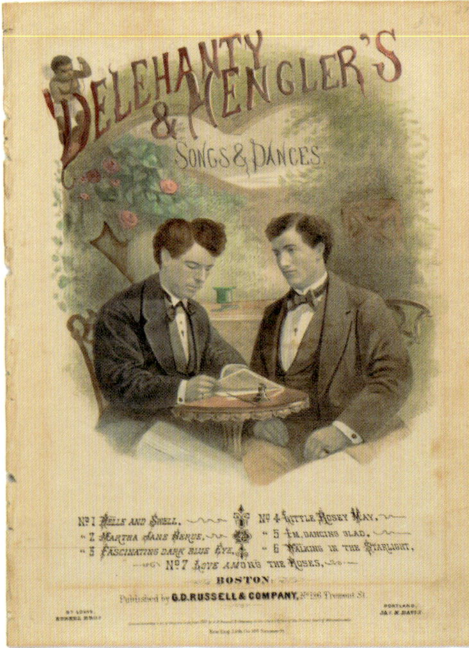

DELEHANTY & HENGLER'S
SONGS & DANCES
BOSTON.
Published by G. D. RUSSELL & COMPANY

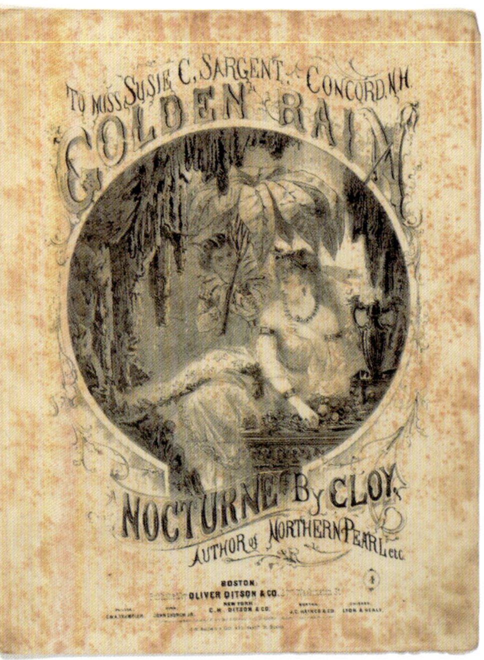

TO MISS SUSIE C. SARGENT, CONCORD N.H.
GOLDEN RAIN
NOCTURNE BY CLOY.
AUTHOR OF NORTHERN PEARL, etc.
BOSTON:
OLIVER DITSON & CO.

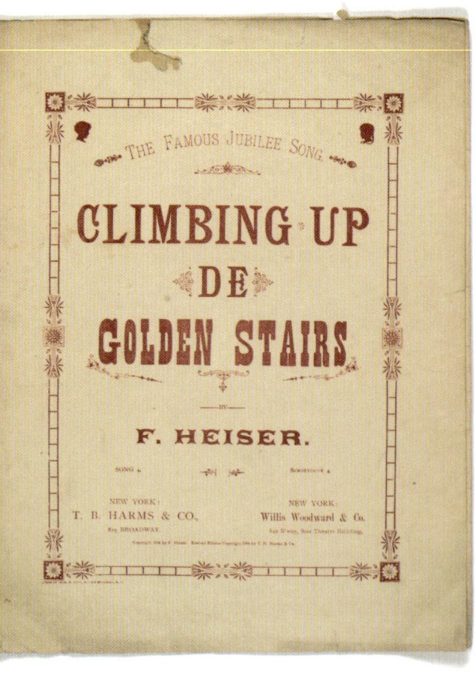

THE FAMOUS JUBILEE SONG.
CLIMBING UP
DE
GOLDEN STAIRS.
F. HEISER.
NEW YORK:
T. B. HARMS & CO.
NEW YORK:
Willis Woodward & Co.

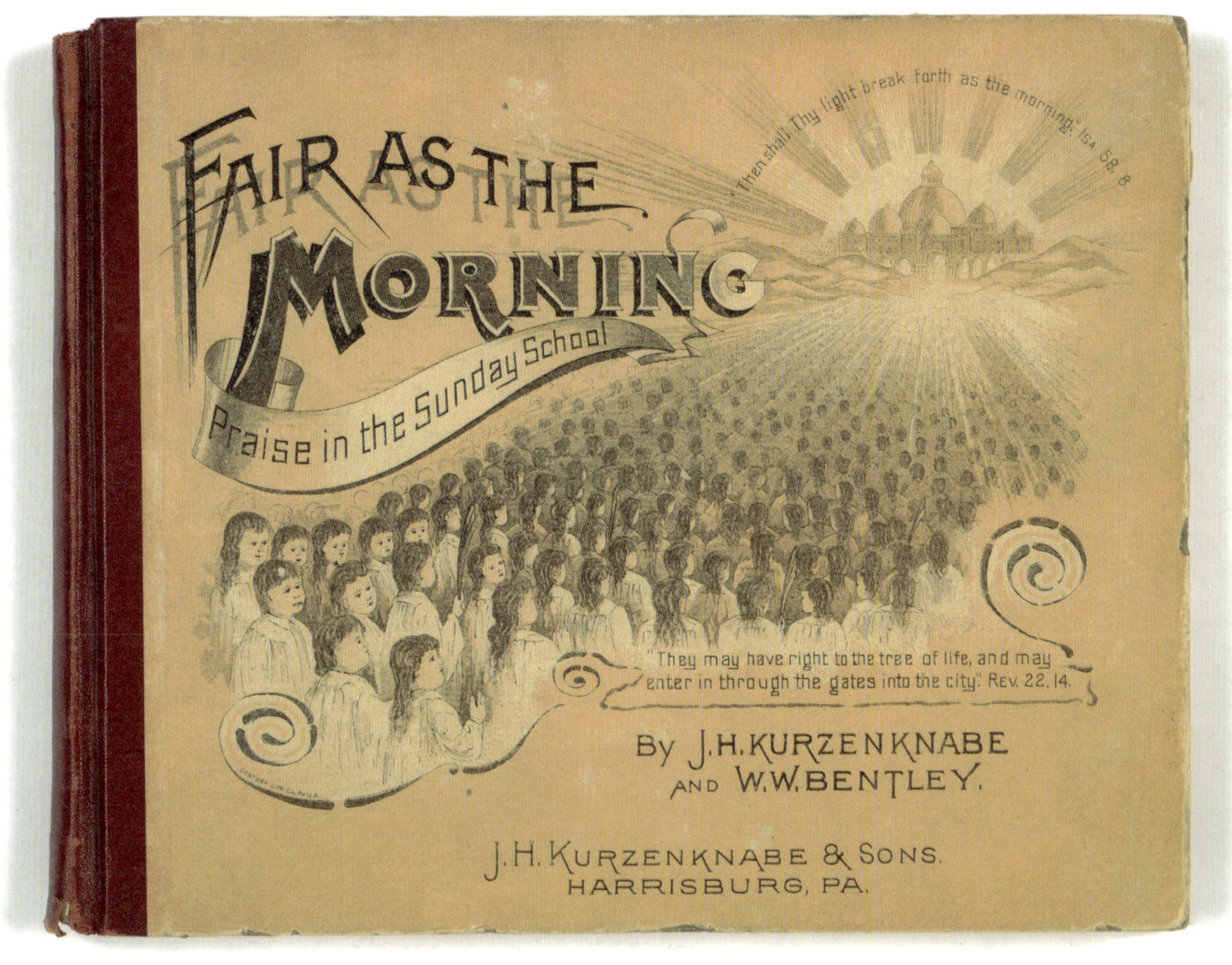

NO TIME LEFT TO START AGAIN
The B (birth) and D (death) of R'n'R

Vess L. Ossman . . . . *The Darkies' Awakening* (George Lansing), Columbia 233, 78, 1906
Columbia Orchestra. . . . . *Darkey's Dream*, Columbia A157, 78, 1908
Gipsy Smith . . . . *Saved By Grace* (George Coles Stebbins and Fanny Jane Crosby),
New World Records NW 224, LP, 1909
Hayden Quartet. . . . . *Where Is My Boy To-Night* (Lowry), Victor 16412, 78, 1909
Trinity Choir . . . . *There Is a Fountain Fill'd with Blood* (Cowper–Mason), Victor 16412, 78, 1909
Matt Keefe . . . . *The Strolling Yodler* (Keefe–Heinsman), Pathe 022151, 78, 1914
Homer Rodeheaver. . . . . *I Am Coming Home* (Rev. A. H. Ackley–B. D. Ackley), Victor 17786, 78, 1915
Brighten the Corner Where You Are (Ina Dudley Ogdon–Chas. H. Gabriel), Victor 17763, 78, 1915
Mr. and Mrs. William Wheeler . . . . *My Jesus As Though Wilt* (Weber–Schmolke), Victor 17940, 78, 1915
Mrs. William Asher and Homer Rodeheaver. . . . . *In the Garden* (C. Austin Miles),
Recorded Anthology of American Music Inc. 224, LP, 1916
Vocalion Military Band. . . . . *Review of the U.S. Fleet* (Erleebach), Aeolian Vocalion 1244, 78, 1916
Amelita Galli-Curci . . . . *Home Sweet Home* (John H. Payne–Henry R. Bishop), Victor 74511, 78, 1917
Billy Sunday Chorus . . . . . . *America (My Country 'Tis of Thee)* (Samuel F. Smith–Henry Carey), Victor 18322, 78, 1917
Sail On (Chas. H. Gabriel), Victor 18322, 78, 1917
Homer Rodeheaver. . . . . *Somebody Cares*, Columbia A2248, 78, 1917
Christ Is All (W. A. Williams), Victor 19452, 78, 1917

Opposite: Sheet music 1846-1884. Above: *Fair as the Morning*, 1891.

Footsteps on the Stairs

BALLAD

SUNG BY

JENNIE KEMPTON

AT

Gottschalks Concerts

Composed by

Elbridge G. B. Holder

BOSTON.
OLIVER DITSON & CO. 277 Washington St.
N. York.
C. H. DITSON & CO.

Lyon & Healy, Chicago.   J. Church Jr. Cinn.   J. C. Haynes & Co. Boston   C. W. A. Trumpler Phila

Enterd according to Act of Congress A 1863 by Firth Son & Co in the Clerks Office of the Dist Court of the South'n Dist of N.Y.

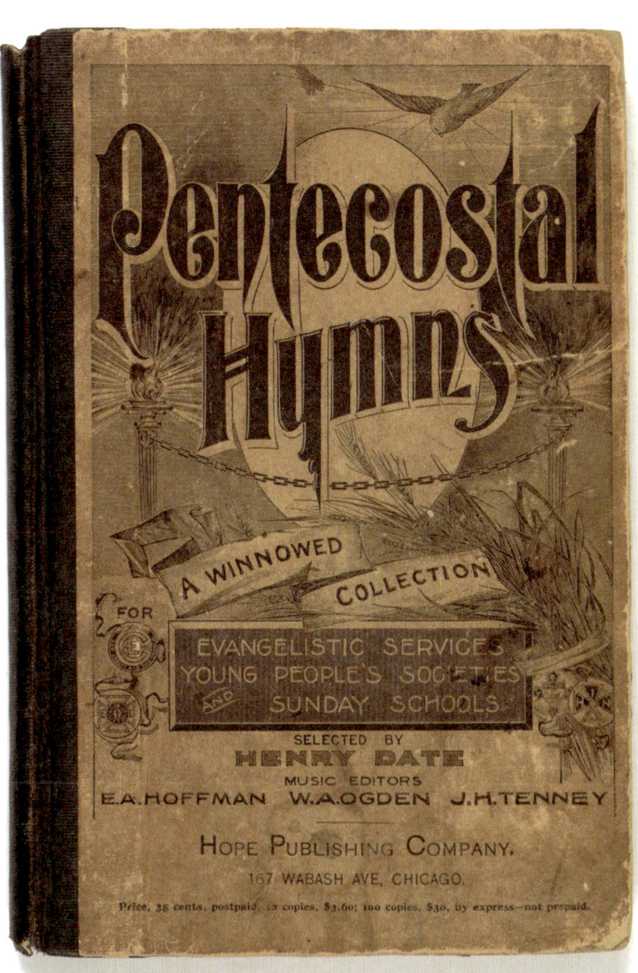
Pentecostal Hymns
A WINNOWED COLLECTION
FOR
EVANGELISTIC SERVICES
YOUNG PEOPLE'S SOCIETIES
AND SUNDAY SCHOOLS
SELECTED BY
HENRY DATE
MUSIC EDITORS
E.A.HOFFMAN   W.A.OGDEN   J.H.TENNEY
HOPE PUBLISHING COMPANY,
167 WABASH AVE, CHICAGO.
Price, 35 cents, postpaid. 12 copies, $3.60; 100 copies, $30, by express—not prepaid.

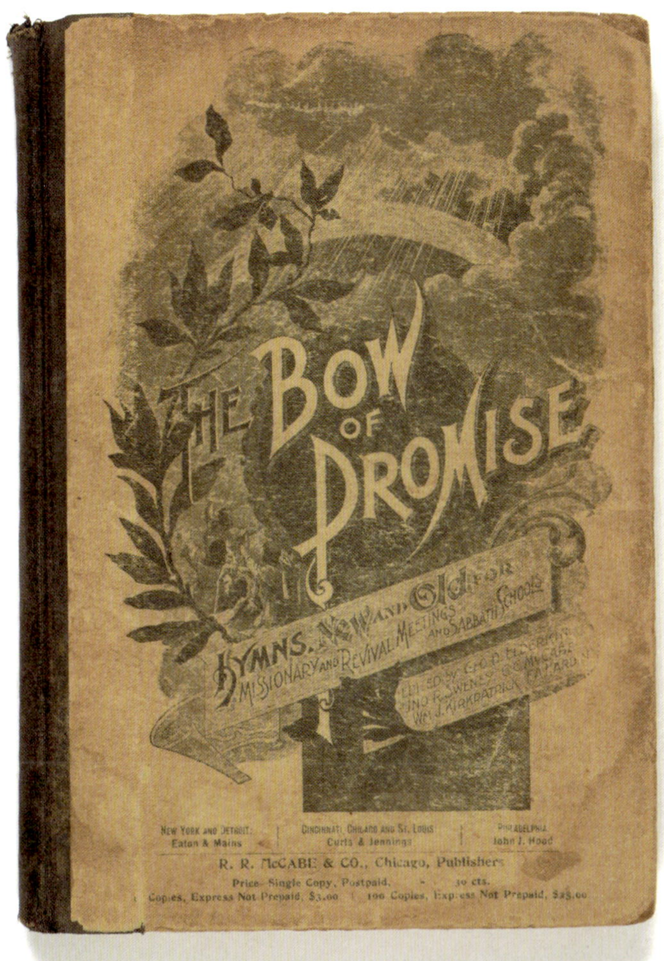
THE BOW OF PROMISE
HYMNS, NEW AND OLD, FOR
MISSIONARY AND REVIVAL MEETINGS AND SABBATH SCHOOLS
EDITED BY GEO. D. ELDERKIN
JNO. R. SWENEY C. C. McCABE
WM. J. KIRKPATRICK E. A. FAZARD
NEW YORK AND DETROIT: CINCINNATI, CHICAGO AND ST. LOUIS   PHILADELPHIA
Eaton & Mains   Curts & Jennings   John J. Hood
R. R. McCABE & CO., Chicago, Publishers
Price—Single Copy, Postpaid,   -   30 cts.
Copies, Express Not Prepaid, $3.00   100 Copies, Express Not Prepaid, $25.00

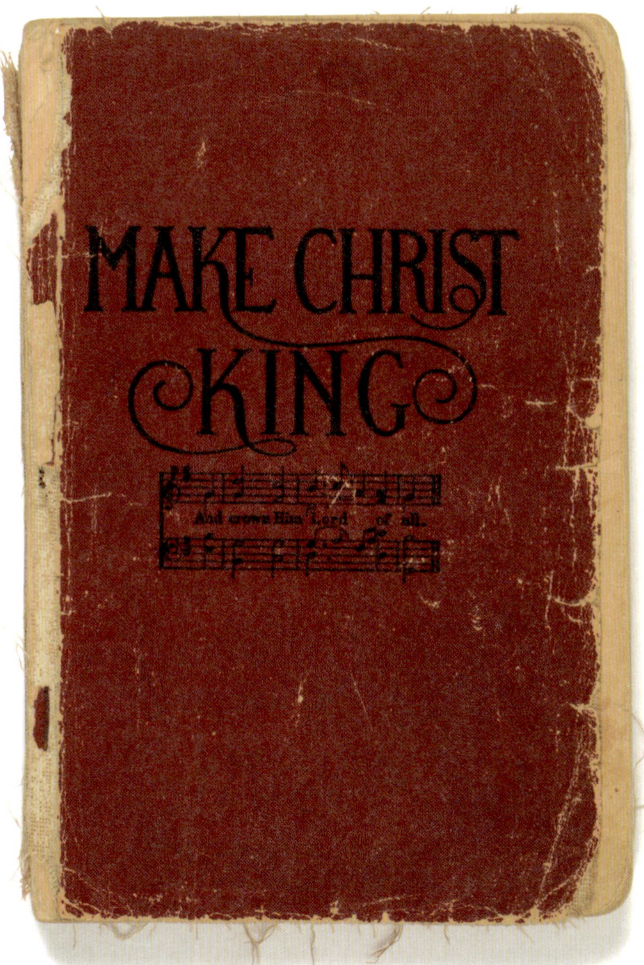
MAKE CHRIST KING
And crown Him Lord of all.

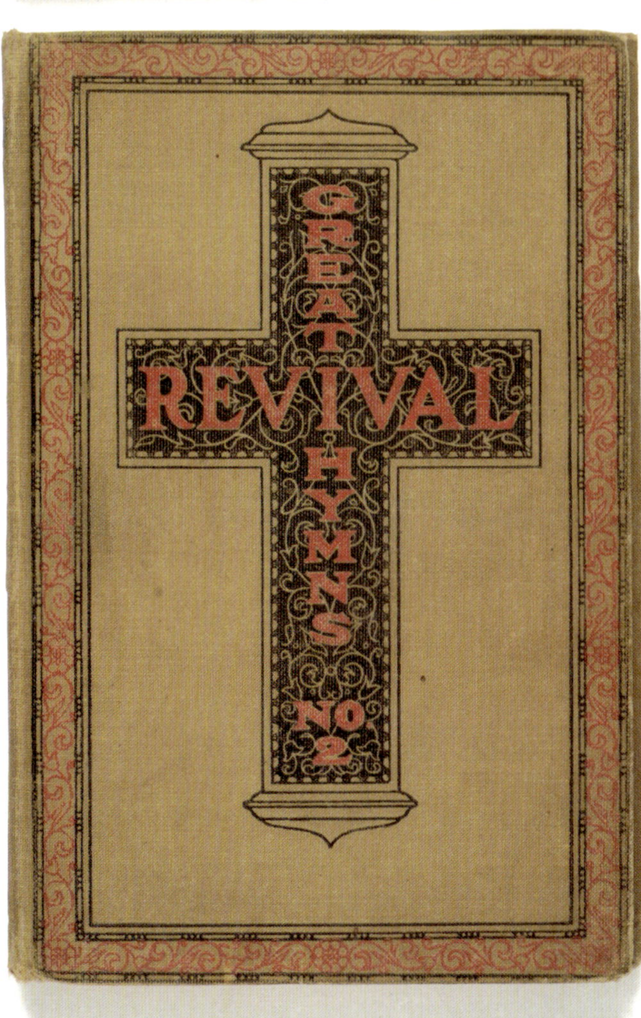
GREAT REVIVAL HYMNS NO 2

"Music Unites the People" 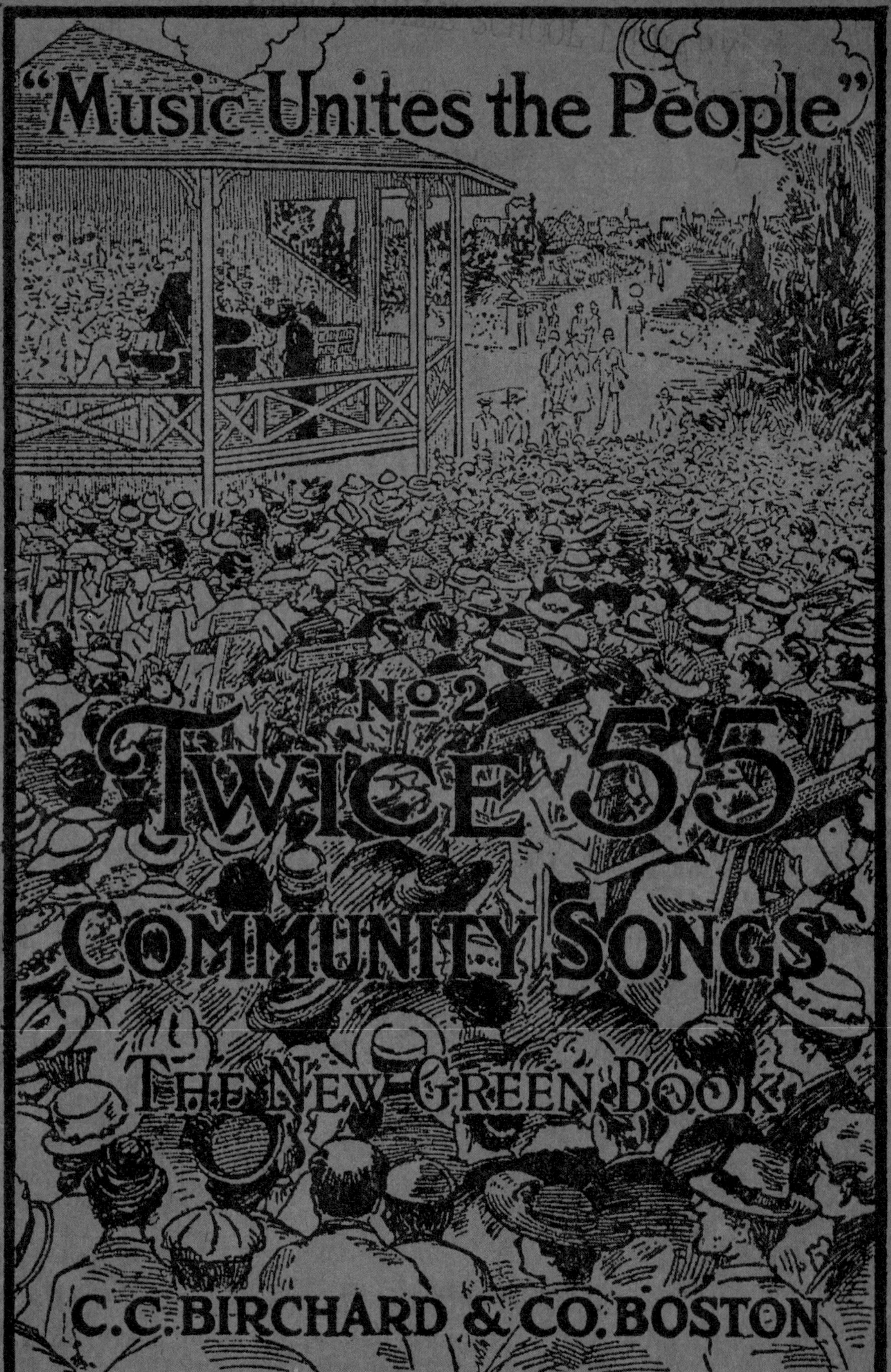
Nº 2
TWICE 55
COMMUNITY SONGS
THE NEW GREEN BOOK
C.C. BIRCHARD & CO. BOSTON
Copyright, 1917, by C. C. Birchard & Company

Homer Rodeheaver. . . . . *Trusting Jesus, That Is All* (Stites–Sankey), Victor 19452, 78, 1917
Howard Kopp. . . . . *Onward Christian Soldiers* (Sullivan), Columbia A2304, 78, 1917
Matt Keefe . . . . *Sleep, Baby, Sleep* (Hadley), Pathe 022151, 78, 1917
Bob Thomas . . . .*The Pickwick Club Tragedy* (Larsan), Grey Gull 4086, 78, 1919
Henry Burr . . . . *Beautiful Ohio* (Earl), Columbia 2701, 78, 1919
Nora Bayes . . . . *Prohibition Blues* (Lardner–Bayes), Columbia 2823, 78, 1919
Taxation Blues (Hess–Rosey–Santly), Columbia 2823, 78, 1919
Reed Miller . . . . *Oh Susanna* (S. Foster), Aeolian Vocalion 14072, 78, 1919
Aeolian Male Quartet . . . . *Plantation Songs*, Aeolian Vocalion 14072, 78, 1920
Lucille Hegamin. . . . .*Jazz Me Blues* (Delaney), Black Swan 2032, 78, 1920
Mamie Smith . . . .*If You Don't Want Me Blues* (Perry Bradford), Okeh 4228, 78, 1920
Mem'ries of You Mammy (Perry Bradford), Okeh 4228, 78, 1920
Original Dixieland Jazz Band. . . . .*Palesteena* (J. R. Robinson–Con Conrad), Victor 18717, 78, 1920
Margie (J. R. Robinson–Con Conrad), Victor 18717, 78, 1920
Oscar Seagle. . . . .*Nearer, My God, to Thee (Bethany)*
(Lowell Mason–Sarah Flower Adams), Recorded Anthology of American Music Inc. 224, LP, 1920

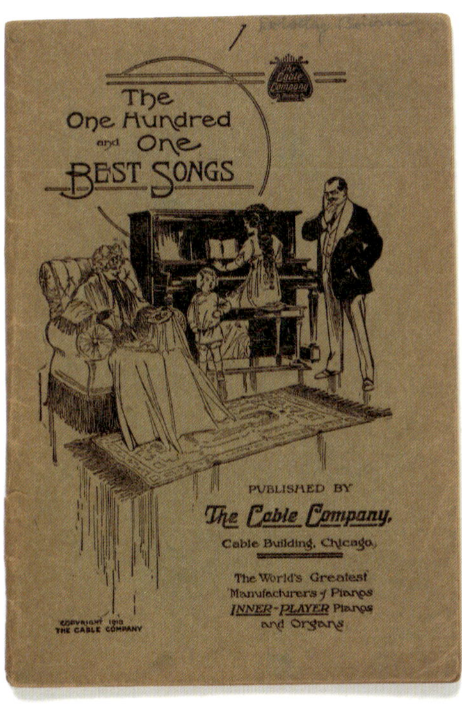
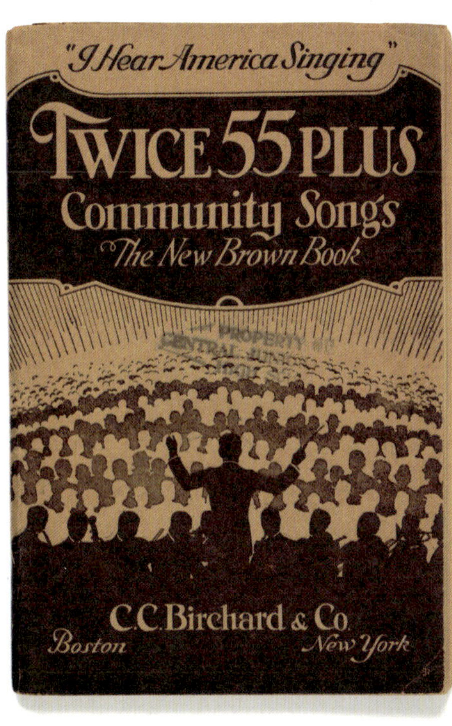
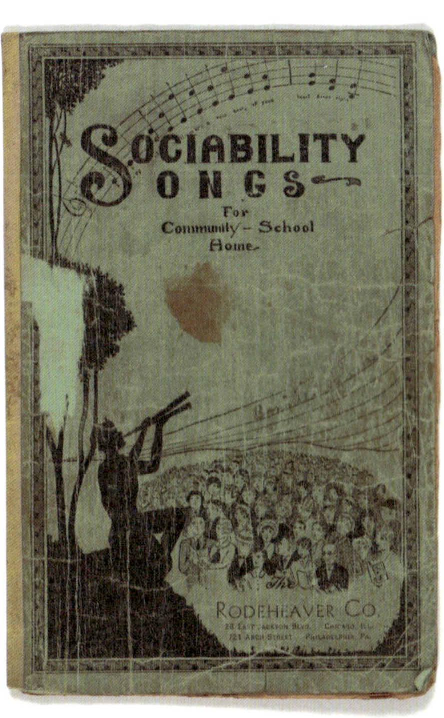

Fisk University Jubilee Singers . . . . *Ezekiel Saw De Wheel*, Columbia 3370, 78, 1921
Lucille Hegamin. . . . . *Arkansas Blues* (Williams), Black Swan 2032, 78, 1921
Noble Sissle . . . . *I'm a Doggone Struttin' Fool* (Ryan–Pinkard), Regal 9158, 78, 1921
I've Got the Red, White and Blues (Clarence Gaskill), Regal 9158, 78, 1921
Southern Serenaders. . . . . *Runnin' Wild* (Woods–Gibbs), Cameo 310, 78, 1922
You've Gotta See Mamma Ev'ry Night (Or You Can't See Mamma at All) (Rose–Conrad), Cameo 310, 78, 1922
Trinity Quartet . . . . *Jesus Lives!* (Gallert–Cox–Gauntlett), Victor 19004, 78, 1922
Albert Campbell. . . . . . .*Henry Burr—I'm Sitting Pretty in a Pretty Little City* (Davis–Baer–Santly), Victor 19180, 78, 1923
Ladd's Black Aces . . . .*You've Got to See Your Mamma Every Night* (Rose–Conrad), Gennett 5035, 78, 1923
Runnin' Wild (Grey–Wood–Gibbs), Gennett 5035, 78, 1923
Mamie Smith . . . .*You've Got to See Mamma Ev'ry Night (Or You Can't See Mamma at All)*
(Billy Rose–Con Conrad), Okeh 4781, 78, 1923
Markels Orchestra. . . . . *By the Shalimar* (F. Magine–D. Delbridge–T. Koehler), Okeh 4826, 78, 1923
Peerless Quartet . . *Alabamy Blacksheep (Won't You Return to My Fold)* (King Zany–Roy Ingraham), Victor 19180, 78, 1923
Tampa Blue Jazz Band . . . .*Maxie Jones* (G. Clark–E. Leslie–P. Wendling), Okeh 4826, 78, 1923
Alf. Taylor (ex-Governor of Tennessee) . . . .*Pharoah's Army Got Drownded*, Victor 19451, 78, 1924
Bessie Smith . . . .*House Rent Blues* (Ted Wallace), Columbia 14032, 78, 1924

Preceding overleaf left: *Footsteps on the Stairs*, 1863. Preceding overleaf right: Hymnals 1894-1913.
Opposite: *Music Unites the People*, 1917. Above: Song books 1911-1929.

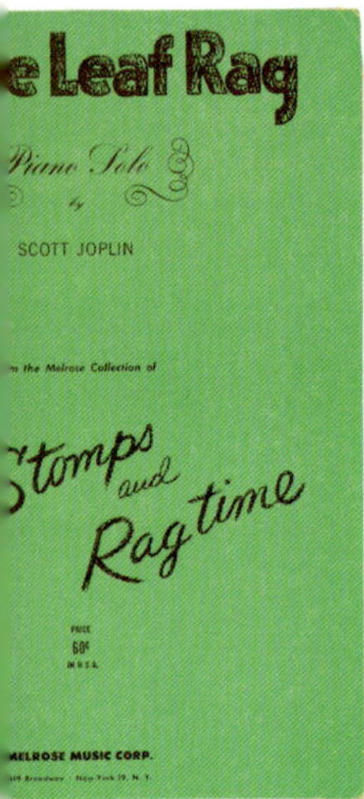
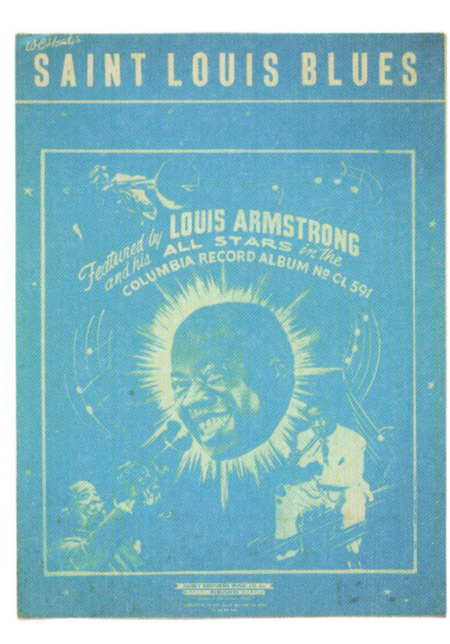
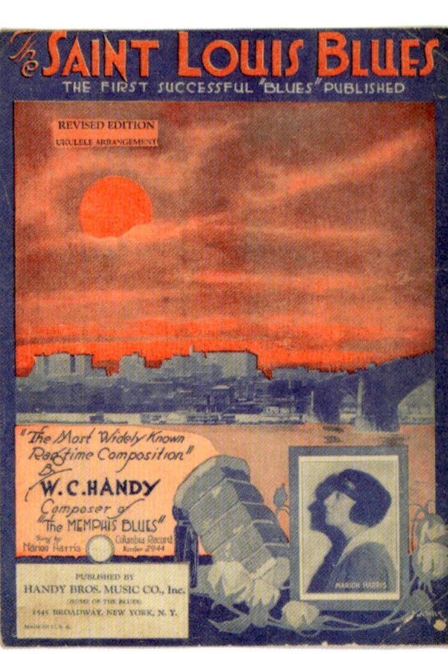
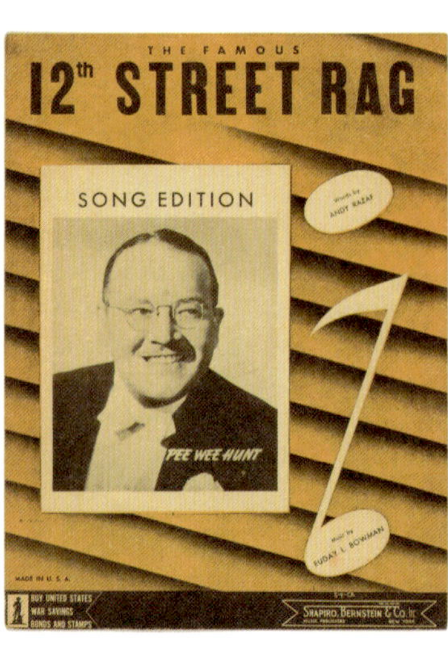
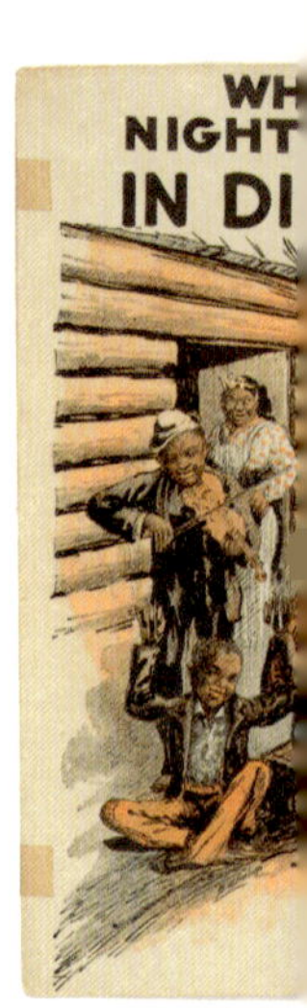

Bessie Smith . . . . *Work House Blues* (Ted Wallace), Columbia 14032, 78, 1924
Woman's Trouble Blues (Jack Gee), Columbia 14060, 78, 1924
Love Me Daddy Blues (Fred W. Longshaw), Columbia 14060, 78, 1924
Ernest Thompson . . . . *In the Baggage Coach Ahead* (Gussie L. Davis), Columbia 216, 78, 1924
The Little Rosebud Casket, Columbia 216, 78, 1924
Ex-Governor Alf. Taylor's Old Lumber Quartet . . . . *Brother Noah Built an Ark*, Victor 19451, 78, 1924
Frank Ferera . . . . *The Farmer's Dream*, Columbia 418, 78, 1924
Riley Puckett . . . . *Just As the Sun Went Down*, Columbia 240, 78, 1924
You'll Never Miss Your Mother 'Til She's Gone, Columbia 240, 78, 1924
Bessie Smith . . . . *Cake Walking Babies (From Home)* (Smith–Troy–Williams), Columbia 35673, 78, 1925
You've Been a Good Ole Wagon (Smith–Balcom), Columbia 35672, 78, 1925
Cold in Hand Blues (Gee–Longshaw), Columbia 35672, 78, 1925
Calvin P. Dixon (Black Billy Sunday) . . . . *The Handwriting on the Wall*, Columbia 14076, 78, 1925
Clean Out Your Wells—Your Water's Muddy, Columbia 14076, 78, 1925
Carl T. Sprague . . . .*Bad Companions*, Victor 19747, 78, 1925
When All the Work's Done This Fall, Victor 19747, 78, 1925
Homer Rodeheaver . . . .*Forgive Me Lord* (A. H. Ackley–B. D. Ackley), Victor 19875, 78, 1925
Mrs. William Asher and Homer Rodeheaver . . . . *The Old Rugged Cross* (George Bennard), Victor 19875, 78, 1925
Sid Harkreader . . . . *Southern Whistling Coon*, Vocalion 5065, 78, 1925
The Dying Girl's Message, Vocalion 5066, 78, 1925
Where Is My Boy To-Night (Lowry), Vocalion 5066, 78, 1925
Uncle Dave Macon . . . . *Watermelon Smilin' on the Vine*, Vocalion 5065, 78, 1925
Vernon Dalhart . . . . *The Letter Edged in Black*, Silvertone 2705, 78, 1925
Zeb Turney's Gal (Lambkin–Robison), Silvertone 2705, 78, 1925
The Runaway Train (Harry Warren–Robert E. Massey), Victor 19684, 78, 1925

Sheet music 1899-1929.

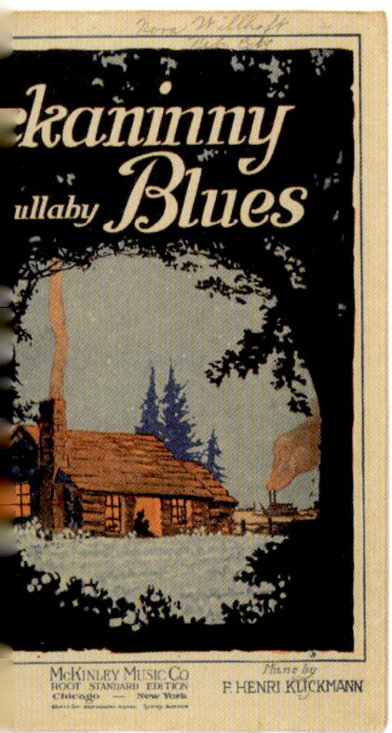
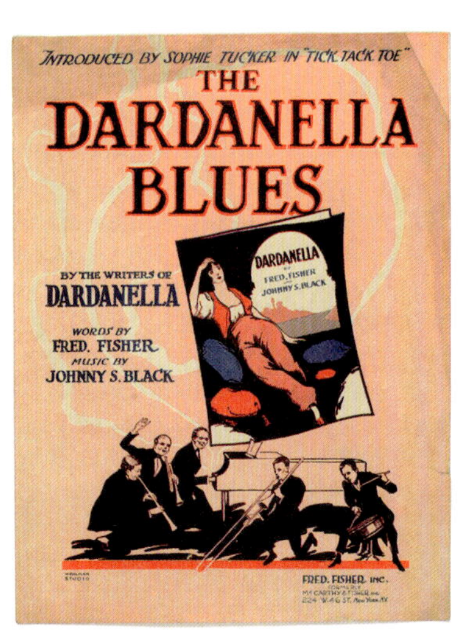
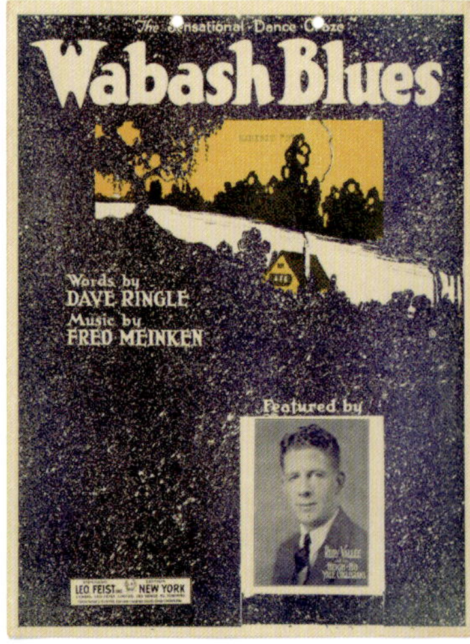
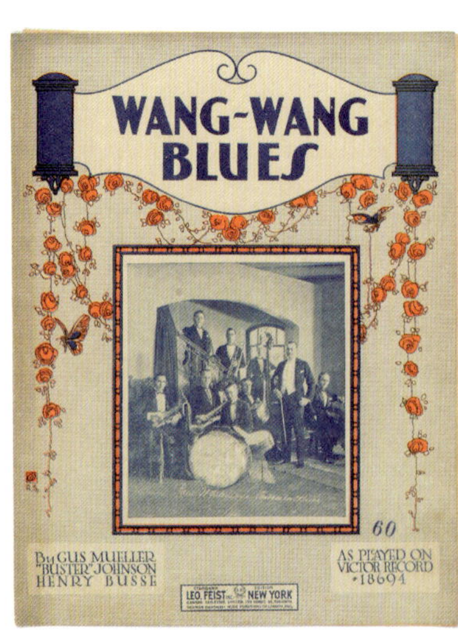
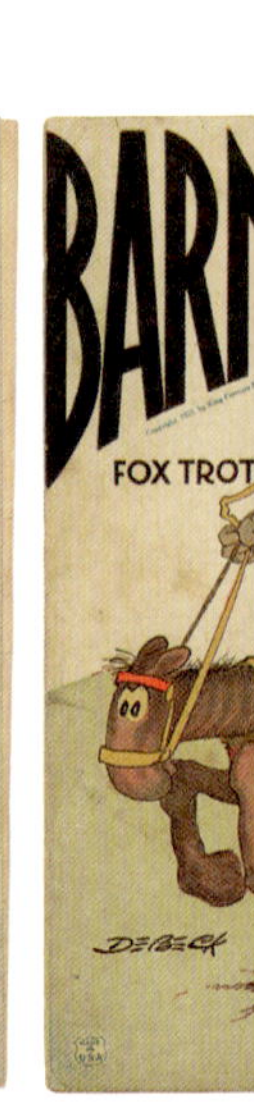

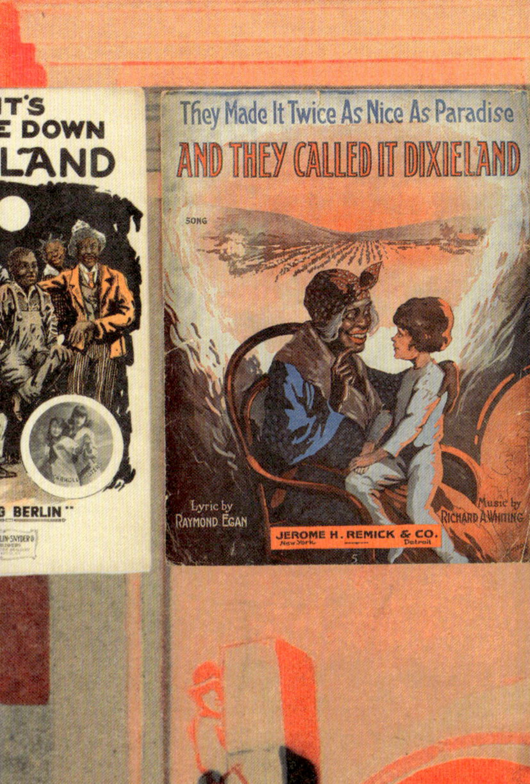
They Made It Twice As Nice As Paradise
AND THEY CALLED IT DIXIELAND
SONG
Lyric by
RAYMOND EGAN
Music by
RICHARD A. WHITING
JEROME H. REMICK & CO.
New York   Detroit

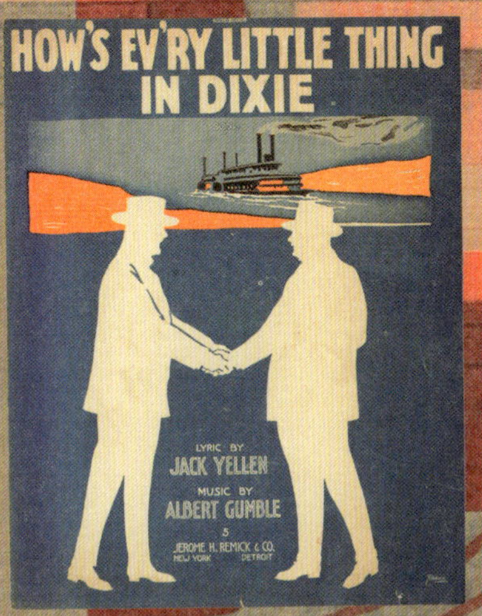
HOW'S EV'RY LITTLE THING
IN DIXIE
LYRIC BY
JACK YELLEN
MUSIC BY
ALBERT GUMBLE
5
JEROME H. REMICK & CO.
NEW YORK   DETROIT

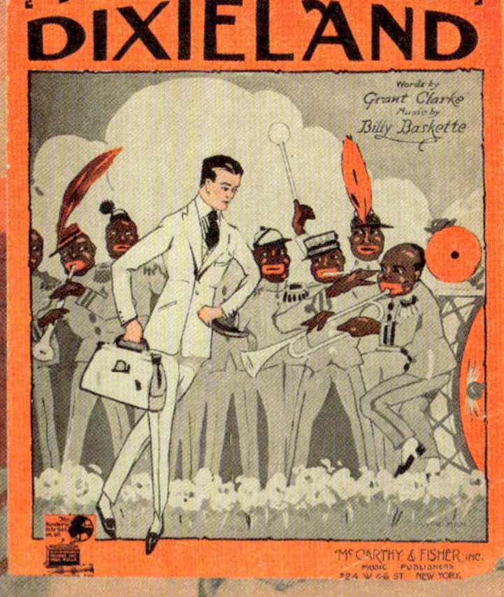
I'LL DANCE MY WAY
RIGHT BACK TO
DIXIELAND
Words by
Grant Clarke
Music by
Billy Baskette
McCARTHY & FISHER, Inc.

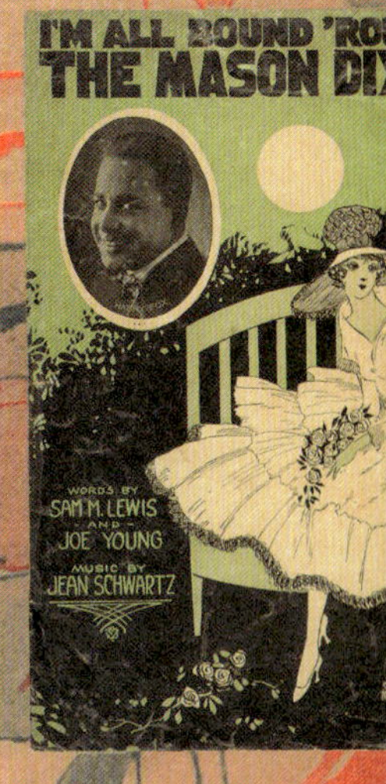
I'M ALL BOUND 'ROUND
THE MASON DIXON
WORDS BY
SAM M. LEWIS
AND
JOE YOUNG
MUSIC BY
JEAN SCHWARTZ

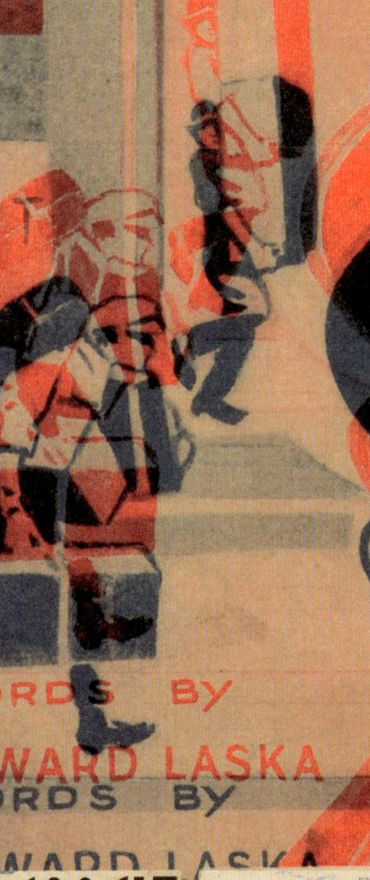
GOOGLE
Song by
BILLY ROSE
AND
CON CONRAD
BY PERMISSION OF DeBeck
CREATOR OF BARNEY GOOGLE
H. REMICK & CO.
Detroit

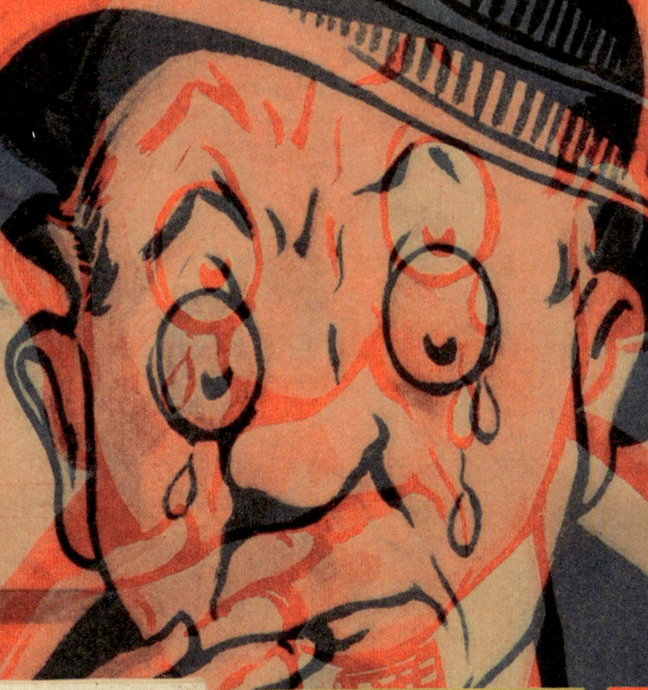
ANDY GUMP
NOVELTY SONG
FOX TROT
ALSO PUBLISHED
for
BAND
and
ORCHESTRA
WORDS AND MUSIC
BY
HAROLD DIXON
DENNI-LANG MUSIC PUB. CO.

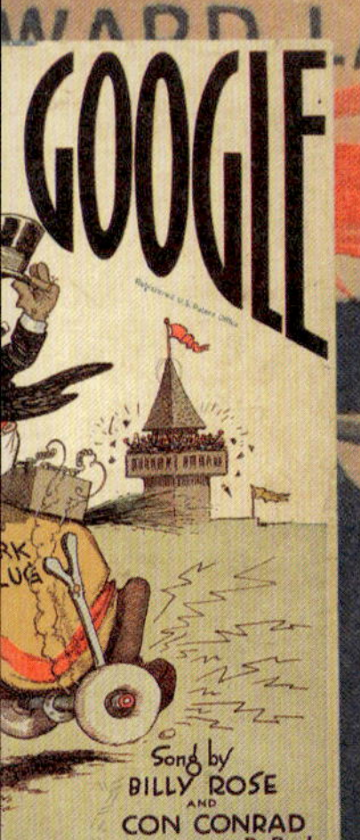

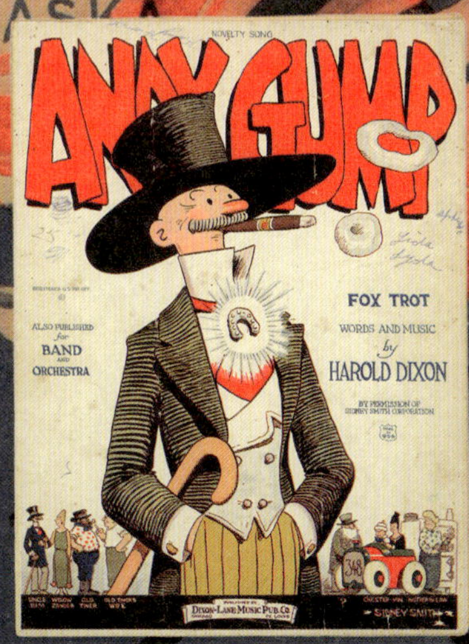

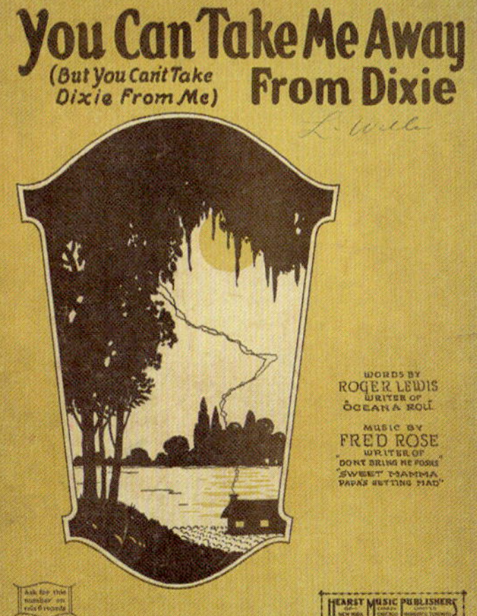
You Can Take Me Away
(But You Can't Take
Dixie From Me)
From Dixie
WORDS BY
ROGER LEWIS
WRITER OF
OCEAN A ROLL
MUSIC BY
FRED ROSE
WRITER OF
"DON'T BRING ME POSIES"
"SWEET MAMMA
PAPA'S GETTING MAD"
HEARST MUSIC PUBLISHERS

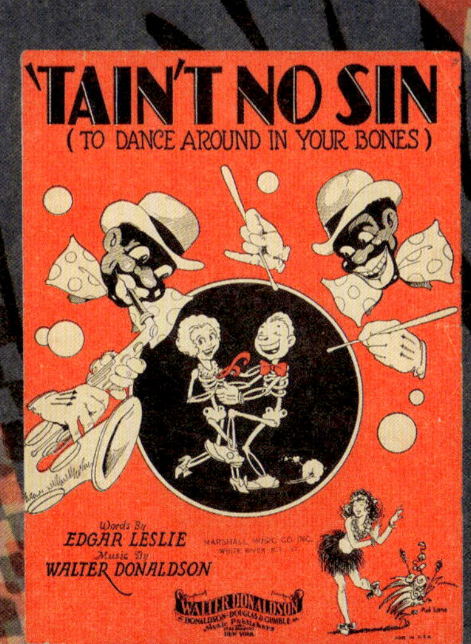
'TAIN'T NO SIN
(TO DANCE AROUND IN YOUR BONES)
WORDS BY
EDGAR LESLIE
MUSIC BY
WALTER DONALDSON

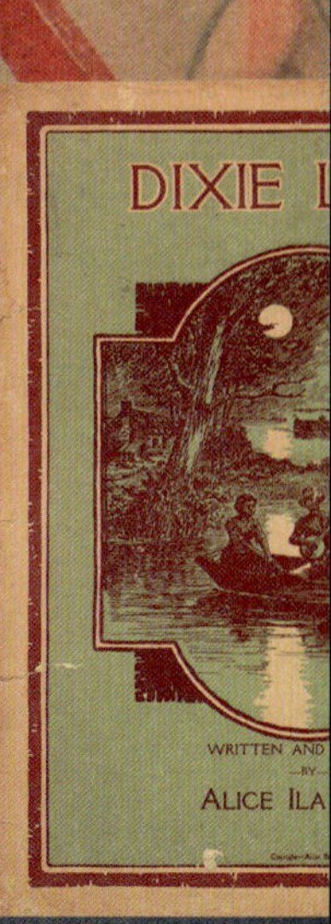
DIXIE
WRITTEN BY
ALICE ILA

Vernon Dalhart . . . . *The Chain Gang Song* (Robert E. Massey), Victor 19684, 78, 1925
Wreck of the '97 (Henry–Whitter), Bell 340, 78, 1925
Prisoner's Song (Massay), Bell 340, 78, 1925
Mother's Grave (Maggie Andrews), Perfect 12228, 78, 1925
Little Rosewood Casket (Maggie Andrews), Perfect 12228, 78, 1925
Arthur Fields . . . . *I Ate the Baloney* (Harry Lee), Supreme 2265, 78, 1926
Bessie Smith . . . . *Young Woman's Blues*, Columbia 35673, 78, 1926
Charlie Poole . . . . *Monkey On a String*, Columbia 15099, 78, 1926
White House Blues, Columbia 15099, 78, 1926
Dixie Jubilee Quintet . . . . *Good News*, Brunswick 3150, 78, 1926
Climbin' Up the Mountain, Children, Brunswick 3150, 78, 1926
Gid Tanner . . . . *Dance All Night with a Bottle in Your Hand*, Columbia 15108, 78, 1926
Hand Me Down My Walking Cane, Columbia 15091, 78, 1926
Watermelon On the Vine, Columbia 15091, 78, 1926
Gid Tanner and Faith Norris . . . . *S-A-V-E-D*, Columbia 15097, 78, 1926
Honey Duke . . . . *Hard Boiled Mama* (Nelson), Supreme 2265, 78, 1926
Kelly Harrell . . . . *Rovin' Gambler*, Montgomery Ward M-4367, 78, 1926
Louis Armstrong . . . . *Come Back Sweet Papa* (Barbarin–Russell), Hot Jazz Club of America 21, 78, 1926
Georgia Grind (Williams), Hot Jazz Club of America 21, 78, 1926
Masters' Hawaiians . . . *I Like Mountain Music* (James Cavanaugh–Frank Weldon), Montgomery Ward M-4367, 78, 1926
Rev. J. M. Gates . . . . *Death Might Be Your Santa Claus*, Okeh 8413, 78, 1926
Paul and Silas in Jail, Okeh 8413, 78, 1926
Death's Black Train Is Coming, Columbia 14145, 78, 1926
Need of Prayer, Columbia 14145, 78, 1926
I'm Going to Heaven If It Takes My Life, Herwin 92004, 78, 1926
I'm So Glad Trouble Don't Last Always, Herwin 92004, 78, 1926
Riley Puckett . . . . *You'd Be Surprised* (Irving Berlin), Columbia 15063, 78, 1926
I'll Never Get Drunk Any More, Columbia 15063, 78, 1926
Smith's Sacred Singers . . . . *Pictures From Life's Other Side* (Vaughn), Columbia 15090, 78, 1926
Texas Pan Handlers . . . . *Better Get Out of My Way* (Carson Robison), Perfect 14615, 78, 1926
The Death of Floyd Collins (P. C. Brockman), Perfect 14615, 78, 1926
Carter Family . . . . *The Poor Orphan Child* (A. P. Carter), Victor 20877, 78, 1927
The Wandering Boy (A. P. Carter), Victor 20877, 78, 1927
Little Log Cabin By the Sea (A. P. Carter), Victor 21074, 78, 1927
Bury Me Under the Weeping Willow (A. P. Carter), Victor 21074, 78, 1927
Deal Family . . . . *I'm a Rolling*, Columbia 15147, 78, 1927
Everybody Will Be Happy Over There, Columbia 15147, 78, 1927
Ernest Stoneman . . . . *Till the Snow Flakes Fall Again*, Victor 20799, 78, 1927
The Old Hickory Cane (Carper–Stoneman), Victor 20799, 78, 1927
Frank and James McCravy . . . . *Will the Circle Be Unbroken* (Gabriel), Brunswick 3779, 78, 1927
When They Ring the Golden Bells (de Marbelle), Brunswick 3779, 78, 1927
I Want to Go There (Sullins), Brunswick 192, 78, 1927
Jacob's Ladder (Arranged by Tillman), Brunswick 192, 78, 1927
Frank Crumit . . . . *Kingdom Coming (and the Year of Jubilo)* (Henry C. Work), Victor 21108, 78, 1927
Bohunkus, Victor 21108, 78, 1927
Jimmie Rodgers . . . . *Treasures Untold* (J. Rodgers–E. T. Cozzens), Victor 21433, 78, 1927
Mother Was a Lady (If Brother Jack Were Here) (Edward B. Marks–Joseph W. Stern), Victor 21433, 78, 1927
King Oliver . . . . *Black Snake Blues*, Vocalion 1112, 78, 1927
Willie, the Weeper, Vocalion 1112, 78, 1927
Lester McFarland and Robert A. Gardner . . . . *Rock of Ages* (Toplady–Hastings), Brunswick 3781, 78, 1927
The Old Rugged Cross (Bennard), Brunswick 3781, 78, 1927
Ma Rainey . . . . *Jelly Bean Blues* (Ma Rainey–Lena Arant), Paramount 12238, 78, 1927
Countin' the Blues, Paramount 12238, 78, 1927
Meade "Lux" Lewis . . . . *Honky Tonk Train Blues*, Bluebird 10175, 78, 1927
Whistlin' Blues, Bluebird 10175, 78, 1927
Scottdale String Band . . . . *Carbolic Rag*, Okeh 45118, 78, 1927
Smith's Sacred Singers . . . . *Life's a Railway to Heaven*, Columbia 15159, 78, 1927
Jesus Prayed, Columbia 15159, 78, 1927
Uncle Dave Macon . . . . *I'se Gwine Back to Dixie*, Vocalion 5157, 78, 1927
Take Me Home Poor Julia, Vocalion 5157, 78, 1927
Vernon Dalhart . . . . *Casey Jones* (Seibert–Newton), Victor 20502, 78, 1927
When the Work's All Done This Fall, Conqueror 7737, 78, 1927
Vernon Dalhart and Carson Robison . . . . *Golden Slippers*, Romeo 464, 78, 1927

Opposite: Sheet music 1907-1936.

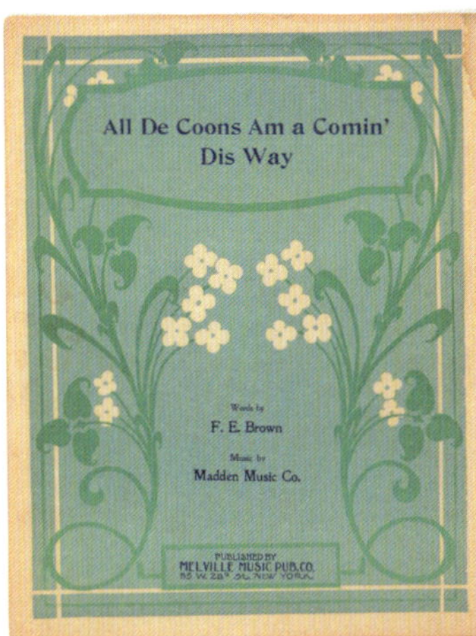
All De Coons Am a Comin'
Dis Way
Words by
F. E. Brown
Music by
Madden Music Co.
PUBLISHED BY
MELVILLE MUSIC PUB. CO.
NEW YORK

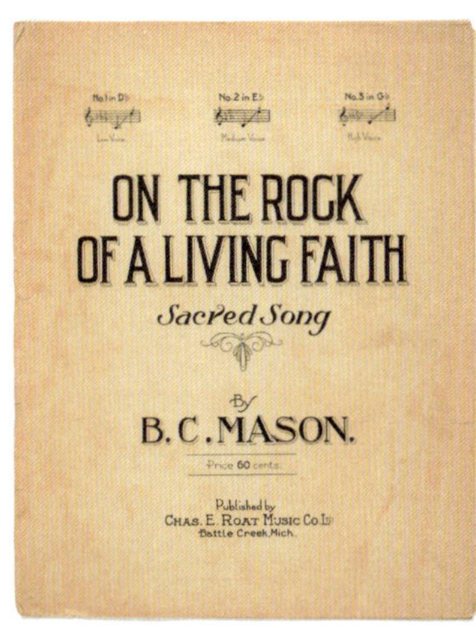
No 1 in D
No 2 in E♭
No 3 in G
ON THE ROCK
OF A LIVING FAITH
Sacred Song
By
B. C. MASON.
Price 50 cents.
Published by
CHAS. E. ROAT MUSIC CO.
Battle Creek, Mich.

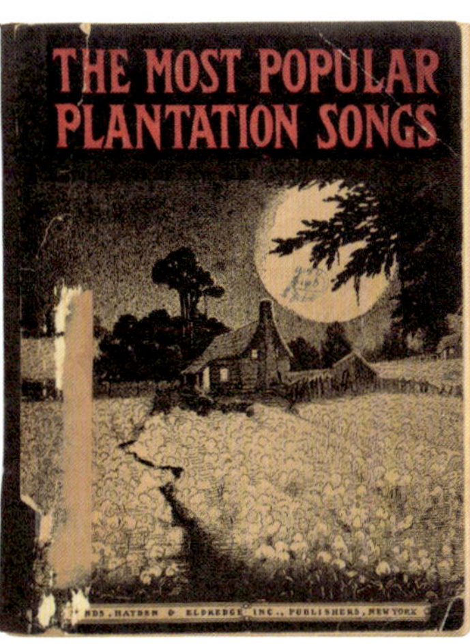
THE MOST POPULAR
PLANTATION SONGS
BROS. HATHON & KLPAEDGE, INC., PUBLISHERS, NEW YORK

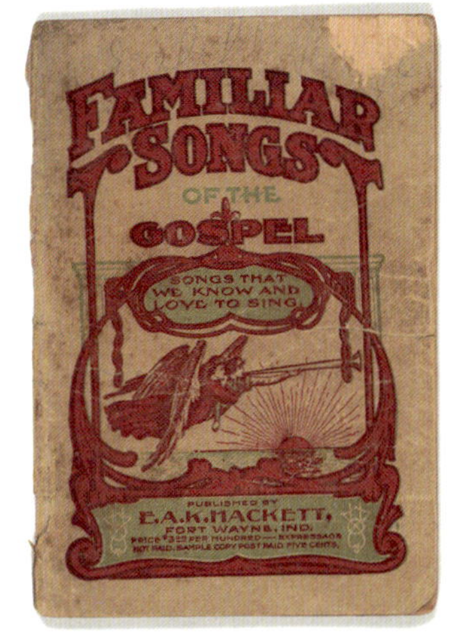
FAMILIAR
SONGS
OF THE
GOSPEL
SONGS THAT
WE KNOW AND
LOVE TO SING
PUBLISHED BY
E. A. K. HACKETT,
FORT WAYNE, IND.

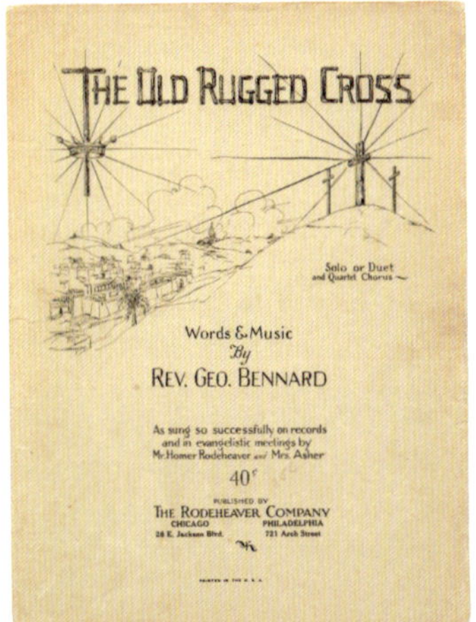
THE OLD RUGGED CROSS
Solo or Duet
and Quartet Chorus
Words & Music
By
REV. GEO. BENNARD
As sung so successfully on records
and in evangelistic meetings by
Mr Homer Rodeheaver and Mrs Asher
40¢
PUBLISHED BY
THE RODEHEAVER COMPANY
CHICAGO   PHILADELPHIA

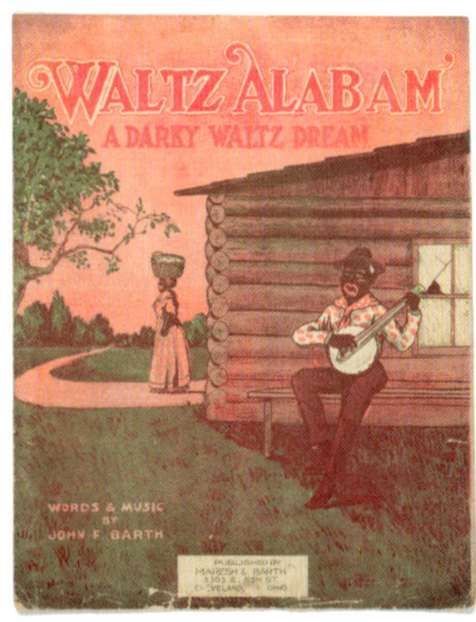
WALTZ ALABAM'
A DARKY WALTZ DREAM
WORDS & MUSIC
BY
JOHN F. GARTH
PUBLISHED BY
HANESH L. SMITH
CLEVELAND, OHIO

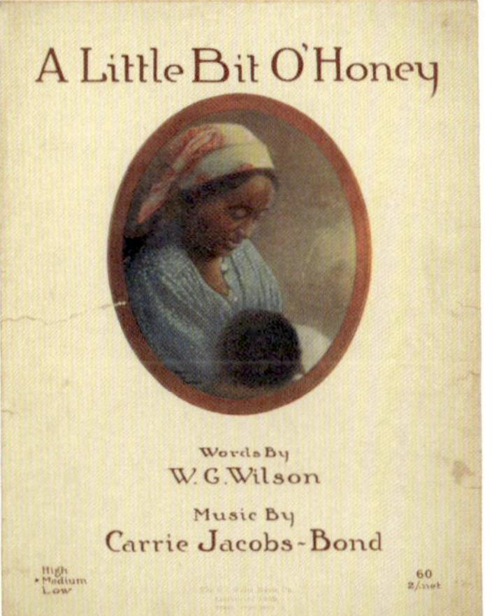
A Little Bit O'Honey
Words By
W. G. Wilson
Music By
Carrie Jacobs-Bond
High
Medium
Low
60
2/net

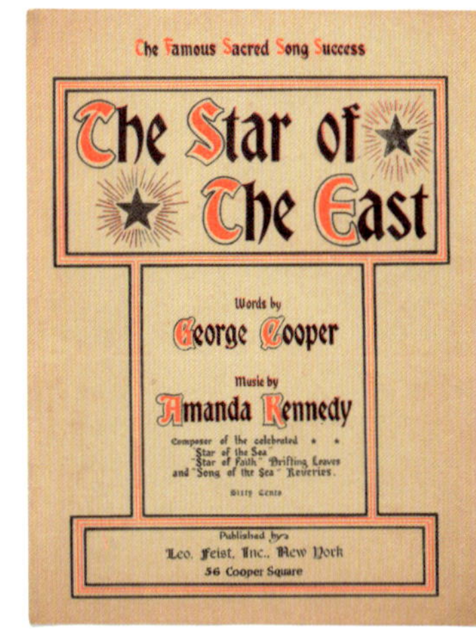
The Famous Sacred Song Success
The Star of
The East
Words by
George Cooper
Music by
Amanda Kennedy
Composer of the celebrated
"Star of the Sea"
"Star of Faith" "Drifting Leaves"
and "Song of the Sea" Reveries.
Sixty Cents
Published by
Leo. Feist, Inc., New York
56 Cooper Square

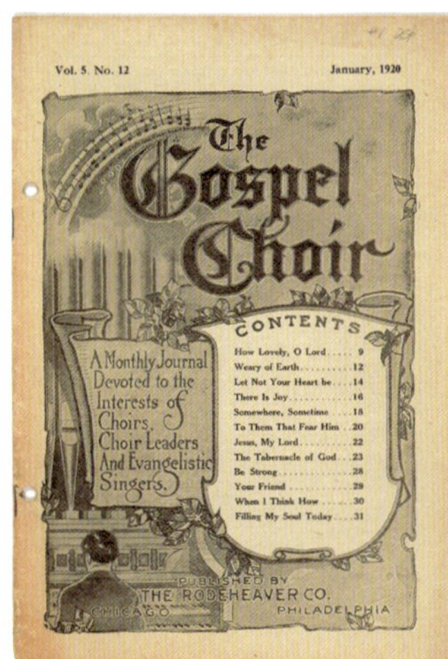
Vol. 5. No. 12   January, 1920
The
Gospel
Choir
A Monthly Journal
Devoted to the
Interests of
Choirs,
Choir Leaders
And Evangelistic
Singers.
CONTENTS
How Lovely, O Lord 9
Weary of Earth 12
Let Not Your Heart be 14
There Is Joy 16
Somewhere, Sometime 18
To Them That Fear Him 20
Jesus, My Lord 22
The Tabernacle of God 23
Be Strong 28
Your Friend 29
When I Think How 30
Filling My Soul Today 31
COPYRIGHTED BY
THE RODEHEAVER CO.
CHICAGO   PHILADELPHIA

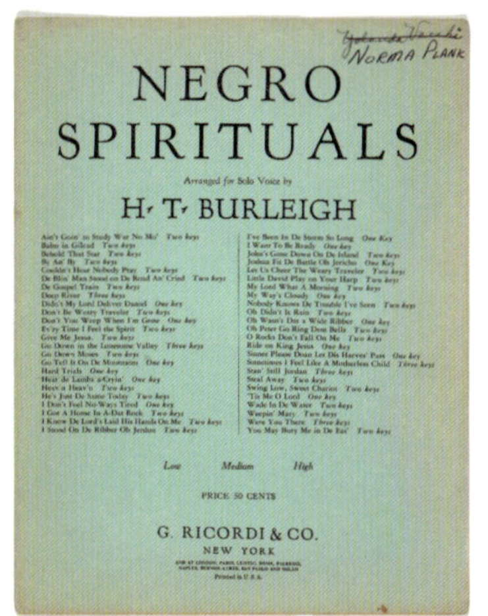
NORMA PLANK
NEGRO
SPIRITUALS
Arranged for Solo Voice by
H. T. BURLEIGH
Low   Medium   High
PRICE 50 CENTS
G. RICORDI & CO.
NEW YORK
Printed in U. S. A.

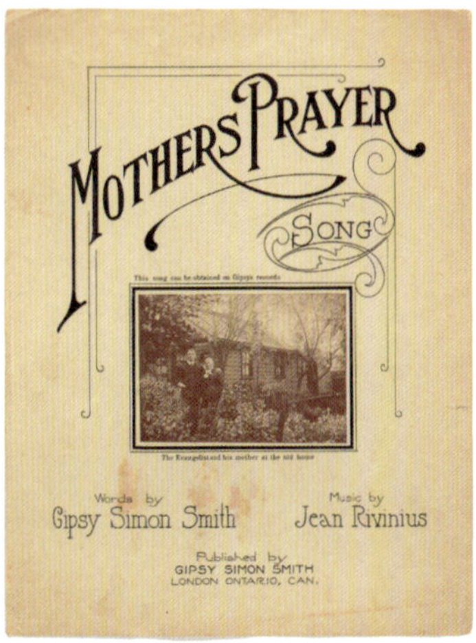
MOTHERS PRAYER
SONG
This song can be obtained on Edison records
Words by
Gipsy Simon Smith
Music by
Jean Rivinius
Published by
GIPSY SIMON SMITH
LONDON ONTARIO, CAN.

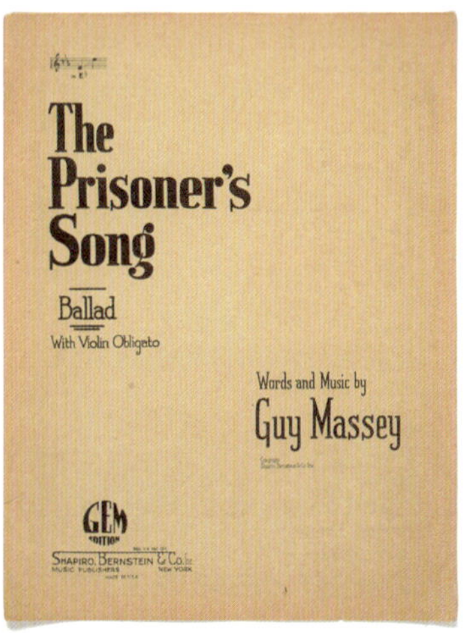
The
Prisoner's
Song
Ballad
With Violin Obligato
Words and Music by
Guy Massey
GEM
SHAPIRO, BERNSTEIN & CO.
MUSIC PUBLISHERS
NEW YORK

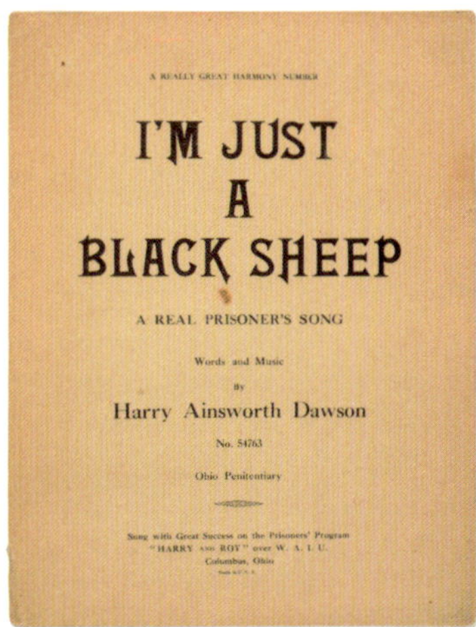
A REALLY GREAT HARMONY NUMBER
I'M JUST
A
BLACK SHEEP
A REAL PRISONER'S SONG
Words and Music
By
Harry Ainsworth Dawson
No. 84763
Ohio Penitentiary
Sung with Great Success on the Prisoners' Program
"HARRY and ROY" over W.A.I.U.
Columbus, Ohio

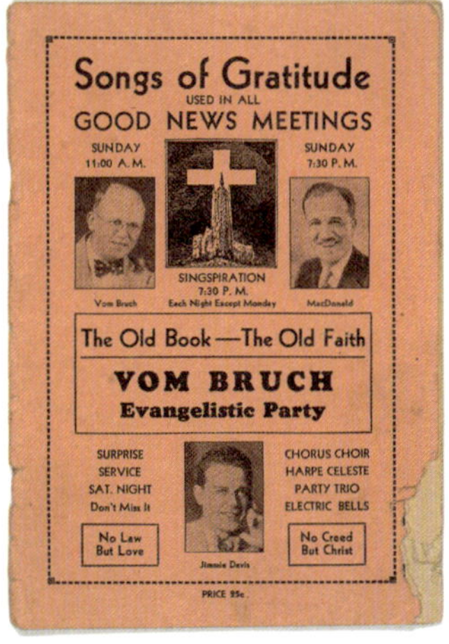
Songs of Gratitude
USED IN ALL
GOOD NEWS MEETINGS
SUNDAY
11.00 A. M.
SUNDAY
7.30 P. M.
SINGSPIRATION
7.30 P. M.
Each Night Except Monday
Vom Bruch   MacDonald
The Old Book — The Old Faith
VOM BRUCH
Evangelistic Party
SURPRISE
SERVICE
SAT. NIGHT
Don't Miss It
CHORUS CHOIR
HARPE CELESTE
PARTY TRIO
ELECTRIC BELLS
Jimmie Davis
No Law
But Love
No Creed
But Christ
PRICE 25c

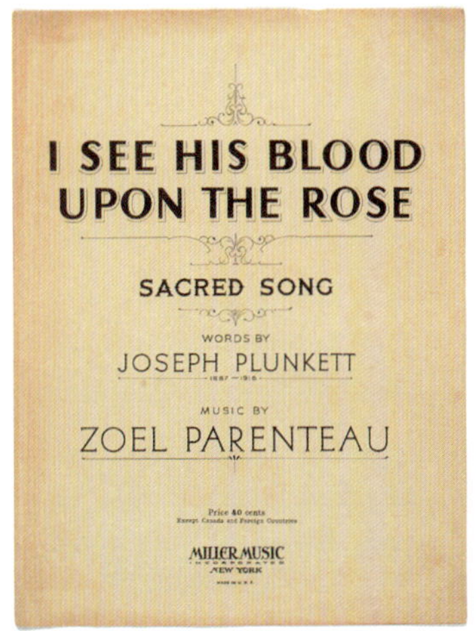
I SEE HIS BLOOD
UPON THE ROSE
SACRED SONG
WORDS BY
JOSEPH PLUNKETT
1887-1916
MUSIC BY
ZOEL PARENTEAU
Price 60 cents
Except Canada and Foreign Countries
MILLER MUSIC

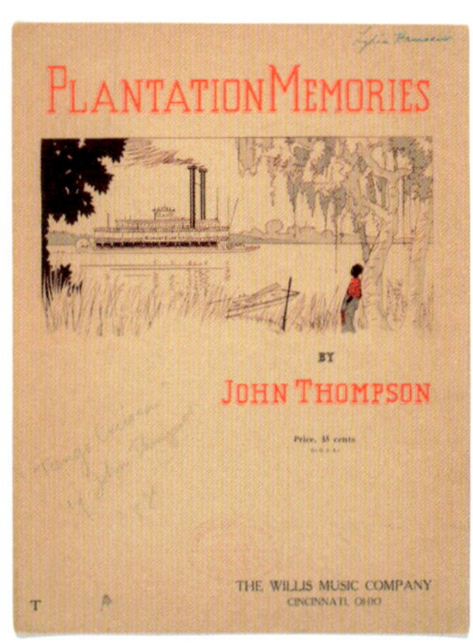
PLANTATION MEMORIES
BY
JOHN THOMPSON
Price. 15 cents.
THE WILLIS MUSIC COMPANY
CINCINNATI, OHIO

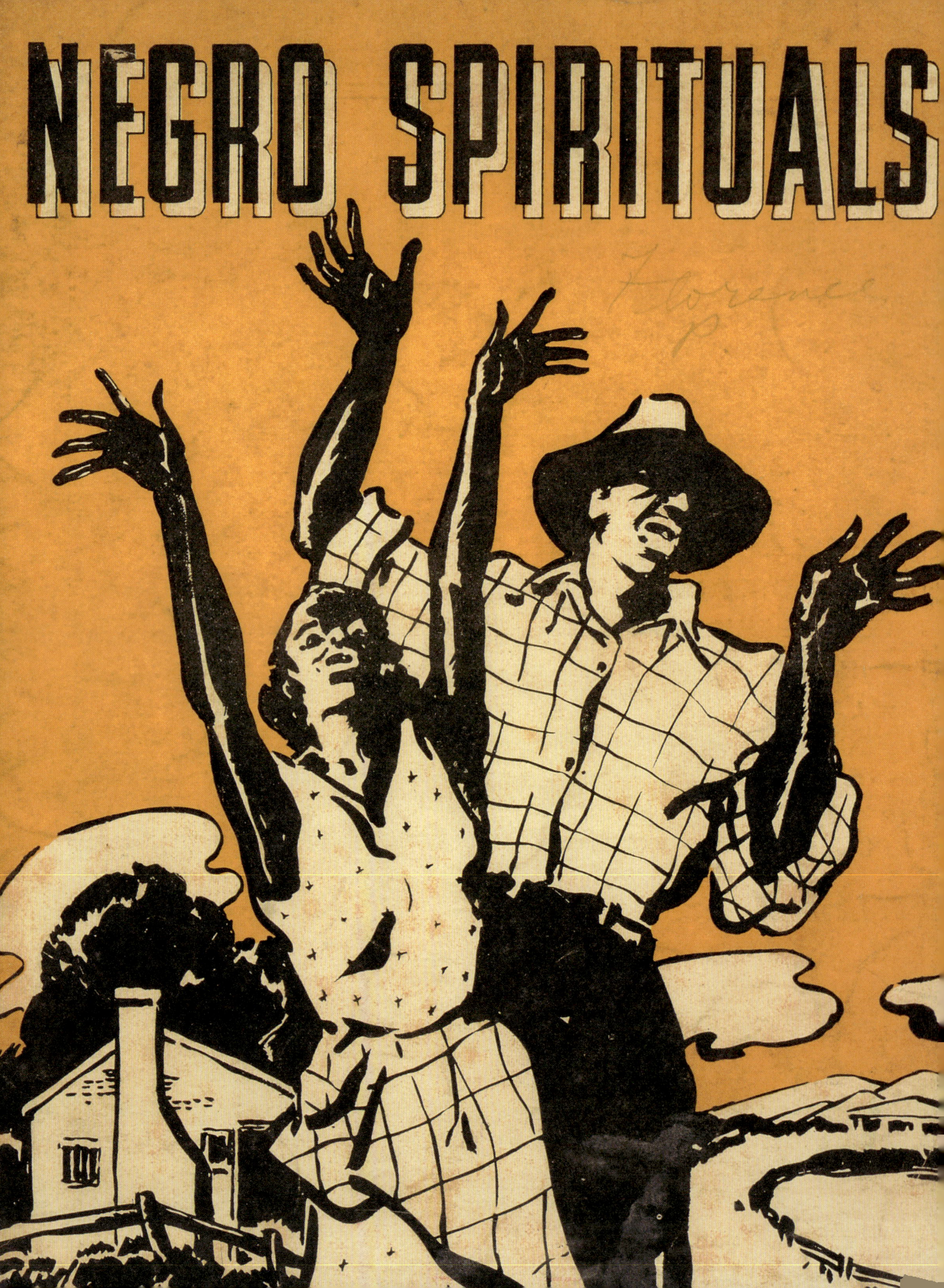

NEGRO SPIRITUALS

Vernon Dalhart and Carson Robison . . . . *My Blue Ridge Mountain Home* (Carson Robison), Romeo 464, 78, 1927
Bessie Smith . . . . *Empty Bed Blues—Part 1* (J. C. Johnson), Columbia 35675, 78, 1928
Empty Bed Blues—Part 2 (J. C. Johnson), Columbia 35675, 78, 1928
Carter Family. . . . . *Anchored in Love* (A. P. Carter), Victor 40036, 78, 1928
I Have No One to Love Me (But the Sailor on the Deep Blue Sea) (A. P. Carter), Victor 40036, 78, 1928
"Doc" Roberts . . . .*She'll Be Comin' 'Round the Mountain*, Montgomery Ward 4990, 78, 1928
Ernest Stoneman. . . . .*In the Shadow of the Pine*, Perfect 12459, 78, 1928
Frank Luther. . . . . *The Bowery Bums* (Samberg), Conqueror 7227, 78, 1928
That Big Rock-Candy Mountain, Conqueror 7227, 78, 1928
Jesse James (Semple), Radiex , 78, 1928
Frankie Wallace . . . . *Way Out on the Mountain* (Rodgers), Conqueror 7163, 78, 1928
Blue Yodel No. 1 (Rodgers), Conqueror 7163, 78, 1928
Jimmie Rodgers. . . . .*Blue Yodel No. II (My Lovin' Gal, Lucille)*, Victor 21291, 78, 1928
The Brakeman's Blues (Yodeling the Blues Away), Victor 21291, 78, 1928
Lonnie Johnson. . . . . *Careless Love*, Okeh 8635, 78, 1928
When You Fall for Some One That's Not Your Own, Okeh 8635, 78, 1928
"MAC" Harry McClintock . . . . *The Bum Song—No. 2*, Victor 21704, 78, 1928
The Big Rock Candy Mountains, Victor 21704, 78, 1928
Hallelujah! I'm a Bum, Victor 21343, 78, 1928
The Bum Song, Victor 21343, 78, 1928
Moran and Mack . . . .*Two Black Crows—Part 1* (Mack), Columbia 935, 78, 1928
Two Black Crows—Part 2 (Mack), Columbia 935, 78, 1928
Rev. J. M. Gates. . . . .*Somebody's Been Stealing*, Bluebird 7936, 78, 1928
Kidnapping, Bluebird 7936, 78, 1928
Texas Alexander (listed as King Oliver). . . . . *Frisco Train Blues*, Temple 526, 78, 1928
Work Ox Blues, Temple 526, 78, 1928
Vernon Dalhart . . . .*The Wreck of the Royal Palm* (Rev. Andrew Jenkins), Perfect 12459, 78, 1928
Bud Billings–Carson Robison. . . . . *Open Up Dem Pearly Gates for Me* (Carson Robison), Victor 40115, 78, 1929
Bush Brothers. . . . .*Endless Glory to the Lamb*, Columbia 15500, 78, 1929
My Happiest Day, Columbia 15500, 78, 1929
Carson Robison and Frank Luther . . . *Left My Gal in the Mountains* (Carson Robison), Montgomery Ward 4990, 78, 1929
Clarence Williams . . . . *Zonky* (Waller–Razaf), Columbia 14488, 78, 1929
You've Got to Be Modernistic (Johnson), Columbia 14488, 78, 1929
Dixie Rag Pickers. . . . . *St. Louis Blues* (Handy), Van Dyke 77023, 78, 1929
John Henry Blues (Handy), Van Dyke 77023, 78, 1929
"Lazy" Larry. . . . .*Barnacle Bill, the Sailor* (Luther–Robison), Romeo 864, 78, 1929
The Bum's Rush (Benjamin Samborg), Romeo 864, 78, 1929
Leake County Revelers. . . . . *Molly Put the Kettle On*, Columbia 15380, 78, 1929
Bring Me a Bottle, Columbia 15380, 78, 1929
Louis Armstrong . . . .*Sweet Savannah Sue* (Razaf–Waller–Brooks), Okeh 41281, 78, 1929
That Rhythm Man (Razaf–Waller–Brooks), Okeh 41281, 78, 1929
Marlow and Young. . . . . *Six Months Ain't Long* (Rutherford–Foster), Champion 15750, 78, 1929
Pie Plant Pete. . . . .*When the Work's All Done This Fall*, Montgomery Ward 4987, 45, 1929
Hand Me Down My Walking Cane, Montgomery Ward 4987, 78, 1929
Rev. J. M. Gates. . . . . *You Midnight Ramblers*, Okeh 8684, 78, 1929
Dead Cat on the Line, Okeh 8684, 78, 1929
Vernon Dalhart . . . . *Flood Song* (Andrew Jenkins), Victor 40075, 78, 1929
Amos Greene . . . .*Blue Yodel No. 6*, Supertone 9710, 78, 1930
Desert Blues, Supertone 9710, 78, 1930
Bud Billings. . . . .*The Prison Fire* (Carson Robison), Victor 40251, 78, 1930
The Old Parlor Organ (Frank Luther–Carson Robison), Victor 40251, 78, 1930
Carson Robison Trio . . . .*Oklahoma Charley*, Conqueror 7734, 78, 1930
Hokum Trio. . . . . *You've Had Your Way* (Robinson), Velvet Tone 7081, 78, 1930
You're Bound to Look Like a Monkey When You Get Old (Hill–Williams), Velvet Tone 7081, 78, 1930
Jimmie Rodgers. . . . .*Pistol Packin' Papa* (Jimmie Rodgers–Waldo O'Neal), Victor 22554, 78, 1930
Those Gambler's Blues (arranged by Jimmie Rodgers), Victor 22554, 78, 1930
Louisiana Rhythm Kings . . . . *Sweet Sue—Just You* (Harris–Young), Brunswick 4953, 78, 1930
Squeeze Me (Williams–Waller), Brunswick 4953, 78, 1930
Pie Plant Pete. . . . . *The Lightning Express*, Supertone 9701, 78, 1930
You'll Find Her with the Angels, Supertone 9701, 78, 1930
Asa Martin. . . . . *The Contented Hobo*, Oriole 8064, 78, 1931
The Wandering Hobo, Oriole 8064, 78, 1931
Claude Davis Trio . . . .*I Don't Want Your Gold or Silver*, Columbia 15740, 78, 1931

Negro Spirituals, 1937.

Claude Davis Trio . . . . *Standing by the Highway*, Columbia 15740, 78, 1931
Frank Welling & John McGhee. . . . .*My Little Mountain Home*, Oriole 8108, 78, 1931
                            The Crime at Quiet Dell (A. H. Grow–Leighten D. Davies), Oriole 8108, 78, 1931
Gene Autry . . . .*True Blue Bill*, Perfect 12695, 78, 1931
                            A Gangster's Warning, Perfect 12695, 78, 1931
Kid Williams . . . .*May I Sleep in Your Barn Tonight, Mister?*, Perfect 160, 78, 1931
Kid Williams & Roy Martin. . . . . *Birmingham Jail*, Perfect 160, 78, 1931
Lester McFarland and Robert A. Gardner . . . . *Don't Lay Me On My Back* (In My Last Sleep) (Arnold–Van Alstyne),
                                                    Brunswick 541, 78, 1931
                      When It's Nightime in Nevada (Clint), Brunswick 541, 78, 1931
The Pickard Family . . . .*Thompson's Old Grey Mule*, Conqueror 7736, 78, 1931
                           The Little Red Caboose, Conqueror 7736, 78, 1931
Ethel Waters . . . *I Can't Give You Anything But Love (Baby)* (Dorothy Fields–Jimmie McHugh), Brunswick 6517, 78, 1932
Frankie and Johnny . . . . *Red Wing* (Frank Welling–John McGhee), Conqueror 7976, 78, 1932
                   Beech Fork Special (Frank Welling–John McGhee), Conqueror 7976, 78, 1932
Mills Brothers, Cab Calloway . . *Doin' the New Low Down* (Dorothy Fields–Jimmie McHugh), Brunswick 6517, 78, 1932
Callahan Brothers . . . . *New Birmingham Jail No. 3*, Perfect 13045, 78, 1934
                    Little Poplar Log House on the Hill (Walter Callahan), Perfect 13045, 78, 1934
Joshua White . . . . *Lord I Want to Die Easy*, Conqueror 8455, 78, 1934
                 Can't Help But Crying Sometime (Clarence Williams), Conqueror 8455, 78, 1934

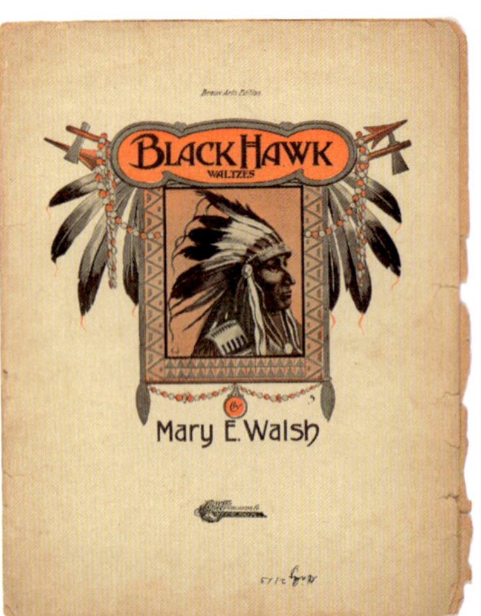

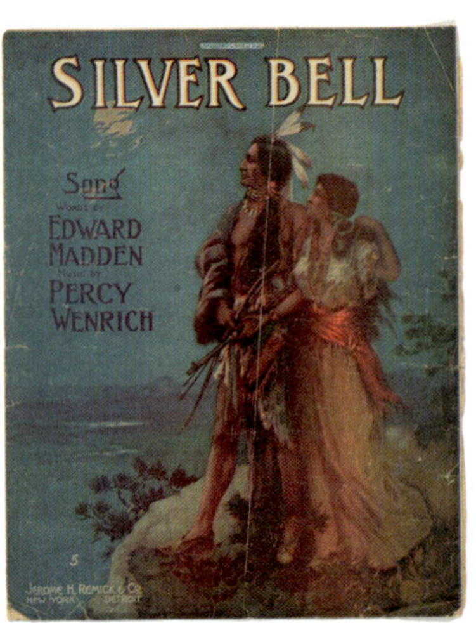

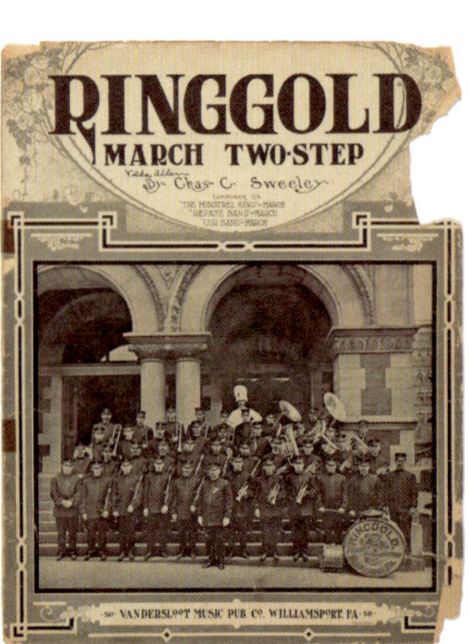

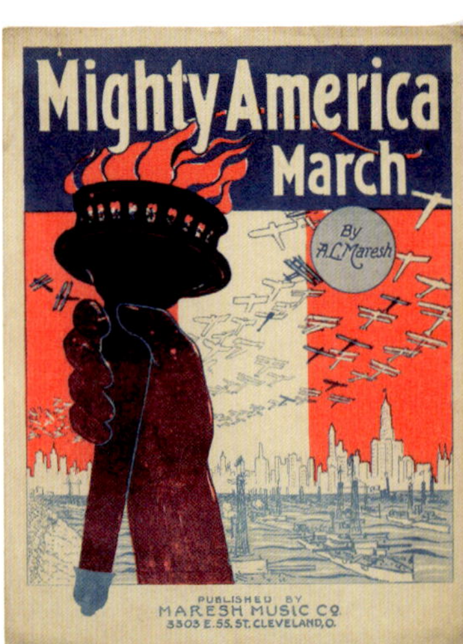

Joshua White . . . . *Leroy Carr and Scrapper Blackwell Mean Mistreater Mama*, Vocalion 02657, 78, 1934
                             Blues Before Sunrise (Carr), Vocalion 02657, 78, 1934
Ranch Boys . . . . *The Strawberry Roan* (Howard–Vincent–Fletcher), Decca 5074, 78, 1934
Bob Wills. . . . . *Good Old Oklahoma*, Vocalion 03086, 78, 1935
Delmore Brothers . . . . *Lorena, the Slave*, Bluebird 5925, 78, 1935
                        Blow Yo' Whistle, Freight Train, Bluebird 5925, 78, 1935
Patsy Montana. . . . . *Ridin' Old Paint*, Conqueror 8575, 78, 1935
                       I Wanna Be a Cowboy's Sweetheart, Conqueror 8575, 78, 1935
Shelton Brothers . . . . *When It's Night Time in Nevada* (Dulmage–O'Reilly–Clint–Pascoe), Decca 5219, 78, 1935
              The Black Sheep (Dulmage–O'Reilly–Clint–Pascoe), Decca 5219, 78, 1935
Uncle Ezra. . . . . *At the Old Maid's Ball* (Irving Berlin), Conqueror 8615, 78, 1935
             They Go Wild Simply Wild Over Me (McCarthy–Fisher), Conqueror 8615, 78, 1935
W. Lee O'Daniel . . . .*San Antonio* (Williams–Van Alstyne), Vocalion 03248, 78, 1935
Anonymous . . . . *The Laughing Record*—No. 1, Okeh 4-6925, 45, orig. 1936
Bob Atcher. *I'm Thinking Tonight of My Blue Eyes* (A. P. Carter), Okeh 4-6925, 45, 1936
Chuck Wagon Gang . . . . *Will You Meet Me Over Yonder?* (Winsett), Columbia 20180, 78, 1936
                          A Beautiful Life (Golden), Columbia 20180, 78, 1936
Doc Hopkins . . . . *The Great Judgment Morning*, Conqueror 8749, 78, 1936
                            The Church of Long Ago, Conqueror 8749, 78, 1936
Georgia White . . . . *I Just Want Your Stingaree*, Decca 48006, 78, 1936

Above: Sheet music 1907-1917

Georgia White . . . . *Alley Boogie* (Bogan), Decca 48006, 78, 1936
Jimmie Davis. . . . . *The Answer to Nobody's Darling But Mine*, Decca 5203, 78, 1936
When a Boy from the Mountains (Weds a Girl from the Valley) (Fred Rose), Decca 5203, 78, 1936
Jimmie Strothers. *We Are Almost Down to the Shore*, Library of Congress AAFS46, 78, 1936
Karl Davis . . . . *I'm S-A-V-E-D*, Conqueror 8660, 78, 1936
Leon's Lone Star Cowboys . . . . *31st Street Blues*, Decca 5280, 78, 1936
China Boy (Dick Winfree–Phil Boutelje), Decca 5280, 78, 1936
Milton Brown. . . . . *Yes Sir!*, Decca 5260, 78, 1936
The Old Gray Mare, Decca 5260, 78, 1936
Billie Holiday . . . . *Born to Love* (Scholl–Jerome), Vocalion 3605, 78, 1937
Georgia White . . . . *Strewin' Your Mess* (Crump–Jones), Decca 7419, 78, 1937
Careless Love (Crump–Jones), Decca 7419, 78, 1937
Light Crust Doughboys . . . . *Just Once Too Often* (Young–Tobias–Stept), Vocalion 03926, 78, 1937
Gig-A-Wig Blues (Marvin Montgomery), Vocalion 03926, 78, 1937
Uncle Dave Macon . . . . *Honest Confession Is Good for the Soul*, Bluebird 7174, 78, 1937
From Jerusalem to Jericho, Bluebird 7174, 78, 1937
Bessie Smith . . . . *Back-Water Blues*, Columbia 3176, 78, 1938
Nobody Knows You When You're Down and Out, Columbia 3176, 78, 1938
Blind Boy Fuller. . . . . *Painful Hearted Man*, Vocalion 04175, 78, 1938
Screaming and Crying Blues, Columbia 37155, 78, 1938

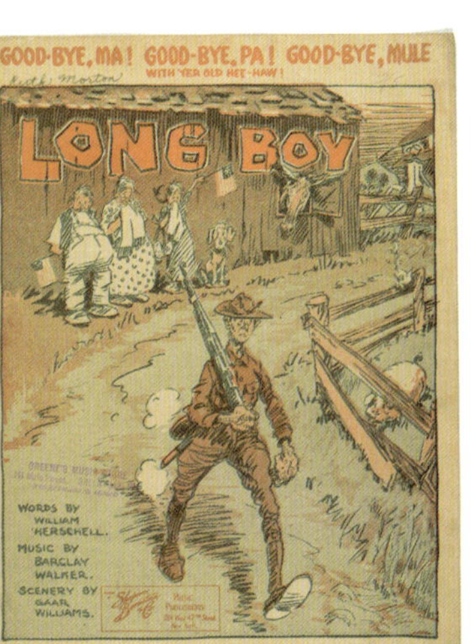

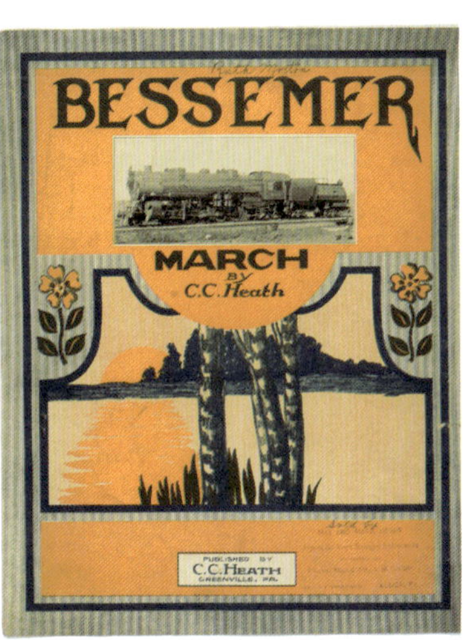

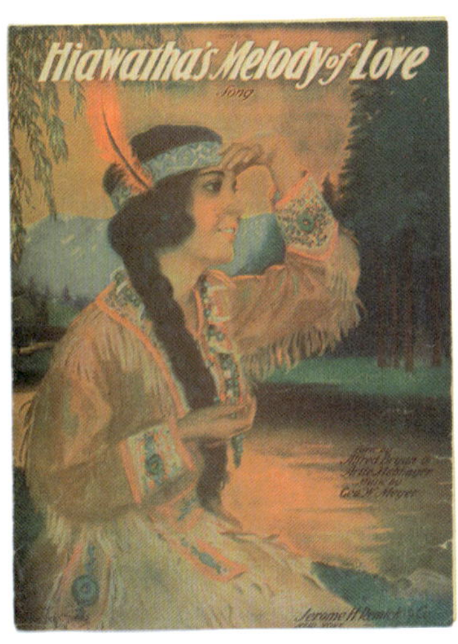

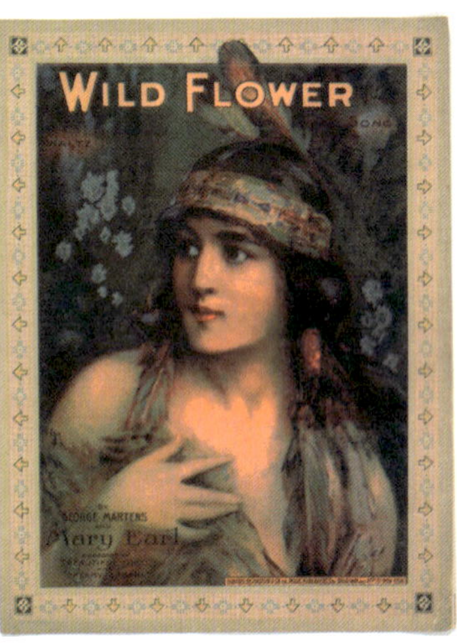

Blind Boy Fuller . . . . *She's a Truckin' Little Baby*, Columbia 37155, 78, 1938
Bob Wills. . . . . *The Convict and the Rose* (Chapin), Columbia 37009, 78, 1938
San Antonio Rose, Columbia 37009, 78, 1938
The Waltz You Saved for Me (Kahn–King–Flindt), Vocalion 04999, 78, 1938
Beaumont Rag, Vocalion 04999, 78, 1938
Rosetta (Hines–Woods), Vocalion 03659, 78, 1938
I'm a Ding Dong Daddy (from Dumas) (Phil Baxter), Vocalion 03659, 78, 1938
Count Basie's Blue Five . . . . *Boogie Woogie* (Pinetop Smith), Columbia 35959, 78, 1938
Frank Croxton . . . . *I Heard the Voice of Jesus Say* (J. W. Bischoff), Columbia 1305, 78, 1938
Joe Turner and Pete Johnson . . . . *Roll 'Em Pete* (Johnson), Columbia 35959, 78, 1938
Light Crust Doughboys . . . . *It Makes No Difference Now* (Tillman–Davis), Vocalion 04559, 78, 1938
Troubles, Vocalion 04559, 78, 1938
Wilf Carter (Montana Slim "The Yodeling Cowboy"). . *Answer to the Swiss Moonlight Lullaby* (Wilf Carter), Regal 3145, 78, 1938
Peerless Quartet . . . . *When the Roll Is Called Up Yonder* (James Black), Columbia 1305, 78, 1938
Roy Acuff. . . . . *Wabash Cannon Ball*, Okeh 04466, 78, 1938
Freight Train Blues, Okeh 04466, 78, 1938
Tampa Red . . . . *I Ain't Fur It* (Hudson Whittaker), Bluebird 34-0711, 78, 1938
You Gonna Miss Me When I'm Gone (Hudson Whittaker), Bluebird 34-0711, 78, 1938
Big Bill . . . . *Don't You Want to Ride* (Broonzy), Okeh 05360, 78, 1939
Dreamy Eyed Baby (Broonzy), Okeh 05360, 78, 1939

Above: Sheet music 1917-1920.

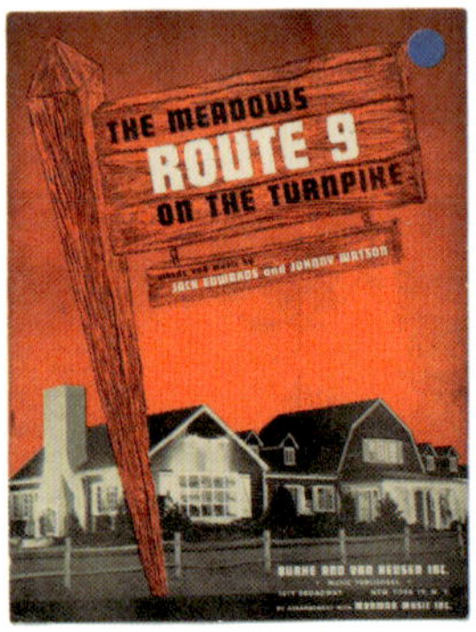
The Meadows
Route 9
on the Turnpike

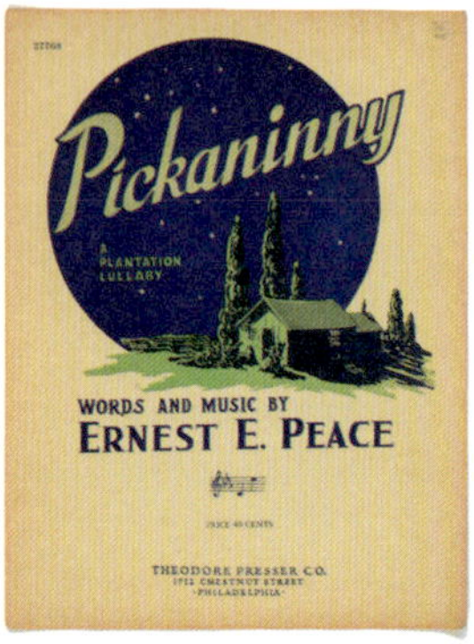
Pickaninny
A Plantation Lullaby
Words and Music by
Ernest E. Peace
Theodore Presser Co.

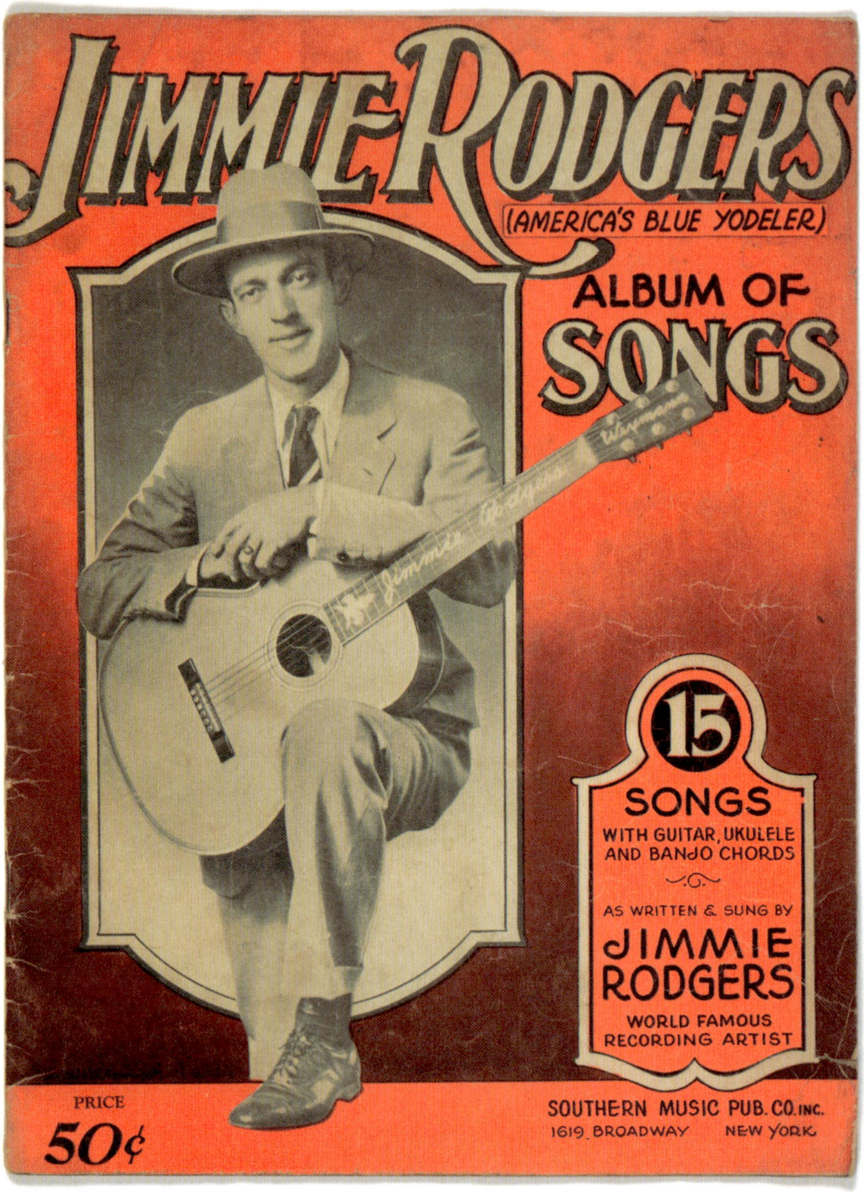
Jimmie Rodgers
(America's Blue Yodeler)
Album of
Songs
15
Songs
With Guitar, Ukulele
and Banjo Chords
As Written & Sung by
Jimmie
Rodgers
World Famous
Recording Artist
Price
50¢
Southern Music Pub. Co. Inc.
1619 Broadway New York

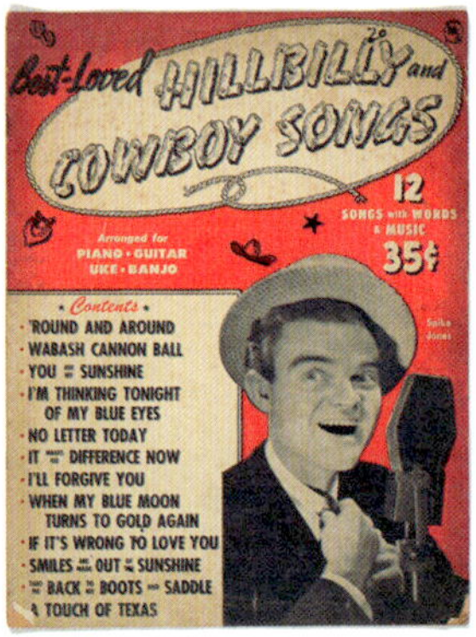
Best-Loved Hillbilly and
Cowboy Songs
12
Songs with Words & Music
35¢
Arranged for
Piano · Guitar
Uke · Banjo
Contents
'Round and Around
Wabash Cannon Ball
You Are My Sunshine
I'm Thinking Tonight
of My Blue Eyes
No Letter Today
It Makes No Difference Now
I'll Forgive You
When My Blue Moon
Turns to Gold Again
If It's Wrong to Love You
Smiles Are Out of Sunshine
Back in the Boots and Saddle
A Touch of Texas

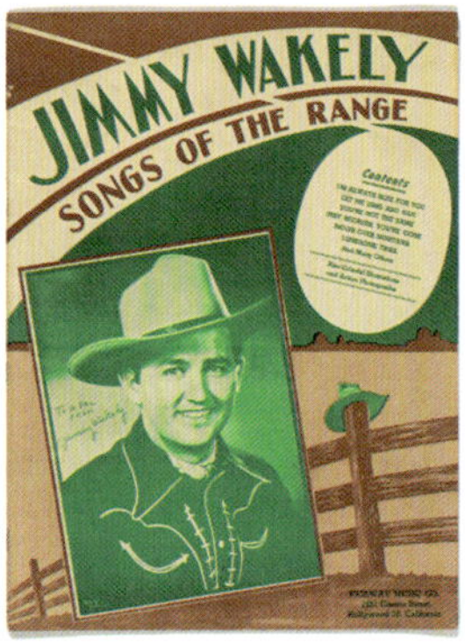
Jimmy Wakely
Songs of the Range

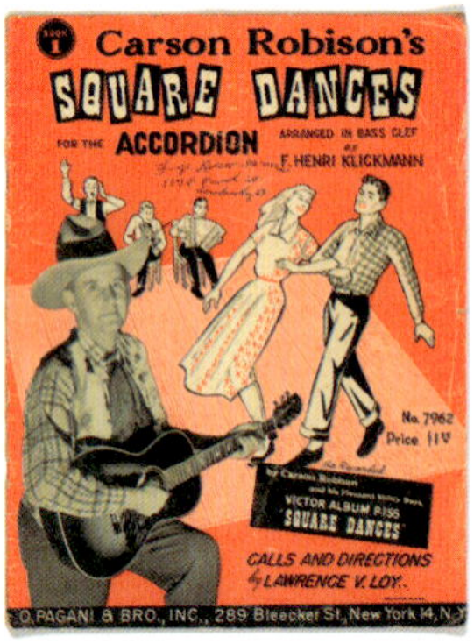
Carson Robison's
Square Dances
for the Accordion
Arranged in Bass Clef
by
F. Henri Klickmann
No. 2982
Victor Album P-155
Square Dances
Calls and Directions
by Lawrence V. Loy
O. Pagani & Bro., Inc., 289 Bleecker St., New York 14, N.Y.

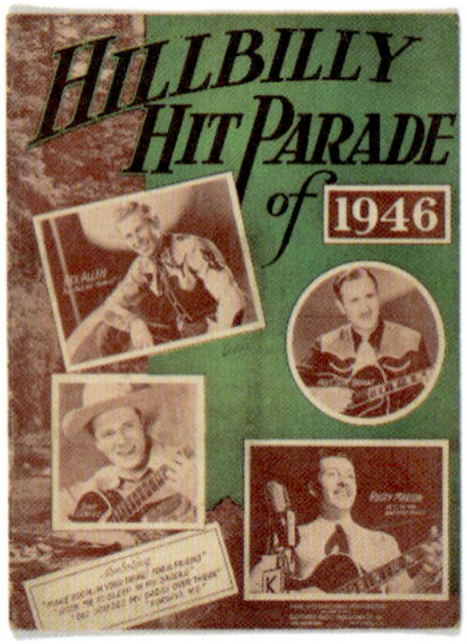
Hillbilly
Hit Parade
of 1946

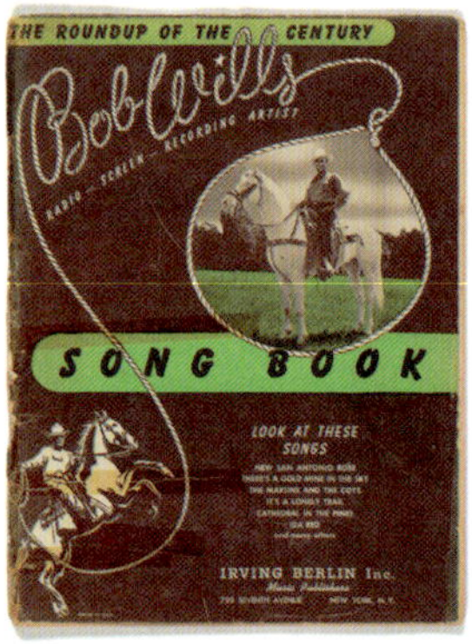
The Roundup of the Century
Bob Wills
Song Book
Look at these songs
Irving Berlin Inc.

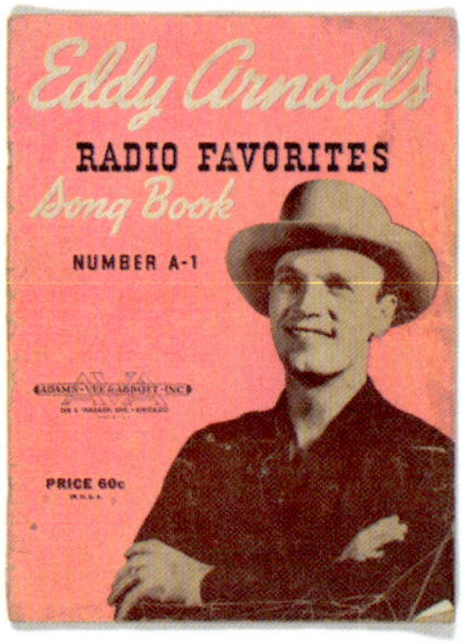
Eddy Arnold's
Radio Favorites
Song Book
Number A-1
Price 60c

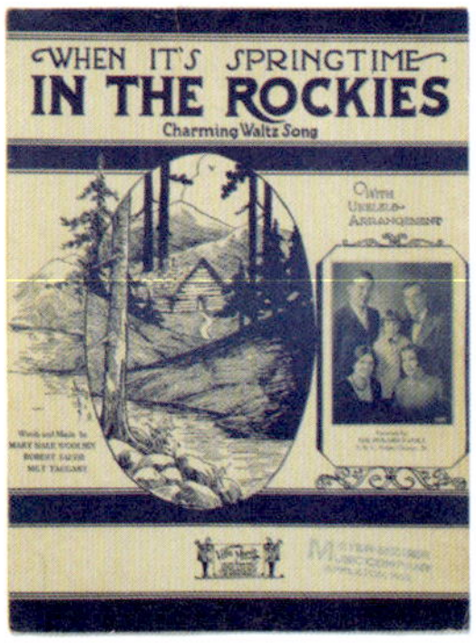
When It's Springtime
In the Rockies
Charming Waltz Song

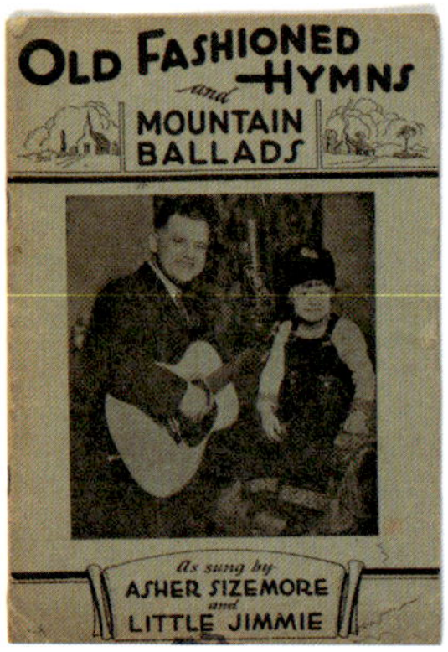
Old Fashioned
and
Hymns
Mountain
Ballads
As sung by
Asher Sizemore
and
Little Jimmie

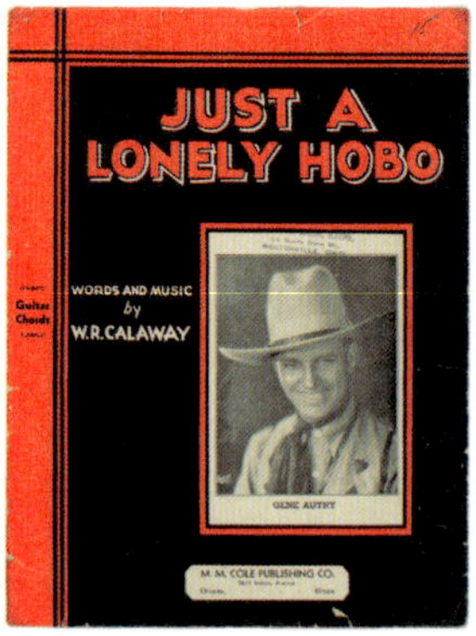
Just a
Lonely Hobo
Words and Music
by
W.R. Calaway
M. M. Cole Publishing Co.

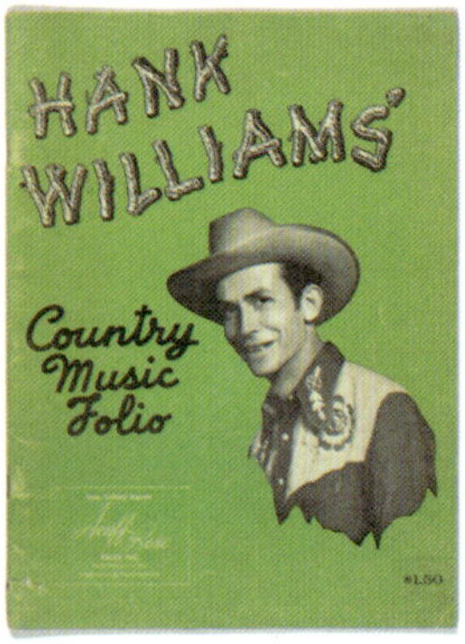
Hank
Williams'
Country
Music
Folio
$1.50

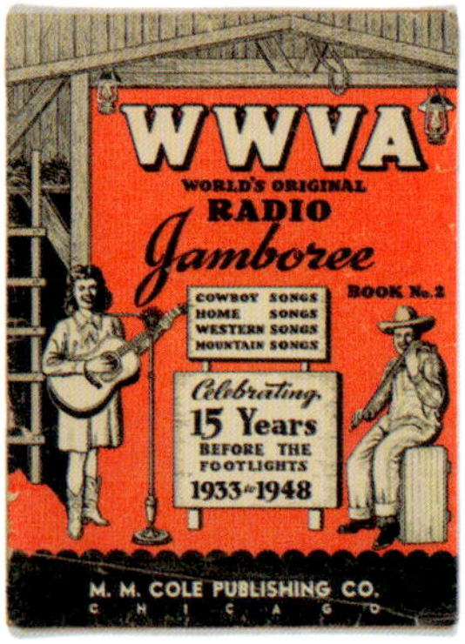
WWVA
World's Original
Radio
Jamboree
Book No. 2
Cowboy Songs
Home Songs
Western Songs
Mountain Songs
Celebrating
15 Years
Before the
Footlights
1933-1948
M. M. Cole Publishing Co.
Chicago

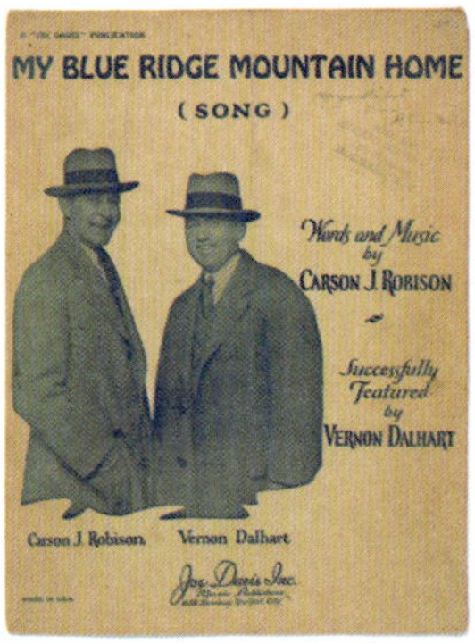
My Blue Ridge Mountain Home
(Song)
Words and Music
by
Carson J. Robison
Successfully
Featured
by
Vernon Dalhart
Carson J. Robison
Vernon Dalhart

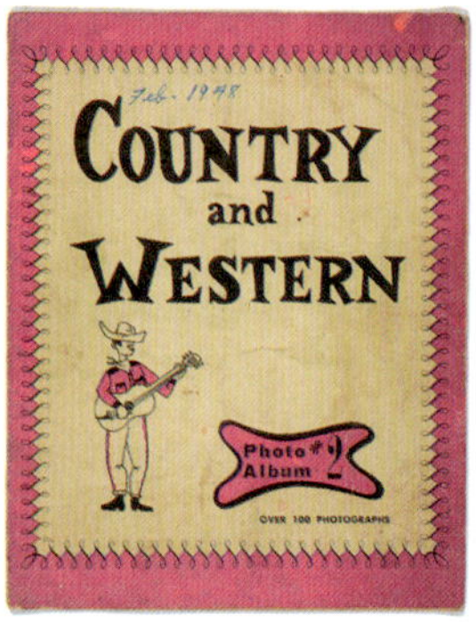
Country
and
Western
Photo Album

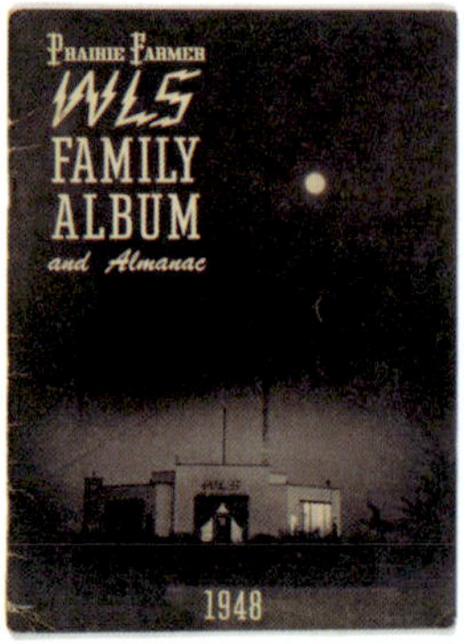
Prairie Farmer
WLS
Family
Album
and Almanac
1948

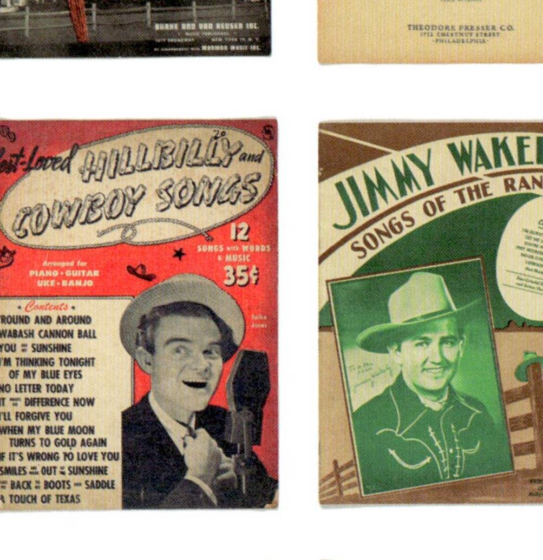

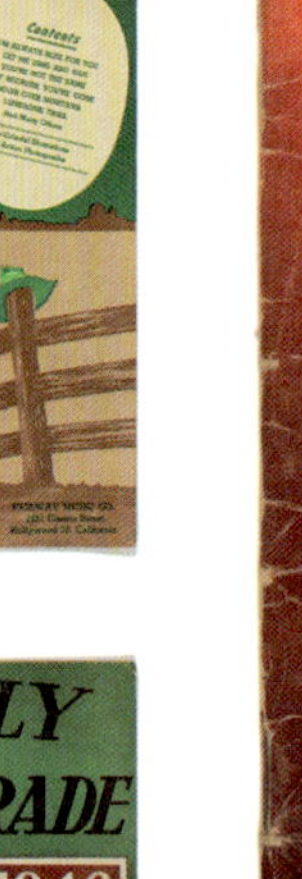

Big Bill . . . .*Oh Yes* (Broonzy), Columbia 37787, 78, 1939
Fightin' Little Rooster (Broonzy), Columbia 37787, 78, 1939
Bob Wills. . . . . *Liza Pull Down the Shades*, Vocalion 04839, 78, 1939
You're Okay (Parrish–Bloom), Vocalion 04839, 78, 1939
Count Basie. . . . . *12th Street Rag* (Sumner–Bowman), Okeh 4886, 78, 1939
Jump for Me, Okeh 4886, 78, 1939
Miss Thing—Part 1 (Basie–Martin), Okeh 4860, 78, 1939
Miss Thing—Part 2 (Basie–Martin), Okeh 4860, 78, 1939
Georgia White . . . . *Fire in the Mountain* (Jones), Decca 7608, 78, 1939
When the Red Sun Turns to Gray (I'll Be Back) (Jones), Decca 7608, 78, 1939
Golden Gate Quartet . . . . *Julius Caesar*, Bluebird 8594, 78, 1939
The Devil with the Devil (Larry Clinton), Bluebird 8594, 78, 1939
Mary Lou Williams. . . . . *Little Joe from Chicago* (Williams–Wells), Columbia 37334, 78, 1939
Pete Johnson. . . . .*Boogie Woogie*, Columbia 37334, 78, 1939
Sister Rosetta Tharpe. . . . . *God Don't Like It*, Decca 2328, 78, 1939
I Looked Down the Line (and I Wondered), Decca 2328, 78, 1939
The Lonesome Road (Gene Austin–Nathaniel Shilkret), Decca 2243, 78, 1939
Rock Me, Decca 2243, 78, 1939
Yas Yas Girl . . . .*Someone to Take Your Place*, Vocalion 04885, 78, 1939
Got a Mind to Ramble, Vocalion 04885, 78, 1939
Art Tatum . . . . *Tiger Rag* (Harry De Costa–D. J. La Rocca), Decca 18051, 78, 1940
Lullaby of the Leaves (Joe Young–Bernice Petkere), Decca 18051, 78, 1940
B. B. King . . . . *Woke Up This Morning (My Baby She Was Gone)* (King–Taub), RPM 380, 78, 1940
Bob Wills. . . . . *Bob Wills' Special*, Columbia 37014, 78, 1940
New San Antonio Rose, Columbia 37014, 78, 1940
Five Soul Stirrers. . . . . *Precious Lord* (Dorsey), W and W BR-103, 78, 1940
Jimmy Yancey . . . . *Bear Trap Blues*, Columbia 37335, 78, 1940
Lead Belly . . . . *Pick a Bale of Cotton*, Victor 27268, 78, 1940
Alabama Bound, Victor 27268, 78, 1940
Ham An' Eggs, Victor 27266, 78, 1940
The Midnight Special, Victor 27266, 78, 1940
Light Crust Doughboys . . . . *Good Gracious Gracie!* (Montgomery), Okeh 05821, 78, 1940
She's Too Young (to Play with the Boys) (Pitts–Campbell–Parker), Okeh 05821, 78, 1940
Lonnie Johnson. . . . . *Get Yourself Together*, Bluebird 8530, 78, 1940
Don't Be No Fool, Bluebird 8530, 78, 1940
Wilf Carter (Montana Slim "The Yodeling Cowboy"). . . . . *Dad's Little Texas Lad* (Wilf Carter), Bluebird 8591, 78, 1940
Thinking (Carter–McBride), Bluebird 8591, 78, 1940
Rushing Family . . . . *Keep on the Firing Line*, White Church 1092, 78, 194?
Tampa Red . . . . *Anna Lou Blues* (Hudson Whittaker), Bluebird 8654, 78, 1940
Don't You Lie to Me (Hudson Whittaker), Bluebird 8654, 78, 1940
You Say We're Through (Hudson Whittaker), Bluebird 8475, 78, 1940
The Way to Get the Low-Down (Hudson Whittaker), Bluebird 8475, 78, 1940
Yodeling Slim Clark . . . . *Yodelin' Mad* (R. Clark), Continental 8050, 78, 194?
Stampede, the Outlaw (R. Clark–Peter Roy), Continental 8050, 78, 194?
B. B. King . . . . *Don't Have to Cry* (King–Taub), RPM 380, 78, 1941
Big Bill . . . . *Going Back to My Plow* (Broonzy), Okeh 06484, 78, 1941
I'm Having So Much Trouble (Broonzy), Okeh 06484, 78, 1941
Double Trouble (Melka), Okeh 06427, 78, 1941
All By Myself, Okeh 06427, 78, 1941
Big Maceo . . . . *Bye, Bye, Baby* (Maceo Merriweather), Bluebird 9012, 78, 1941
Poor Kelly Blues (Maceo Merriweather), Bluebird 9012, 78, 1941
Bob Wills. . . . .*My Life's Been a Pleasure* (Ashlock), Columbia 37025, 78, 1941
Champion Jack Dupree. . . . .*Dupree Shake Dance*, Columbia 37335, 78, 1941
Hour of Charm All Girl Orchestra . . . .*In the Garden* (Miles), Columbia 36366, 78, 1941
Holy, Holy, Holy (Heber–Dykes), Columbia 36366, 78, 1941
Jay McShann. . . . .*Confessin' the Blues—Part 1* (Walter Brown–Jay McShann), Decca 48008, 78, 1941
Confessin' the Blues—Part 2 (Walter Brown–Jay McShann), Decca 48008, 78, 1941
Jazz Gillum . . . .*Me and My Buddy*, Bluebird 8872, 78, 1941
That's What Worries Me, Bluebird 8872, 78, 1941
Lil Green . . . . *What's the Matter with Love?* (Fred Walker), Bluebird B-8754, 78, 1941
County Boy Blues (Willie Broonzy), Bluebird B-8754, 78, 1941
If I Didn't Love You (Joe McCoy), Bluebird 8865, 78, 1941
Hello Babe (Joe McCoy), Bluebird 8865, 78, 1941

Opposite: Song books, sheet music and promotional material 1929-1948.

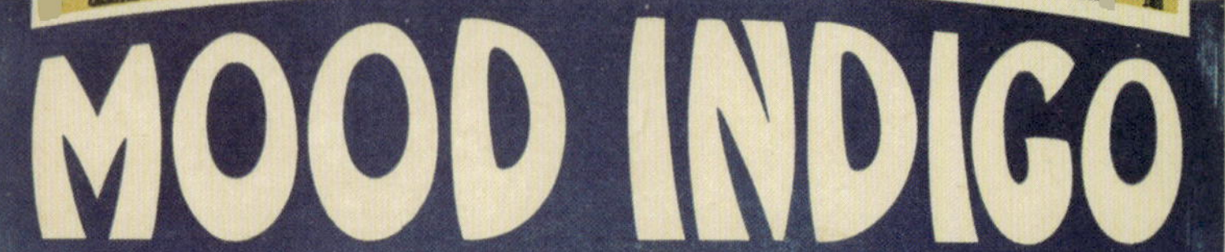

MOOD INDIGO
WORDS AND MUSIC BY
DUKE ELLINGTON-IRVING MILLS AND ALBANY BIGARD

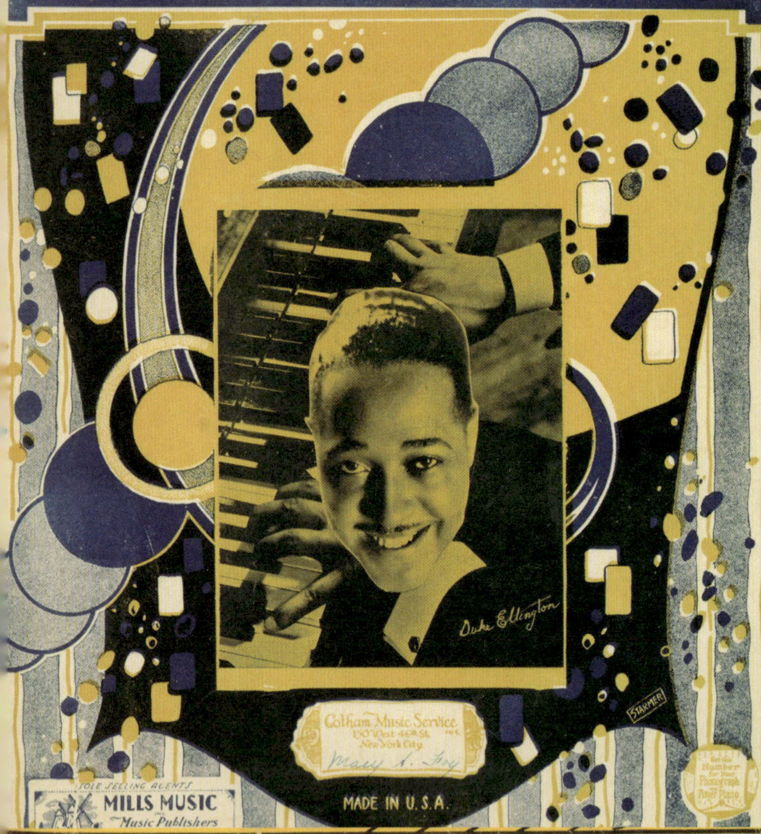

Duke Ellington
Gotham Music Service
New York City
SOLE SELLING AGENTS
MILLS MUSIC
Music Publishers
MADE IN U.S.A.

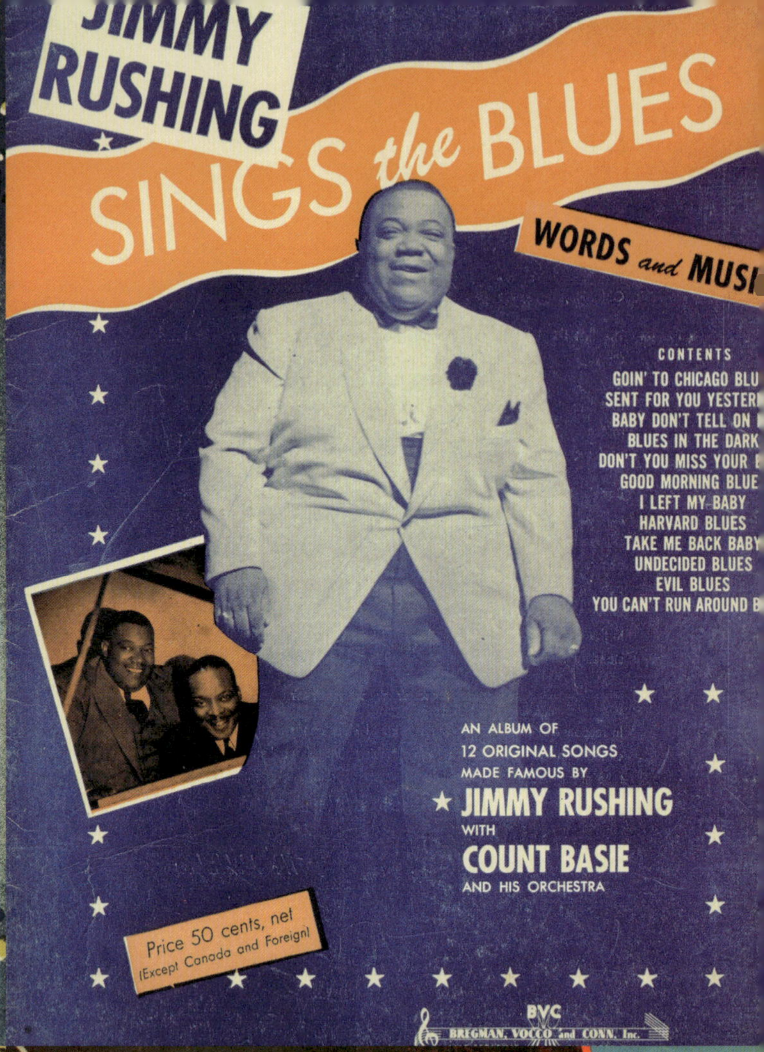

JIMMY RUSHING
SINGS the BLUES
WORDS and MUSI
CONTENTS
GOIN' TO CHICAGO BLU
SENT FOR YOU YESTERN
BABY DON'T TELL ON
BLUES IN THE DARK
DON'T YOU MISS YOUR
GOOD MORNING BLUE
I LEFT MY BABY
HARVARD BLUES
TAKE ME BACK BABY
UNDECIDED BLUES
EVIL BLUES
YOU CAN'T RUN AROUND B
AN ALBUM OF
12 ORIGINAL SONGS
MADE FAMOUS BY
JIMMY RUSHING
WITH
COUNT BASIE
AND HIS ORCHESTRA
Price 50 cents, net
(Except Canada and Foreign)
BVC
BREGMAN, VOCCO and CONN, Inc.

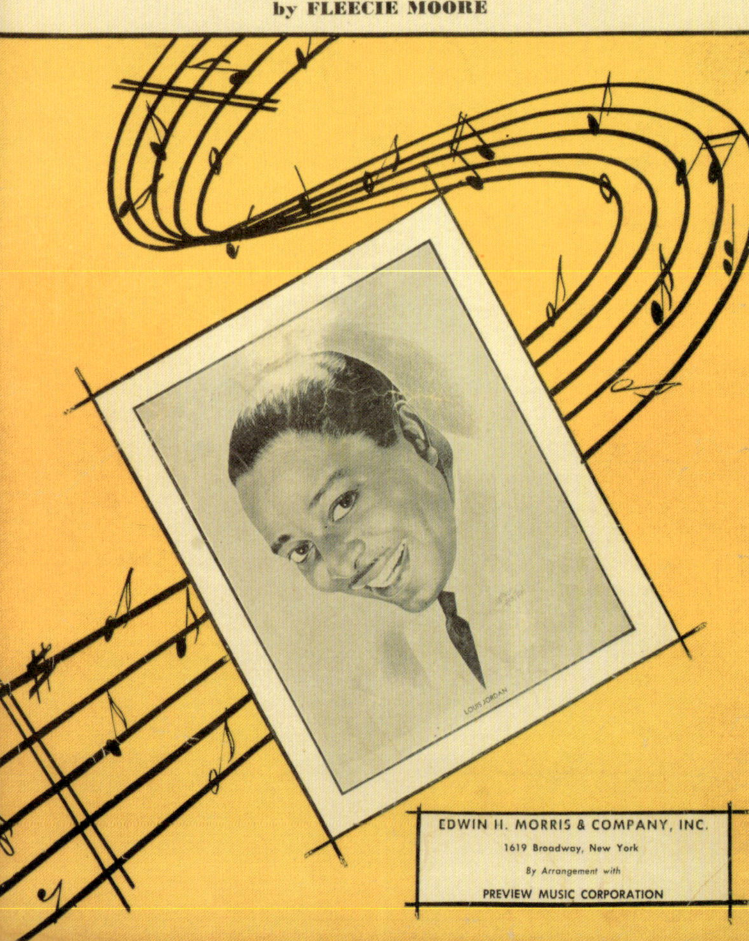

CALDONIA
(What Makes Your Big Head So Hard?)
by FLEECIE MOORE
LOUIS JORDAN
EDWIN H. MORRIS & COMPANY, INC.
1619 Broadway, New York
By Arrangement with
PREVIEW MUSIC CORPORATION

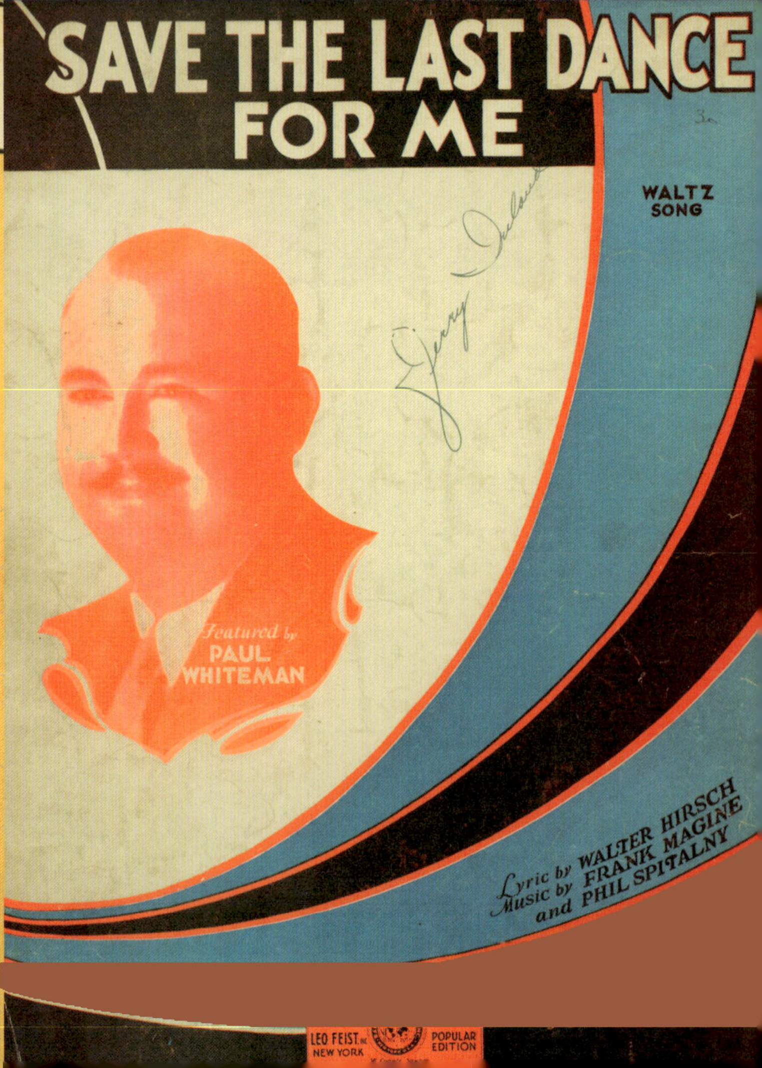

SAVE THE LAST DANCE
FOR ME
WALTZ SONG
Featured by
PAUL WHITEMAN
Lyric by WALTER HIRSCH
Music by FRANK MAGINE
and PHIL SPITALNY
LEO FEIST INC
NEW YORK
POPULAR EDITION

Louis Jordan . . . . *Pinetop's Boogie Woogie* (Pinetop Smith), Decca 25394, 78, 1941
Lucky Millinder . . . . *That's All* (Rosetta Tharpe), Decca 18496, 78, 1941
Memphis Minnie . . . . *Can't Afford to Lose My Man* (Lawlar), Okeh 06288, 78, 1941
    Me and My Chauffeur Blues (Lawlar), Okeh 06288, 78, 1941
    It Was You Baby (Lawler), Okeh 06624, 78, 1941
    I'm Not a Bad Girl (Lawler), Okeh 06624, 78, 1941
Pete Johnson and Albert Ammons . . . . *Movin' the Boogie*, Victor 27507, 78, 1941
    Foot Pedal Boogie, Victor 27507, 78, 1941
    Sixth Avenue Express, RCA Victor 27506, 78, 1941
    Pine Creek, RCA Victor 27506, 78, 1941
Peter Cleighton (Doctor Clayton) . . . . *Love Is Gone*, Okeh 06375, 78, 1941
    '41 Blues, Okeh 06375, 78, 1941
Roosevelt Sykes (The Honey Dripper) . . . . *Sugar Babe Blues*, Okeh 6709, 78, 1941
    Training Camp Blues, Okeh 6709, 78, 1941
Sam Price . . . . *Things 'Bout Coming My Way* (Johnson–Williams), Decca 8557, 78, 1941
    Just Jivin' Around, Decca 8557, 78, 1941
Sister Rosetta Tharpe . . . . *Stand By Me* (Thomas A. Dorsey), Decca 8548, 78, 1941
    There Is Something Within Me (Katie Bell–Sister Rosetta Tharpe), Decca 8548, 78, 1941
The Prairie Ramblers . . . . *I'll Love You Till I Die* (Hurt–Taylor), Okeh 06576, 78, 1941
    Darling, Do You Love Another? (Hurt–Taylor), Okeh 06576, 78, 1941
Tony Hollins . . . . *Tease Me Over Blues*, Okeh 06523, 78, 1941
    Traveling Man Blues, Okeh 06523, 78, 1941
Big Bill . . . . *Hard Hearted Woman*, Columbia 37196, 78, 1942
    I'm Gonna Move to the Outskirts of Town (Weldon), Columbia 37196, 78, 1942
Bob Wills . . . . *Liberty*, Columbia 37926, 78, 1942
Brownie McGhee . . . . *Workingman's Blues*, Okeh 6698, 78, 1942
    Step It Up and Go—No. 2 (J. B. Long), Okeh 6698, 78, 1942
Carol Chapelle . . . . *I Won't Give It Away*, Party Record Company 10, 78, 1942
    Shake Your Can, Party Record Company 10, 78, 1942
Kelley Pace . . . . *Holy Babe—Part 2*, Library of Congress AAFS49, 78, 1942
Lonnie Johnson . . . . *He's a Jelly-Roll Baker*, Bluebird 9006, 78, 1942
    When You Feel Low Down, Bluebird 9006, 78, 1942
Savannah Churchill . . . . *Fat Meat Is Good Meat* (Irene Higginbotham), Celebrity 2003, 78, 1942
    Tell Me Your Blues An' I Will Tell You Mine (Irene Higginbotham), Celebrity 2003, 78, 1942
Tampa Red . . . . *My First Love Blues* (Hudson Whittaker), Bluebird 34-0700, 78, 1942
    Let Me Play with Your Poodle (Hudson Whittaker), Bluebird 34-0700, 78, 1942
    Maybe Some Day (Hudson Whittaker), RCA Victor 20-1988, 78, 1942
    Crying Won't Help You (Hudson Whittaker), RCA Victor 20-1988, 78, 1942
Big Bill . . . . *What's Wrong with Me* (Melka), Okeh 6705, 78, 1943
    Night Watchman Blues (Broonzy), Okeh 6705, 78, 1943
Coleman Hawkins . . . . *Stumpy*, Signature 28102, 78, 1943
    How Deep Is the Ocean (Irving Berlin), Signature 28102, 78, 1943
Cliff Bruner . . . . *My Pretty Blonde* (Link Davis), Decca 46033, 78, 1944
    I'll Try Not to Cry (Clif Bruner–Moon Mullican), Decca 46033, 78, 1944
Coleman Hawkins . . . . *Step On It*, Manor 1036, 78, 1944
    Memories of You, Manor 1036, 78, 1944
Cootie Williams . . . . *Red Blues–F.T.* (Haggart), Hit 7084, 78, 1944
    Things Ain't What They Used to Be (Ellington–Persons), Hit 7084, 78, 1944
Hank D'Amico Sextet . . . . *Gone at Dawn–Blues* (Bill Simon), National 9003, 78, 1944
Jimmy Noone . . . . *High Society*, Carousel 2501, 78, 1944
King Radio . . . . *I'll Be a Colored Hitler* (Norman Span), Decca 34007, 78, 1944
Lord Invader . . . . *The Soldiers Came and Broke Up My Life* (Rupert Grant), Decca 34007, 78, 1944
Memphis Minnie . . . . *I'm So Glad* (Lawlar), Columbia 37295, 78, 1944
    Mean Mistreater Blues (Lawlar), Columbia 37295, 78, 1944
    Love Come and Go (Lawler), Okeh 6733, 78, 1944
    When You Love Me (Lawler), Okeh 6733, 78, 1944
Pvt. Cecil Gant . . . . *I Wonder*, National 9003, 78, 1944
Red Foley . . . . *Smoke on the Water* (Earl Nunn–Zeke Clements), Decca 6102, 78, 1944
Sister Rosetta Tharpe . . . . *Strange Things Happening Every Day*, Decca 8669, 78, 1944
    Two Little Fishes and Five Loaves of Bread (Bernie Hanighen), Decca 8669, 78, 1944
Soul Stirrers . . . . *Walk Around* (R. H. Harris), New World Records NW 224, LP, orig. 1944
Bailes Brothers . . . . *As Long as I Live* (Acuff), Columbia 36932, 78, 1945
    Searching for a Soldier's Grave (Acuff), Columbia 36932, 78, 1945

Opposite: Sheet music and song books 1931-1945.

Bailes Brothers . . . . *I Want to Be Loved (But Only by You)* (W. Bailes–J. Bailes), Columbia 37341, 78, 1945
The Drunkard's Grave (W. Bailes–J. Bailes), Columbia 37341, 78, 1945
Barney Bigart Sextet . . . . *Sweet Marijuana Brown* (Leonard Feather), Black & White 13, 78, 1945
Blues for Art's Sake (Bigard–Tatum), Black & White 13, 78, 1945
Bill Monroe . . . . *Rocky Road Blues*, Columbia 20013, 78, 1945
Kentucky Waltz, Columbia 20013, 78, 1945
Bill Samuels . . . . *Jockey Blues* (Samuels–Jones), Mercury 2003, 78, 1945
Bob Wills . . . . *You Should Have Thought of That Before* (Browne), Columbia 37824, 78, 1945
Buchanan Brothers . . . . *(When I Put on My) Long White Robe* (Bob Miller), RCA Victor 20-1953, 78, 1945
Shut That Gate (Dick James–Ted Daffan), RCA Victor 20-1953, 78, 1945
Buster Bennett Trio . . . . *Reefer Head Woman*, Columbia 36873, 78, 1945
Coleman Hawkins . . . . *Bean-A-Re-Bop* (Hawkins–Jones), Alladin 3006, 78, 1945
Cootie Williams . . . . *Salt Lake City Bounce* (Johnson–Hastings), Capitol 237, 78, 1945
Juice Head Baby (Williams–Daylie), Capitol 237, 78, 1945
Cozy Cole's All Stars . . . . *Willow Weep for Me* (Ann Ronell), Continental 6001, 78, 1945
Take It On Back (C. Cole–W. P. Thomas–C. Hart), Continental 6001, 78, 1945
Helen Humes . . . . *Be-Baba-Luba*, Philo PV106, 78, 1945
Jack Guthrie . . . . *Oklahoma Hills*, Capitol 201, 78, 1945
Pvt. Cecil Gant . . . . *Cecil's Mop Mop*, Gilt-Edge 500, 78, 1945
You're Going to Cry, Gilt-Edge 507, 78, 1945
Cecil Knows Better Now, Gilt-Edge 507, 78, 1945
Roy Acuff . . . . *I Heard a Silver Trumpet* (Fred Rose), Okeh 6735, 78, 1945
Sippie Wallace . . . . *Bedroom Blues* (S. Wallace–W. Thomas), Mercury 2010, 78, 1945
Buzz Me (D. Baxter–F. More), Mercury 2010, 78, 1945
Slim Gaillard . . . . *Voot Boogie*, Queen 4159, 78, 1945
Queen Boogie, Queen 4159, 78, 1945
Tennessee Ramblers . . . . *Beaty Steel Blues* (Cecil Campbell), Super Disc 1004, 78, 1945
Tex Ritter . . . . *Green Grow the Lilacs* (Traditional), Capitol 206, 78, 1945
Wiley (Walker) and Gene (Sullivan) . . . .*Forgive Me*, Columbia 36869, 78, 1945
Wynonie "Mr. Blues" Harris . . . . *Around the Clock—Part 1*, Philo P103, 78, 1945
Around the Clock—Part 2, Philo P103, 78, 1945
Wynonie "Blues" Harris . . . . *Wynonie's Blues*, Apollo 362, 78, 1945
Somebody Changed the Lock on My Door (William Weldon), Apollo 362, 78, 1945
Albert Ammons . . . . *Boogie Woogie at the Civic Opera*, Mercury 8007, 78, 1946
Arthur "Big Boy" Crudup . . . . *So Glad You're Mine*, RCA Victor 20-1949, 78, 1946
Ethel Mae, RCA Victor 20-1949, 78, 1946
Bill Monroe . . . . *Will You Be Loving Another Man* (Monroe–Flatt), Columbia 37565, 78, 1946
Blue Moon of Kentucky, Columbia 37888, 78, 1946
Goodbye Old Pal, Columbia 37888, 78, 1946
Bob Wills . . . .*The Kind of Love I Can't Forget* (Wills–Ashlock), Columbia 37926, 78, 1946
Fat Boy Rag (Wills–Barnard), Columbia 37824, 78, 1946
Charlie Linville . . . .*I Gotta Gallop into Gallop* (C. Linville–Cargill), King 642, 78, 1946
Bake Them Hoe Cakes Brown, King 642, 78, 1946
Cootie Williams . . . . *Wrong Neighborhood* (Hall–Merrell), Capitol 289, 78, 1946
Let's Do the Whole Thing or Nothing at All (Johnson–Williams–Johnson), Capitol 289, 78, 1946
Count Basie . . . .*Patience and Fortitude* (Warren–Moore Jr.), Columbia 36946, 78, 1946
The Mad Boogie (Basie–Harding), Columbia 36946, 78, 1946
Cumberland Mountain Folks . . . . *The Tramp on the Street* (G. Cole–H. Cole), Columbia 37559, 78, 1946
Deacon Tom Foger . . . .*I'm Gonna Walk Right in and Make Myself at Home*, Diamond 2026, 78, 1946
Anyhow, Diamond 2026, 78, 1946
Working on the Building, Diamond 2027, 78, 1946
Delmore Brothers . . . . *Hillbilly Boogie* (Rabon Delmore), King 527, 78, 1946
I'm Sorry I Caused You to Cry (Alton Delmore), King 527, 78, 1946
Elder Charles Beck . . . .*Delilah*, Eagle 102, 78, 1946
Blow, Gabriel, Eagle 101, 78, 1946
Ella Mae Morse . . . . *Hey Mr. Postman* (Ray–Weston), Capitol 251, 78, 1946
Ethel Waters . . . . *You Took My Man* (Leonard Feather), Continental 10008, 78, 1946
Floyd Tillman . . . . *Go Out and Find Sombody New*, Columbia 37221, 78, 1946
Fred Kirby . . . . *Atomic Power*, Sonora 7008, 78, 1946
Freddie Slack . . . .*The House of Blue Lights* (Raye–Slack), Capitol 251, 78, 1946
Golden Gate Quartet . . . . *Shadrack* (MacGimsey), Columbia 27236, 78, 1946
Grandpa Jones . . . . *Steppin' Out Kind* (Syd Nathan), King 513, 78, 1946
Hank Penny . . . .*Flamin' Mamie* (Rex Martin), King 534, 78, 1946

Opposite: *Who Threw the Overalls in Mistress Murphy's Chowder* (The Texas Rangers), 1937.

Who Threw the Overalls in Mistress Murphy's Chowder

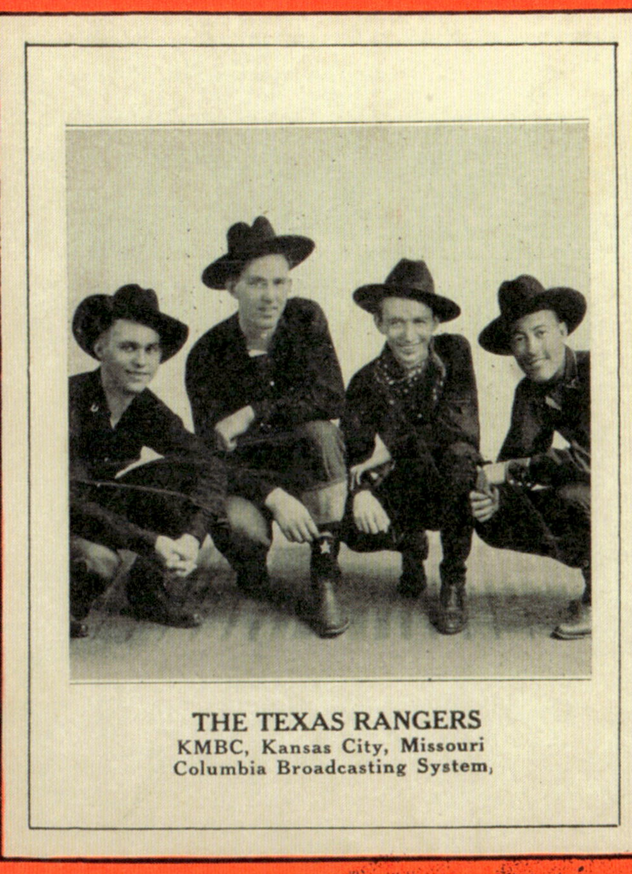

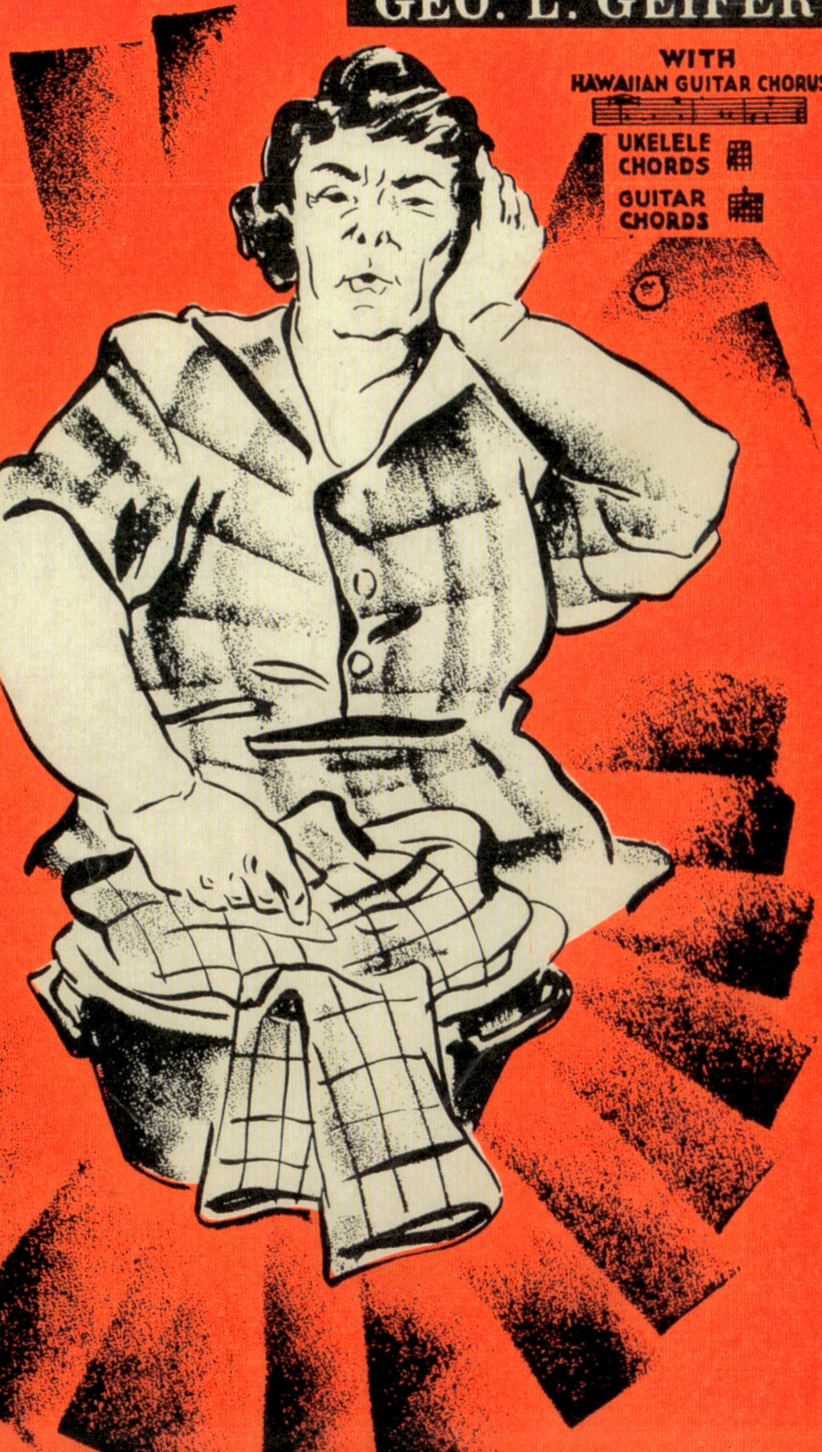

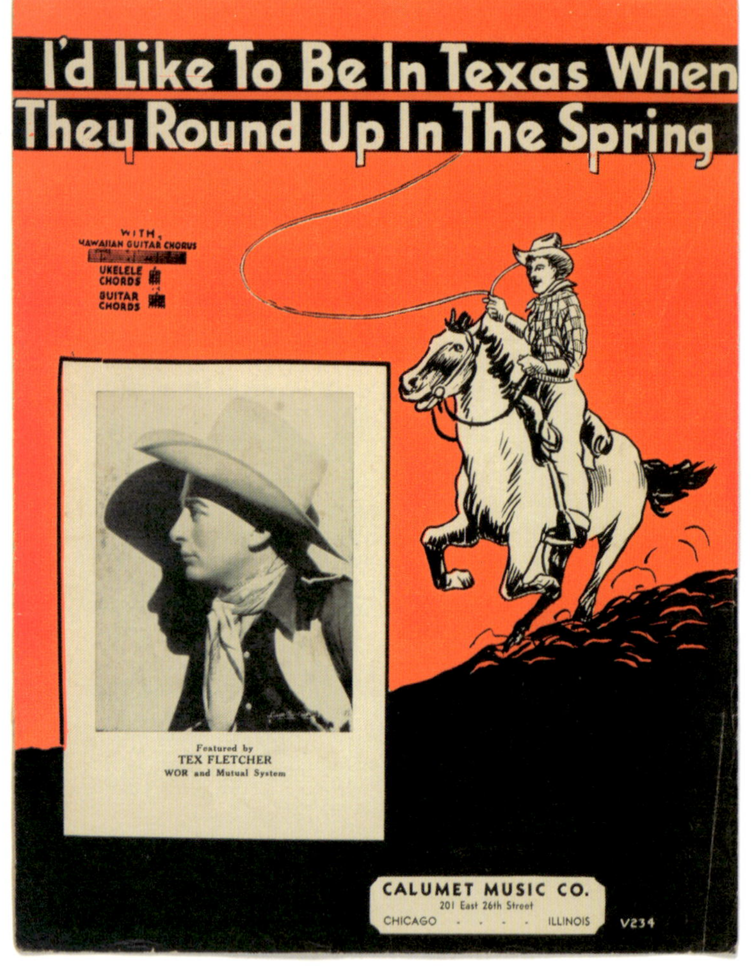

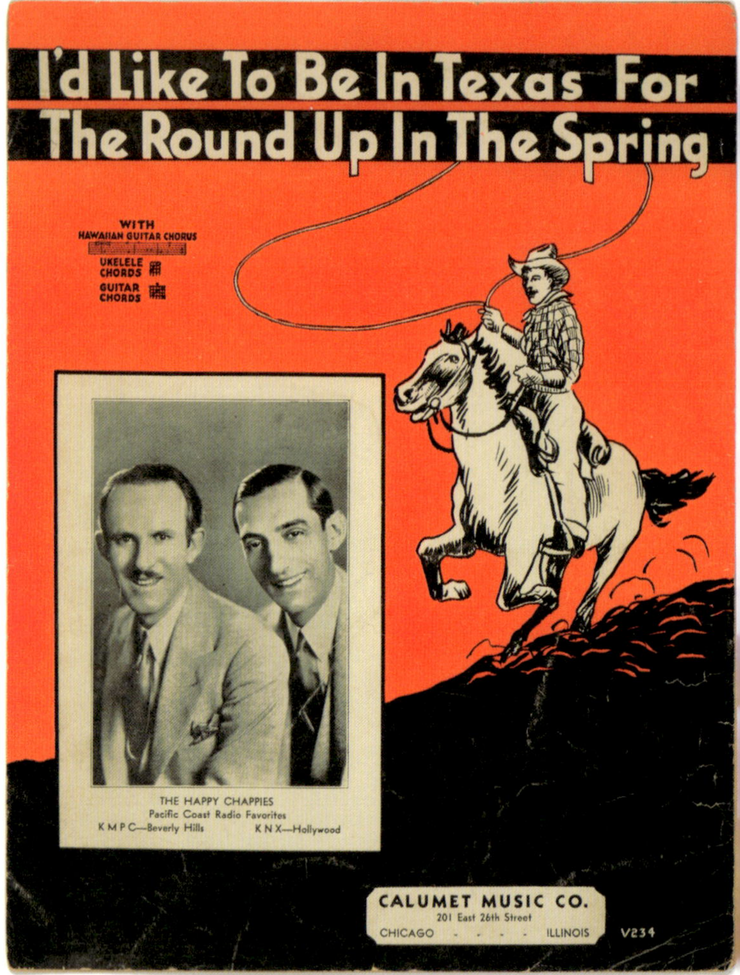

Joe Liggins . . . . "Tanya," Exclusive 231, 78, 1946
Josh White . . . . .Jelly, Jelly (Earl Hines–Billy Eckstein), Decca 23582, 78, 1946
Back Water Blues (Bessie Smith), Decca 23582, 78, 1946
Lester Young . . . . .She's Funny That Way (Niel Moret), Aladdin 138, 78, 1946
Lester's Be-Bop Boogie, Aladdin 138, 78, 1946
Louis Jordan . . . . That Chick's Too Young to Fry (Tommy Edward–Jimmy Hilliard), Decca 23610, 78, 1946
Choo Choo Ch'Boogie (Vaughn Horton–Denver Darling–Milton Gabler), Decca 23610, 78, 1946
I Know What You're Puttin' Down (Louis Jordan–Bud Allen), Decca 23901, 78, 1946
Memphis Jimmy . . . . .Drifting (Charles Brown), RCA Victor 34-0478, 78, 1946
Roy Acuff. . . . . That Glory Bound Train (Odell McLeod), Columbia 36974, 78, 1946
All the World Is Lonely Now (Mel Foree), Columbia 36974, 78, 1946
Sister Bernice Dobson . . . . .If I Can Just Make It In, Diamond 2027, 78, 1946
Sonny Boy Williamson . . . . .Early in the Morning, RCA Victor 20-1875, 78, 1946
You're an Old Lady, RCA Victor 20-1875, 78, 1946
Tampa Red .I Can't Get Along with You (Hudson Whittaker), RCA Victor 34-0478, 78, 1946
Ted Daffan. . . . . .Broken Vows, Columbia 37087, 78, 1946
Shut That Gate (Daffan–D. James), Columbia 37087, 78, 1946
Texas Ruby . . . . .The Old Home (Earls), Columbia 37075, 78, 1946
Thomas Family . . . . .I Ain't Gonna Study War No More, Majestic 11009, 78, 1946
Wynonie Harris . . . . Hey! Ba-Ba-Re-Bop—Part 1 (Lionel Hampton–Curley Hammer), Hamp-Tone 100, 78, 1946
Hey! Ba-Ba-Re-Bop—Part 2 (Lionel Hampton–Curley Hammer), Hamp-Tone 100, 78, 1946
Albert Ammons . . . . Tuxedo Boogie (H. Young), Mercury 8087, 78, 1947
Bear Den Boogie (H. Young), Mercury 8087, 78, 1947
Hiroshima (Young), Mercury 8063, 78, 1947
S. P. Blues (Young), Mercury 8063, 78, 1947
Big Bill . . . . .Saturday Evening Blues (Broonzy), Columbia 37314, 78, 1947
What Can I Do (Broonzy), Columbia 37314, 78, 1947
Bill Carlisle's Kentucky Boys . . . . .Sparkling Blue Eyes, Decca 46045, 78, 1947
Wabash Cannon Ball, Decca 46045, 78, 1947
Bill Monroe . . . . .Sweetheart You Done Me Wrong, Columbia 20423, 78, 1947

Above: *I'd Like to Be in Texas When They Round Up in the Spring* (Tex Fletcher/The Happy Chappies), 1937.

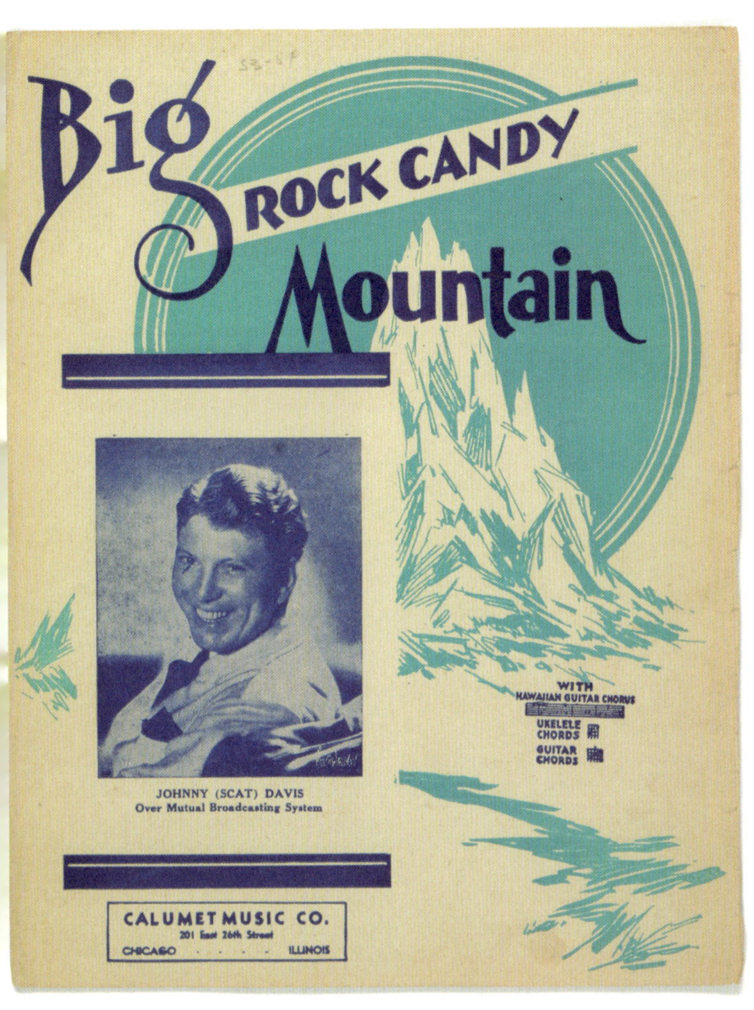

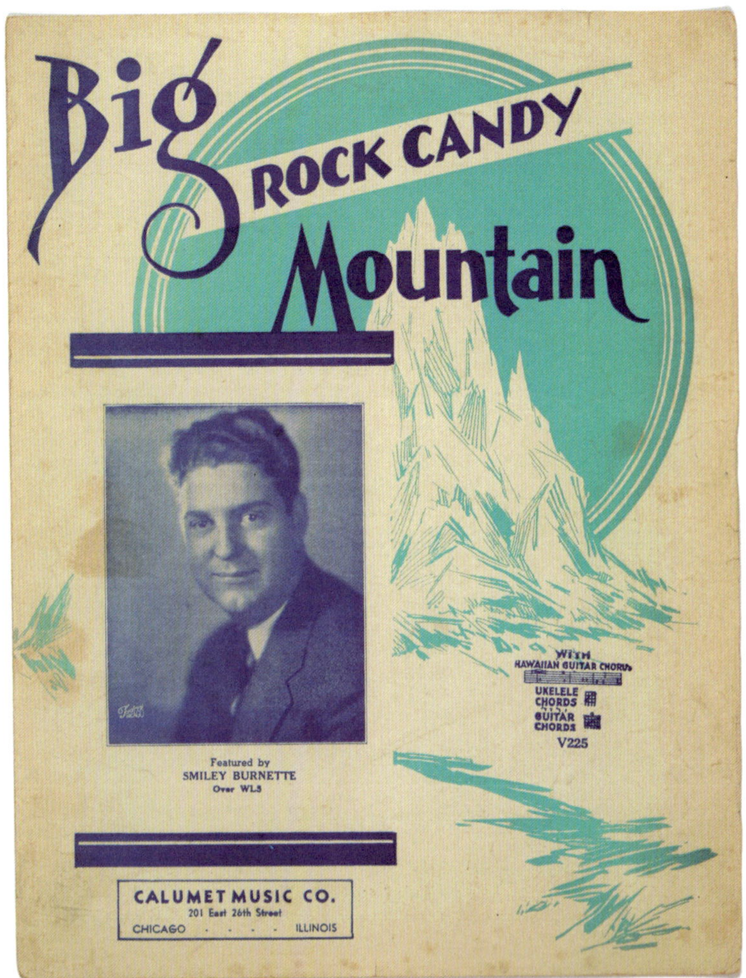

Bill Monroe . . . . *My Rose of Old Kentucky*, Columbia 20423, 78, 1947
Mansions for Me, Columbia 37294, 78, 1947
Mother's Only Sleeping, Columbia 37294, 78, 1947
Bill Moore . . . . *We're Gonna Rock*, Savoy 666, 78, 1947
Harlem Parade, Savoy 666, 78, 1947
Bob Wills . . . . *Liberty*, Columbia 37926, 78, 1947
I'm Gonna Be Boss from Now On (Wills–Ashlock), Columbia 37205, 78, 1947
There's a Big Rock in the Road (Fred Rose), Columbia 37205, 78, 1947
Delmore Brothers . . . . *I'm Leavin' You* (Alton Delmore), Decca 46043, 78, 1947
Honey I'm Ramblin' Away (Alton Delmore), Decca 46043, 78, 1947
Effie Smith. . . . .*It's Been So Long* (Criner–Smith), Miltone 218, 78, 1947
Answer to R. M. Blues (Reed–Perkins–Powell–Criner), Miltone 218, 78, 1947
I'm in the Groove Tonight, Gem 7, 78, 1947
Famous Bluejay Singers . . . *Caanan Land* (A. H. Windom), Recorded Anthology of American Music Inc. 224, LP, 1947
Four Knights . . . . *He'll Understand and Say Well Done*, Decca 48018, 78, 1947
Helen Humes. . . . . *He May Be Your Man*, Philo 105, 78, 1947
Blue Prelude (Joe Bishop–Gordon Jenkins), Philo 105, 78, 1947
Homer & Jethro. . . . . *Groundhog* (Traditional), King 596, 78, 1947
Over the Rainbow (Harburg–Arlen), King 596, 78, 1947
Illinois Jacquet, Flip Phillips, Bill Harris, Howard McGhee,
Jo Jones, Ray Brown, Hank Jones . . . .*Mordido—Part 5* (Shrdlu), Mercury 11014, 78, 1947
Ivory Joe Hunter . . . .*Pretty Mamma Blues*, 4 Star 1254, 78, 1947
Jazz at the Philharmonic All Stars . . . .*Mordido—Part 2* (Shrdlu), Mercury 11014, 78, 1947
Mordido—Part 5 (Shrdlu), Mercury 2451, 78, 1947
Johnson Family. . . . . *Cabin in the Valley of the Pines* (Brumley), Columbia 37225, 78, 1947
I'll Reap My Harvest in Heaven (Jenkins), Columbia 37225, 78, 1947
King's Sacred Quartette . . . .*Turn Your Radio On*, King 674, 78, 1947
This World Can't Stand Long, King 674, 78, 1947
Les Paul. . . . .*Guitar Boogie* (Arthur Smith), Decca 23903, 78, 1947
Steel Guitar Rag (L. McAuliffe–Merle Travis–Cliff Stone), Decca 23903, 78, 1947

Above: *Big Rock Candy Mountain* (Johnny "Scat" Davis/Smiley Burnette), 1937.

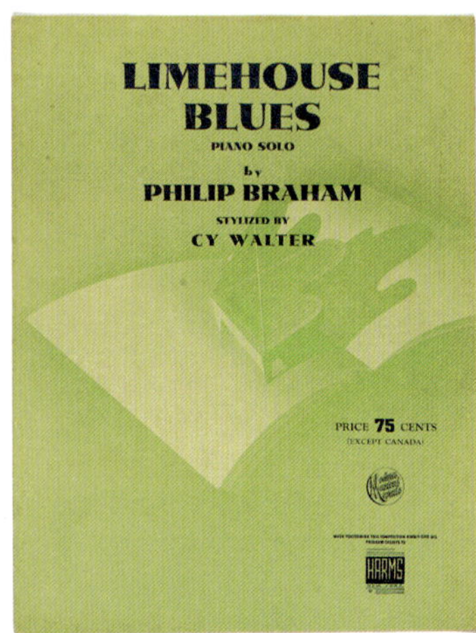
LIMEHOUSE
BLUES
PIANO SOLO
by
PHILIP BRAHAM
STYLIZED BY
CY WALTER
PRICE 75 CENTS
(EXCEPT CANADA)
HARMS

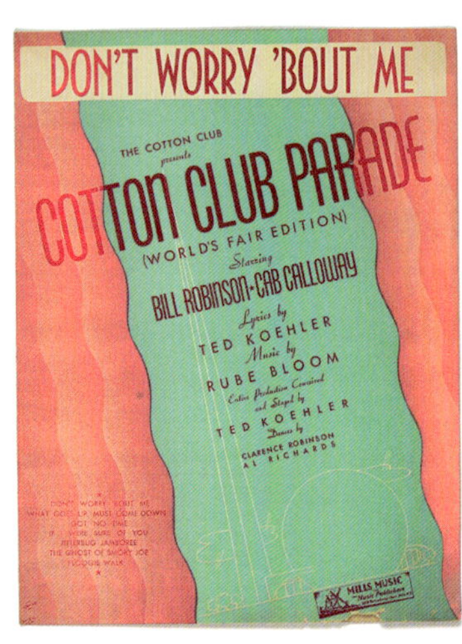
DON'T WORRY 'BOUT ME
THE COTTON CLUB
presents
COTTON CLUB PARADE
(WORLD'S FAIR EDITION)
Starring
BILL ROBINSON · CAB CALLOWAY
Lyrics by
TED KOEHLER
Music by
RUBE BLOOM
Entire Production Conceived and Staged by
TED KOEHLER
Dances by
CLARENCE ROBINSON
AL RICHARDS
MILLS MUSIC

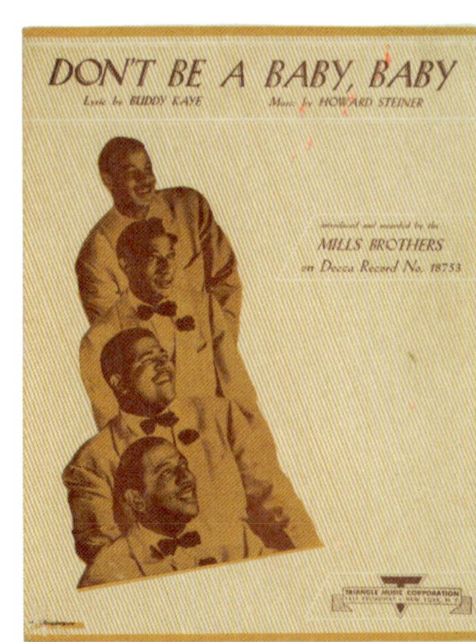
DON'T BE A BABY, BABY
Lyric by BUDDY KAYE   Music by HOWARD STEINER
Introduced and recorded by the
MILLS BROTHERS
on Decca Record No. 18753

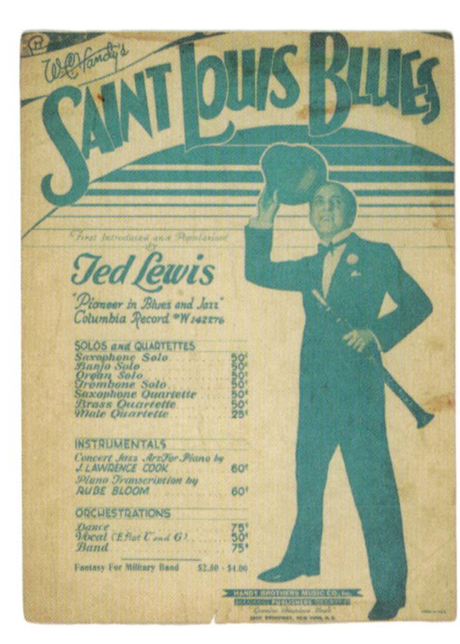
W.C. Handy's
SAINT LOUIS BLUES
First Introduced and Popularized
Ted Lewis
"Pioneer in Blues and Jazz"
Columbia Record No. 142270
SOLOS and QUARTETTES
Saxophone Solo
Banjo Solo
Organ Solo
Trombone Solo
Saxophone Quartette
Brass Quartette
Male Quartette
INSTRUMENTALS
Concert Jazz Arr. for Piano by
J. LAWRENCE COOK
Piano Transcription by
RUBE BLOOM
ORCHESTRATIONS
Dance
Vocal (Eflat and G)
Band

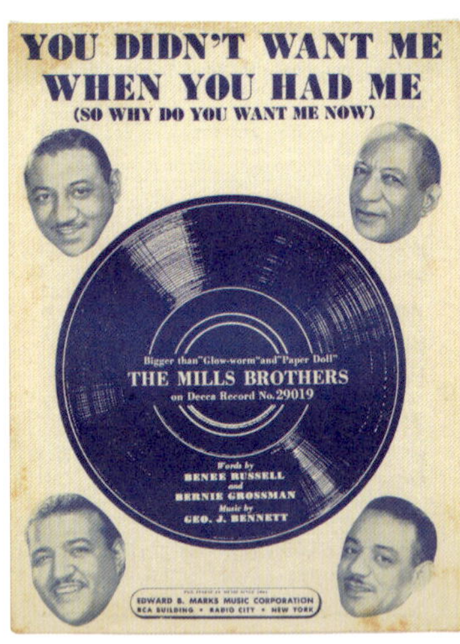
YOU DIDN'T WANT ME
WHEN YOU HAD ME
(SO WHY DO YOU WANT ME NOW)
Bigger than "Glow-worm" and "Paper Doll"
THE MILLS BROTHERS
on Decca Record No. 29019
Words by
RENEE RUSSELL
and
BERNIE GROSSMAN
Music by
GEO. J. BENNETT
EDWARD B. MARKS MUSIC CORPORATION
RCA BUILDING · RADIO CITY · NEW YORK

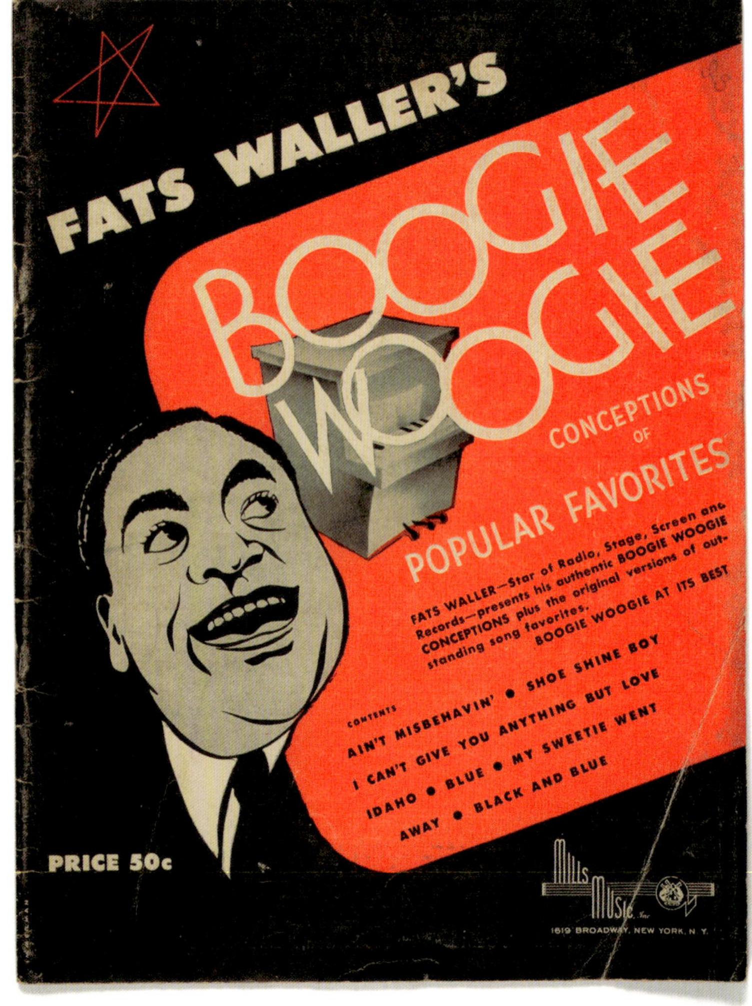
FATS WALLER'S
BOOGIE
WOOGIE
CONCEPTIONS
OF
POPULAR FAVORITES
FATS WALLER—Star of Radio, Stage, Screen and
Records—presents his authentic BOOGIE WOOGIE
CONCEPTIONS plus the original versions of out-
standing song favorites.
BOOGIE WOOGIE AT ITS BEST
CONTENTS
AIN'T MISBEHAVIN' · SHOE SHINE BOY
I CAN'T GIVE YOU ANYTHING BUT LOVE
IDAHO · BLUE · MY SWEETIE WENT
AWAY · BLACK AND BLUE
PRICE 50c
Mills Music, Inc.
1619 BROADWAY, NEW YORK, N. Y.

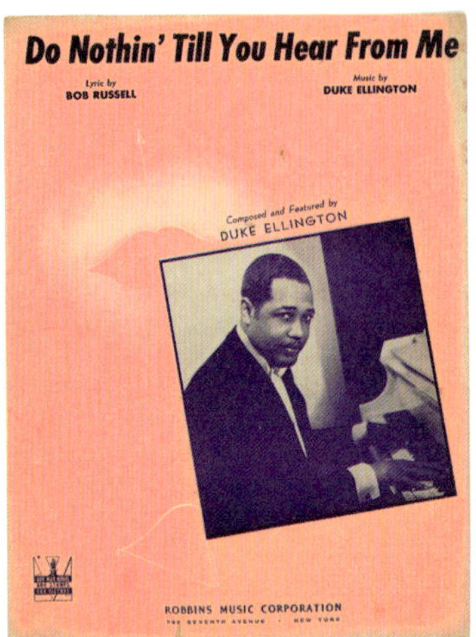
Do Nothin' Till You Hear From Me
Lyric by
BOB RUSSELL
Music by
DUKE ELLINGTON
Composed and Featured by
DUKE ELLINGTON
ROBBINS MUSIC CORPORATION
799 SEVENTH AVENUE · NEW YORK

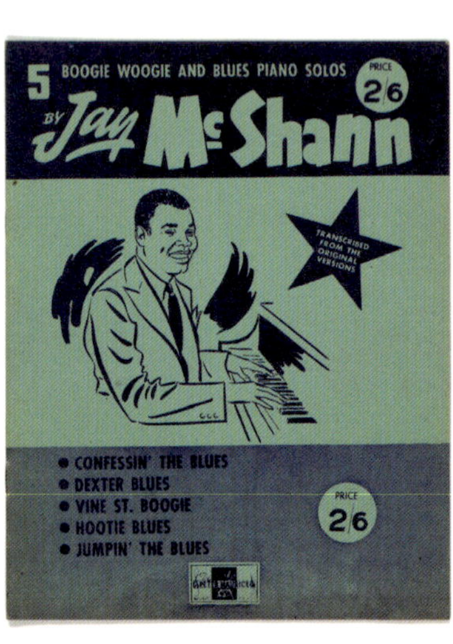
5
BOOGIE WOOGIE AND BLUES PIANO SOLOS
PRICE 26
By Jay McShann
TRANSCRIBED FROM THE
ORIGINAL VERSIONS
· CONFESSIN' THE BLUES
· DEXTER BLUES
· VINE ST. BOOGIE
· HOOTIE BLUES
· JUMPIN' THE BLUES
PRICE 26

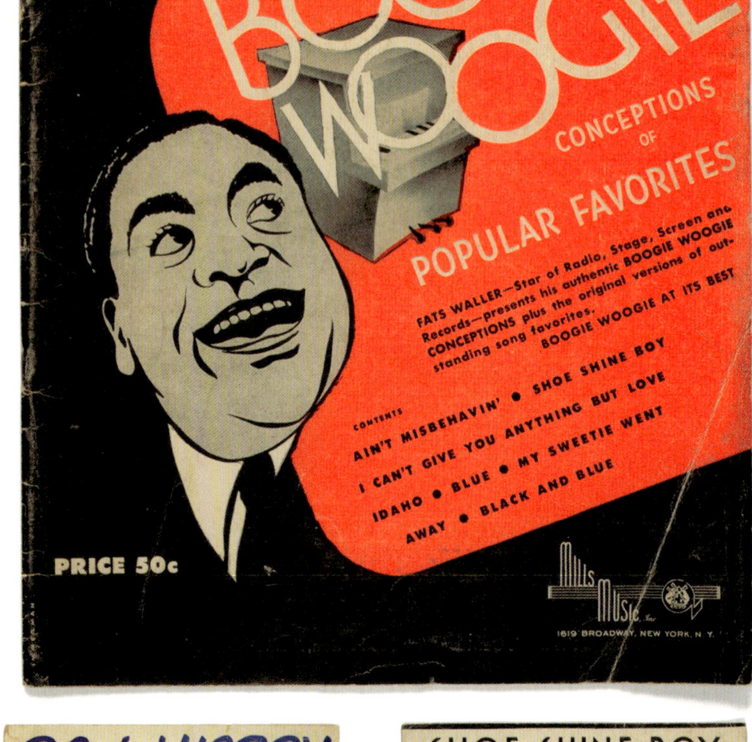

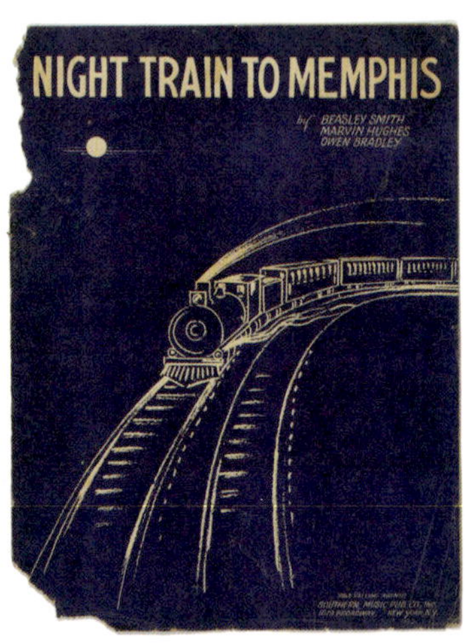
NIGHT TRAIN TO MEMPHIS
by BEASLEY SMITH
MARVIN HUGHES
OWEN BRADLEY

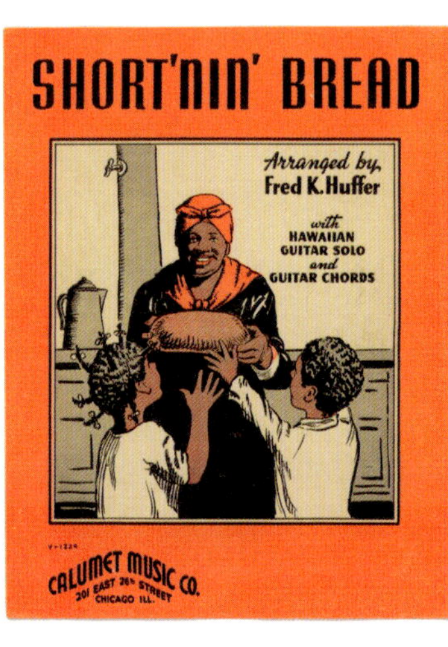
SHORT'NIN' BREAD
Arranged by
Fred K. Huffer
with
HAWAIIAN
GUITAR SOLO
and
GUITAR CHORDS
CALUMET MUSIC CO.
20 EAST 26 STREET
CHICAGO, ILL.

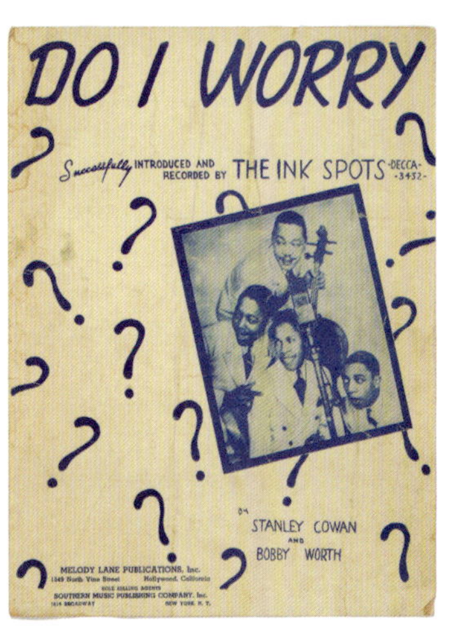
DO I WORRY
Successfully INTRODUCED AND
RECORDED BY THE INK SPOTS DECCA-3432
by
STANLEY COWAN
AND
BOBBY WORTH
MELODY LANE PUBLICATIONS, Inc.
1540 Sixth Vine Street   Hollywood, California
SOLE SELLING AGENTS
SOUTHERN MUSIC PUBLISHING COMPANY, Inc.
1619 BROADWAY   NEW YORK, N. Y.

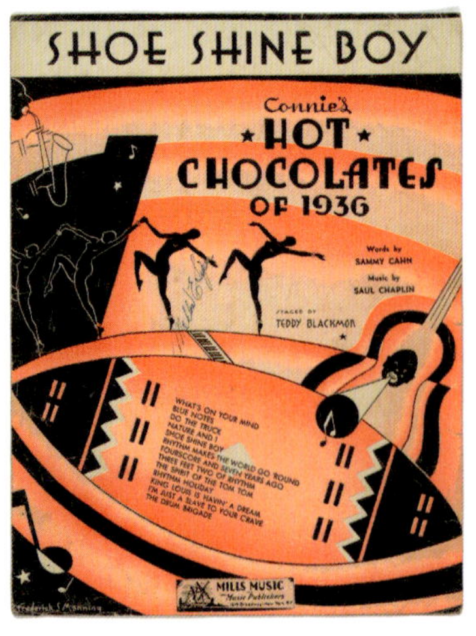
SHOE SHINE BOY
Connie's
HOT
CHOCOLATES
OF 1936
Words by
SAMMY CAHN
Music by
SAUL CHAPLIN
Staged by
TEDDY BLACKMAN
MILLS MUSIC

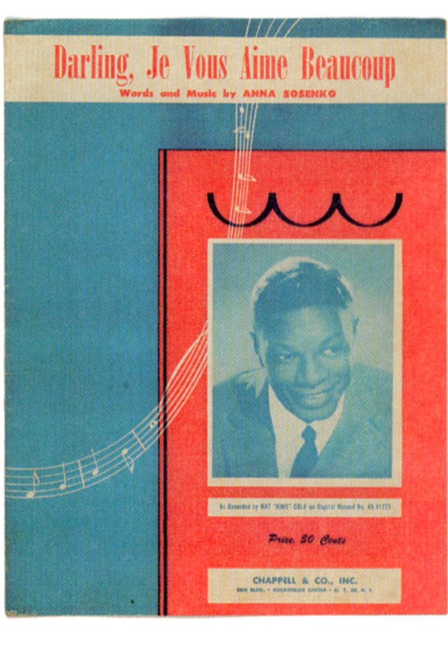
Darling, Je Vous Aime Beaucoup
Words and Music by ANNA SOSENKO
As Recorded by NAT "KING" COLE on Capitol Record No. 15-11211
Price 30 Cents
CHAPPELL & CO., INC.
RKO BLDG., RADIO CITY, NEW YORK, N. Y.

"Lightnin'" Hopkins . . . . *Katie Mae Blues* (Sam Hopkins), Aladdin 167, 78, 1947
That Mean Old Twister (Sam Hopkins), Aladdin 167, 78, 1947
Fast-Mail Rambler, Aladdin 204, 78, 1947
Thinkin' and Worryin', Aladdin 204, 78, 1947
Lonnie Johnson . . . . *What a Woman*, King 4201, 78, 1947
Louis Jordan . . . .*Roamin' Blues* (Ben Lorre–Jeff Dane–Louis Jordan), Decca 24571, 78, 1947
Have You Got the Gumption (Billy Austin–Sheldon Smith), Decca 24571, 78, 1947
Lowell Fulson . . . . *Jelly, Jelly* (E. Hines–B. Eckstine), Trilon 185, 78, 1947
Mean Woman Blues, Trilon 185, 78, 1947
Merle Travis . . . . *So Round, So Firm, So Fully Packed* (Travis–Stone–Kirk), Capitol 349, 78, 1947
Nellie Lutcher . . . .*Hurry On Down*, Capitol 40002, 78, 1947
Roberta Martin Singers . . *Yield Not to Temptation* (Horatio Palmer), Recorded Anthology of American Music Inc. 224, LP, 1947
Rosetta Howard . . . .*When I Been Drinking* (Broonzy), Columbia 37573, 78, 1947
Ebony Rhapsody (Johnston–Coslow), Columbia 37573, 78, 1947
Roy Milton . . . . *Train Blues* (Bartley–Milton), Specialty SP524, 78, 1947
Sister Rosetta Tharpe . . . . *Don't Take Everybody to Be Your Friend* (Rosetta Tharpe–Katie Bell), Decca 48025, 78, 1947
When I Move to the Sky, Decca 48025, 78, 1947
This Train, Decca 48043, 78, 1947
Oh, When I Come to the End of My Journey (Arr.: Sister Rosetta Tharpe), Decca 48043, 78, 1947
Precious Memories, Decca 48070, 78, 1947
Beams of Heaven, Decca 48070, 78, 1947
Sons of the Pioneers . . . .*Out in Pioneertown* (Tim Spencer), RCA Victor 20-2484, 78, 1947
Tex Williams . . . . *Smoke! Smoke! Smoke!* (That Cigarette) (Merle Travis–Tex Williams), Capitol 40001, 78, 1947
The Three Flames . . . . *Open the Door, Richard* (McVea–F. Clark–Howell), Columbia 37268, 78, 1947
Two Gospel Keys . . . . *Can't No Grave Hold My Body Down* (Daniel–Jones), Apollo 137, 78, 1947
Jesus Met the Woman at the Well (Daniel–Jones), Apollo 137, 78, 1947
Wesley Tuttle . . . .*I'm Writing a Letter to Heaven* (Bill Boyd–Doris Mayer), Capitol 40104, 78, 1947
Zeke Manners . . . . *Fat Man Blues* (Bill Cahan–Zeke Manners), RCA Victor 20-2139, 78, 1947
Carter Family . . . .*Lay My Head Beneath the Rose* (W. Madison–J. Falkenstein), Decca 46005, 78, 1948
Jealous Hearted Me (A. P. Carter), Decca 46005, 78, 1948
Clyde McCoy . . . . *Sugar Blues* (Williams–Fletcher), Decca 381, 78, 1948
Tear It Down (Williams–Fletcher), Decca 381, 78, 1948
Delmore Brothers . . . . *Take It to the Captain* (Jim Scott), King 718, 78, 1948
Peach Tree Street Boogie (Neely–King–Rickie), King 718, 78, 1948
Earl Bostic . . . .*Earl's Rumboogie*, Gotham 154, 78, 1948
845 Stomp, Gotham 154, 78, 1948
Hal Singer Sextette . . . . *Corn Bread*, Savoy 671, 78, 1948
Hootie McShann . . . . *I Love You Just the Same* (Witherspoon–Tate), Modern 20-637, 78, 1948
Ivory Joe Hunter . . . . *Pretty Mamma Blues*, Pacific 637, 78, 1948
"I Don't Want No Cheese No More" (Just Leave Me Out of This Trap) (Wolfe–Hunter), Pacific 637, 78, 1948
Jay McShann . . . . *Hot Biscuits*, Downbeat 165, 78, 1948
Slow Drag Blues, Downbeat 165, 78, 1948
John Lee Hooker . . . . *Boogie Chillen* (Hooker), Modern Hollywood 7006, 78, 1948
"Lightnin'" Hopkins . . . .*Moonrise Blues*, Aladdin 3077, 78, 1948
Honey Honey Blues, Aladdin 3077, 78, 1948
Lonnie Johnson . . . . *Happy New Year, Darling*, King 4251, 78, 1948
Backwater Blues, King 4251, 78, 1948
Maddox Bros. & Rose . . . . *When God Dips His Love in My Heart*, 4 Star 1301, 78, 1948
He Will Set Your Fields on Fire, 4 Star 1301, 78, 1948
Mahalia Jackson . . . .*God's Gonna Separate the Wheat from the Tares*, Coral 65001, 78, 1948
Keep Me Every Day, Coral 65001, 78, 1948
Orioles . . . .*It's Too Soon to Know* (Deborah–Chessler), Natural 5000, 78, 1948
Barbra Lee (Deborah–Chessler), Natural 5000, 78, 1948
Rambler Trio . . . .*Guitar Boogie* (Arthur Smith), Super Disc 1004, 78, 1948
Red Ingle . . . . *Cigareets, Whuskey and Wild Wild Women*
(Tim Spencer, arranged by Carling–Washburne), Capitol 15045, 78, 1948
Roy Hogsed . . . . *Cocaine Blues* (T. J. "Red" Arnall), Capitol 40120, 78, 1948
"T" Texas Tyler . . . .*Deck of Cards*, 4 Star 2s-9-(a), 78, 1948
Tex Ritter . . . . *I Can't Get My Foot Off the Rail* (Pete Purvis), Capitol 40036, 78, 1948
Ward Singers . . . .*I Need Thee Every Hour*, Savoy 4017, 78, 1948
Surely God Is Able, Savoy 4017, 78, 1948
Wynonie Harris . . . . *Good Rockin' Tonight* (Brown), King 4210, 78, 1948
Good Morning Mr. Blues, King 4210, 78, 1948

Opposite: Sheet music and song book 1936-1942.

Wynonie Harris . . . . *Lollipop Mama* (B. Brown), King 4226, 78, 1948
Blow Your Brains Out, King 4226, 78, 1948
Big Jay McNeely. . . . . *Blow Big Jay* (Cecil McNeely), Exclusive 90x, 78, 1949
Brown's Ferry Four . . . . *I've Made a Covenant with My Lord* (Arnold), King 785, 78, 1949
Chubby "Hip Shakin" Newsom. . . . . *Close to Train Time* (Brown), DeLuxe 3213, 78, 1949
Deacon McNeeley's Blue Jays. . . . . *Artie's Jump* (C. J. McNeeley), Savoy 685, 78, 1949
The Deacon's Hop (C. J. McNeeley), Savoy 685, 78, 1949
Delmore Brothers . . . . *Goin' Back to the Blue Ridge Mountains* (Jim Scott), King 803, 78, 1949
Blues Stay Away from Me (Delmore–Raney–Delmore–Glover), King 803, 78, 1949
Jimmie Dickens. . . . . *Take an Old Cold 'Tater (and Wait)* (Bartlett), Columbia 20548, 78, 1949
Louis Jordan . . . . *Saturday Night Fish Fry–Part 1* (Louis Jordan–Ellis Walsh), Decca 24725, 78, 1949
Saturday Night Fish Fry–Part 2 (Louis Jordan–Ellis Walsh), Decca 24725, 78, 1949
Maddox Bros. & Rose. . . . .*I Just Steal Away and Pray* (Stevenson), 4 Star X-51, 78, 1949
I'd Rather Have Jesus (Stevenson), 4 Star X-51, 78, 1949
Maddox Brothers. . . . . *Sally Let Your Bangs Hang Down*, 4 Star 1398, 78, 1949
You've Been Talking in Your Sleep (Hank Locklin), 4 Star 1398, 78, 1949
Memphis Slim . . . .*Slim's Boogie*, King 4312, 78, 1949
A Letter Home, King 4312, 78, 1949
Rosetta Tharpe . . . .*Daniel in the Lion's Den (He Locked the Lion's Jaw)* (Traditional),
Recorded Anthology of American Music Inc. 224, LP, 1949
Roy Brown. . . . .*Rockin' at Midnight*, DeLuxe 3212, 78, 1949
Judgement Day Blues, DeLuxe 3212, 78, 1949
Shelton Brothers . . . . *When They Baptized Sister Lucy Lee*, King 780, 78, 1949
Sister Rosetta Tharpe. . . . . *Move On Up a Little Higher*—Part 1, Decca 48093, 78, 1949
Move On Up a Little Higher—Concluded, Decca 48093, 78, 1949
Stuart Hamblen. . . . . *Sheepskin Corn and a Wrinkle on a Horn*, Columbia 20674, 78, 1949
T-Bone Walker . . . . *First Love Blue* (John "Shifty" Henry), Capitol 57-70042, 78, 1949

Below: Detail of *Hank Snow "The Singing Ranger,"* 1949.

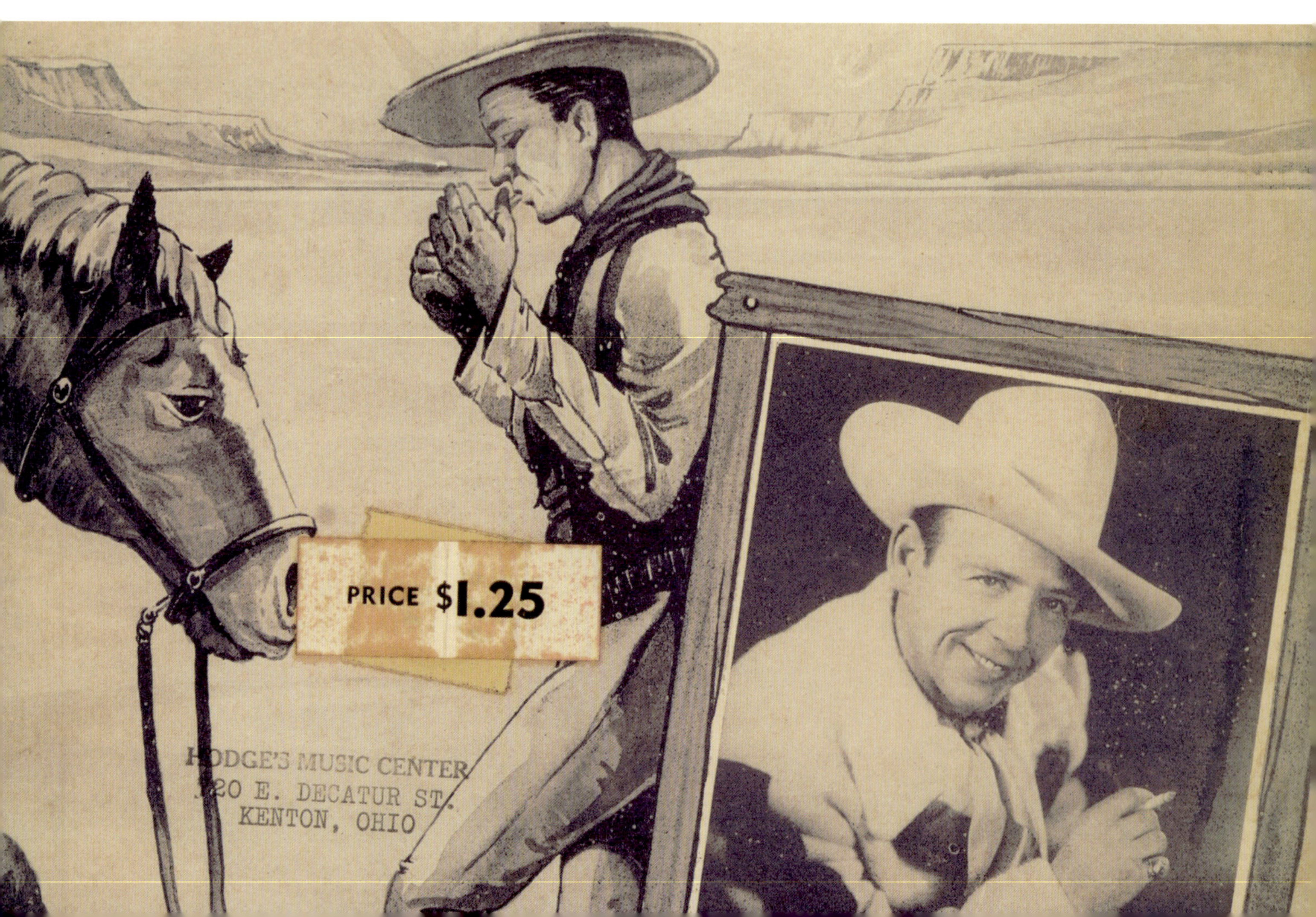

T-Bone Walker . . . . *T-Bone Shuffle* (John "Shifty" Henry), Capitol 57-70042, 78, 1949
Wilma Lee & Stoney Cooper . . . . *Moonlight on West Virginia* (R. Parker–E. Parker), Columbia 20607, 78, 1949
On the Banks of the River (D. Lewis), Columbia 20607, 78, 1949
All American Quartet . . . . *You Sho' Do Need Him Now*, All American Quartet 1101, 78, 1950
Arkie Shibley . . . . *Hot Rod Race* (G. Wilson), Gilt-Edge 5021, 78, 1950
Beale St. Gang . . . . *Back Alley Blues* (A. M. Brunner), Savoy 731, 78, 1950
Charles Brown Trio . . . . *Trouble Blues*, Aladdin 3024, 78, 1950
Honey Keep Your Mind on Me (Porter Roberts–Allan Roberts), Aladdin 3024, 78, 1950
Dominos . . . . *Sixty-Minute Man* (Ward–Marks), Federal 12022, 78, 1950
Do Something for Me (Ward–Marks), Federal 12001, 78, 1950
Chicken Blues (Ward–Marks), Federal 12001, 78, 1950
Eddie "Cleanhead" Vinson . . . . *Peas and Rice* (Milton Larkin), King 4414, 78, 1950
If You Don't Think I'm Sinking (Look What a Hole I'm In) (Ott–Mann–Glover), King 4414, 78, 1950
Famous Blue Jay Singers of Birmingham, Alabama . . . . *I Feel Like My Time Ain't Long*, Decca 48150, 78, 1950
Jesus Hits Like the Atom Bomb (Lee V. McCullom), Decca 48150, 78, 1950
Fats Domino . . . . *Every Night About This Time*, Imperial 5099, 78, 1950
Korea Blues (A. Young–D. Bartholomew), Imperial 5099, 78, 1950
Great Gildersleeve . . . . *Gerald McBoing-Boing—Side 1* (Dr. Seuss), Capitol CAS-3054, 78, 1950
Gerald McBoing-Boing—Side 2 (Dr. Seuss), Capitol CAS-3054, 78, 1950
Hank Penny . . . . *I'm Gonna Have My Picture Taken*, King 902, 78, 1950
Remington Ride (Herb Remington), King 902, 78, 1950
Hank Snow "The Singing Ranger" . . . . *With This Ring I Thee Wed* (S. Nelson–J. Rollins–E. Nelson, Jr.),
RCA Victor 21-0328, 78, 1950
I'm Moving On (Clarence E. Snow), RCA Victor 21-0328, 78, 1950
Ivory Joe Hunter . . . . *Gimme a Pound O' Ground Round* (Samuels), MGM 10733, 78, 1950
Lying Woman, King 4405, 78, 1950
Jimmy Liggins . . . . *Answer to Tear Drop Blues*, Specialty 362, 78, 1950

Below: Detail of *My Bucket's Got a Hole in It* (Hank Williams), 1950.

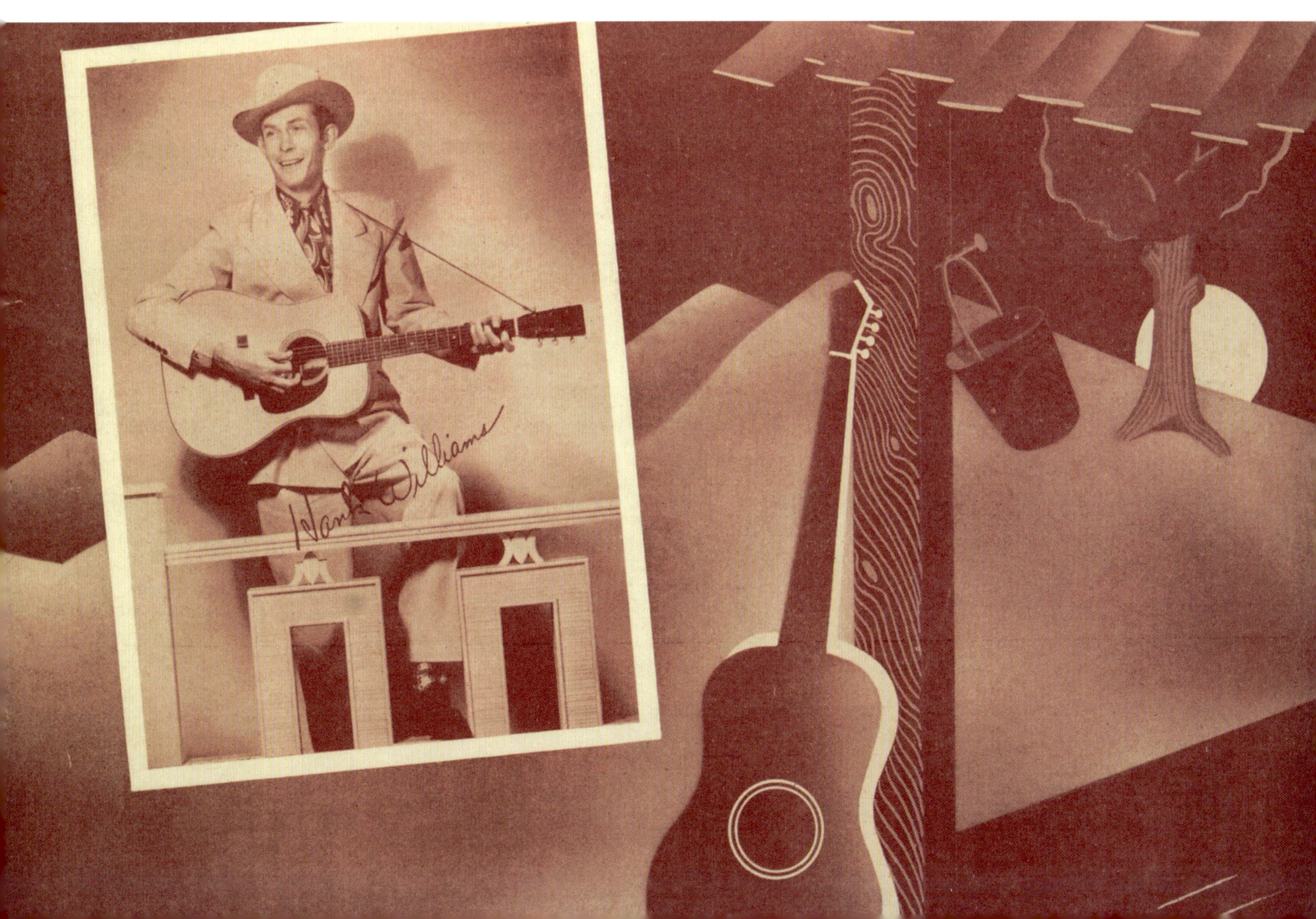

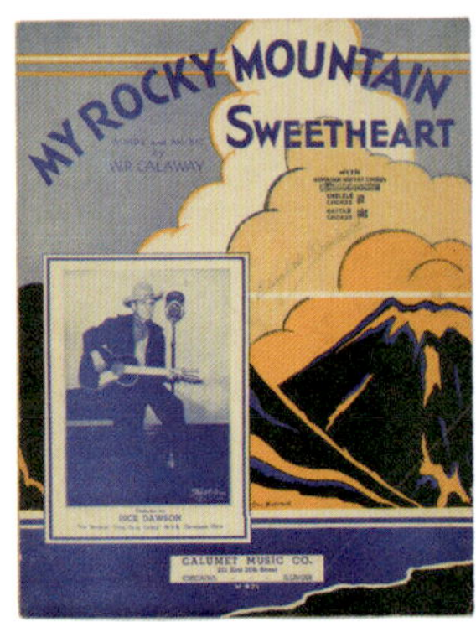

MY ROCKY MOUNTAIN
SWEETHEART
by
BOB CALAWAY
CALUMET MUSIC CO.
CHICAGO ILLINOIS

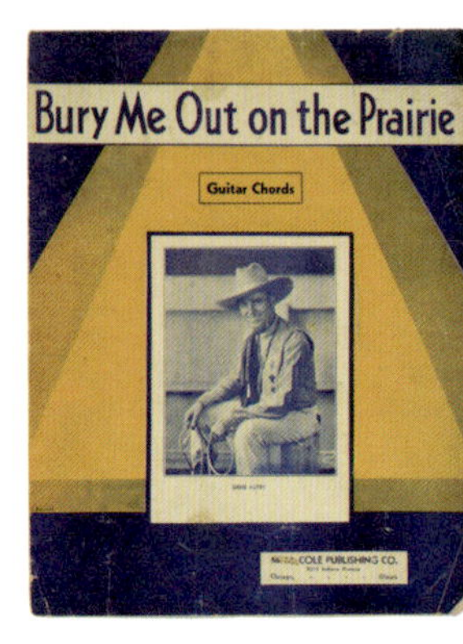

Bury Me Out on the Prairie
Guitar Chords
M.M. COLE PUBLISHING CO.

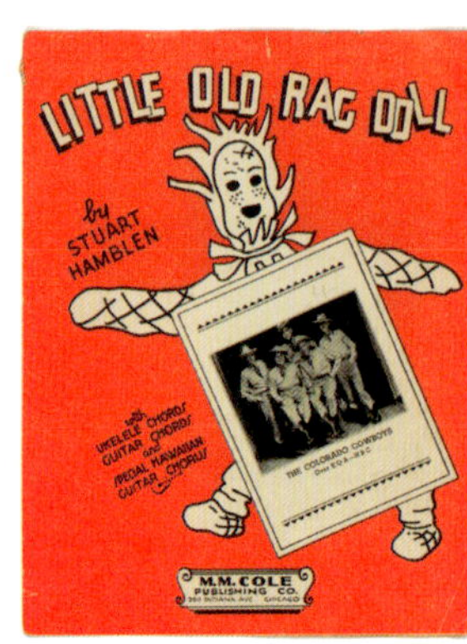

LITTLE OLD RAG DOLL
by
STUART HAMBLEN
UKELELE CHORDS
GUITAR CHORDS
SPECIAL HAWAIIAN
GUITAR CHORUS
THE COLORADO COWBOYS
M.M. COLE
PUBLISHING CO.

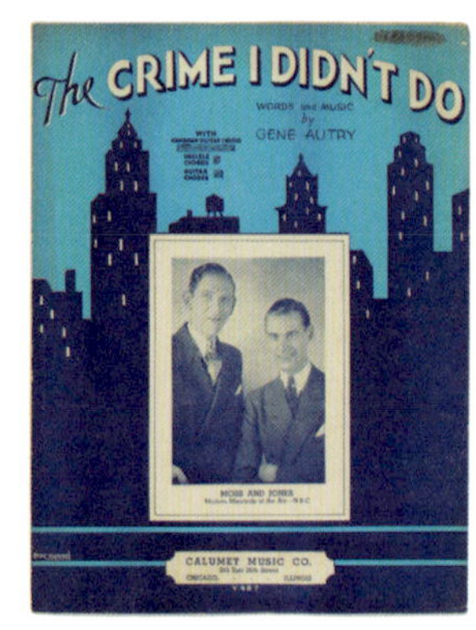

The CRIME I DIDN'T DO
WORDS and MUSIC
by
GENE AUTRY
BOB AND JONES
CALUMET MUSIC CO.
CHICAGO ILLINOIS

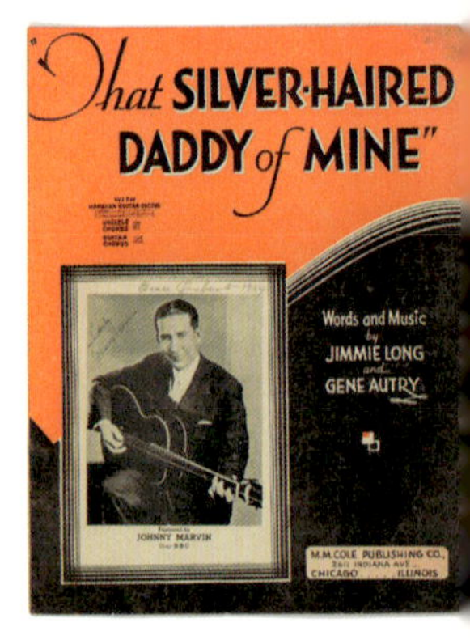

"That SILVER-HAIRED
DADDY of MINE"
Words and Music
by
JIMMIE LONG
and
GENE AUTRY
JOHNNY MARVIN
M.M. COLE PUBLISHING CO.
CHICAGO ILLINOIS

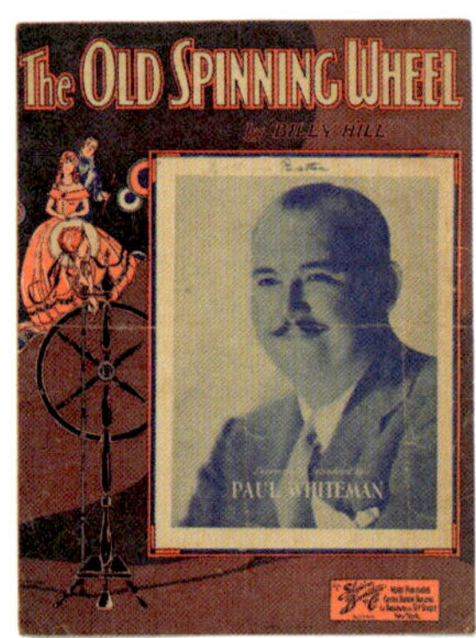

The OLD SPINNING WHEEL
PAUL WHITEMAN

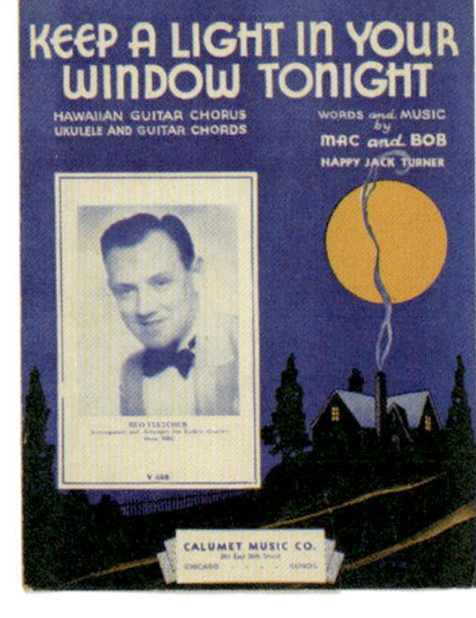

KEEP A LIGHT IN YOUR
WINDOW TONIGHT
HAWAIIAN GUITAR CHORUS
UKULELE AND GUITAR CHORDS
WORDS and MUSIC
by
MAC and BOB
HAPPY JACK TURNER
CALUMET MUSIC CO.
CHICAGO ILLINOIS

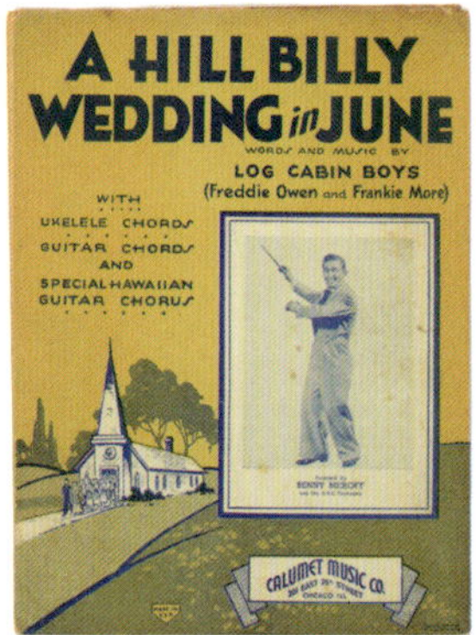

A HILL BILLY
WEDDING in JUNE
WORDS and MUSIC by
LOG CABIN BOYS
(Freddie Owen and Frankie More)
WITH
UKELELE CHORDS
GUITAR CHORDS
AND
SPECIAL HAWAIIAN
GUITAR CHORUS
CALUMET MUSIC CO.

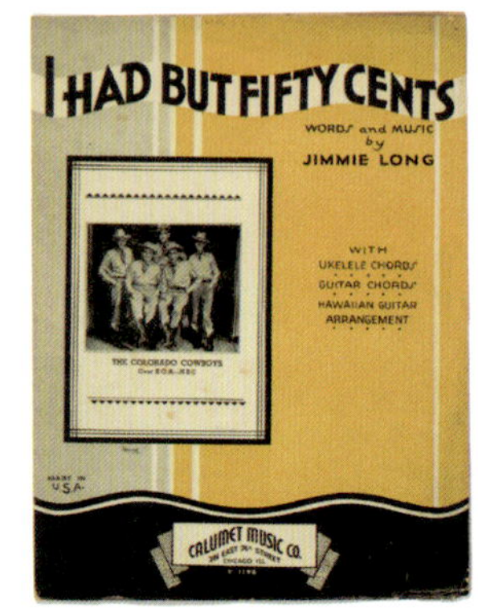

I HAD BUT FIFTY CENTS
WORDS and MUSIC
by
JIMMIE LONG
WITH
UKELELE CHORDS
GUITAR CHORDS
AND
HAWAIIAN GUITAR
ARRANGEMENT
THE COLORADO COWBOYS
MADE IN
U.S.A.
CALUMET MUSIC CO.

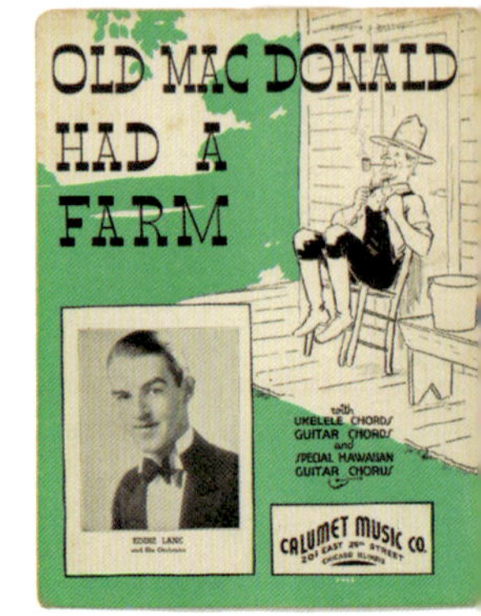

OLD MAC DONALD
HAD A
FARM
UKELELE CHORDS
GUITAR CHORDS
AND
SPECIAL HAWAIIAN
GUITAR CHORUS
EDDIE LANE
and His Orchestra
CALUMET MUSIC CO.
CHICAGO ILLINOIS

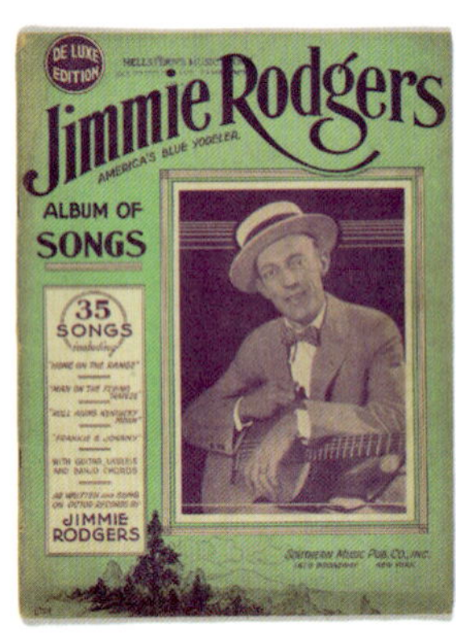

DE LUXE
EDITION
Jimmie Rodgers
AMERICA'S BLUE YODELER
ALBUM OF
SONGS
35
SONGS
JIMMIE RODGERS
SOUTHERN MUSIC PUB. CO., INC.
NEW YORK

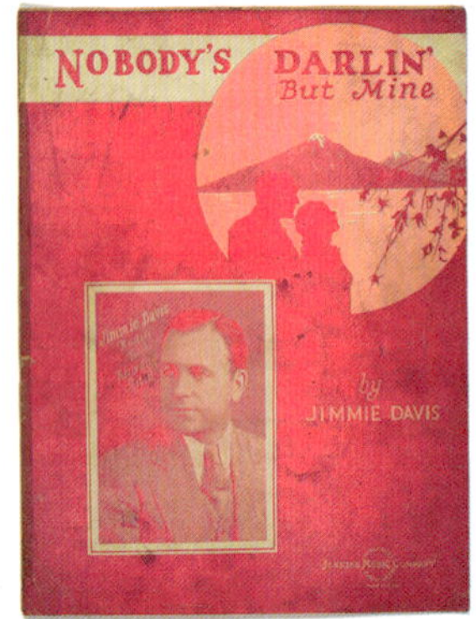

NOBODY'S DARLIN'
But Mine
by
JIMMIE DAVIS

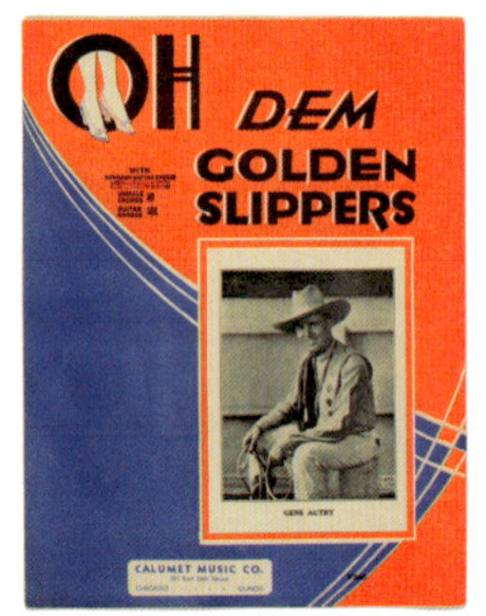

OH DEM
GOLDEN
SLIPPERS
GENE AUTRY
CALUMET MUSIC CO.
CHICAGO ILLINOIS

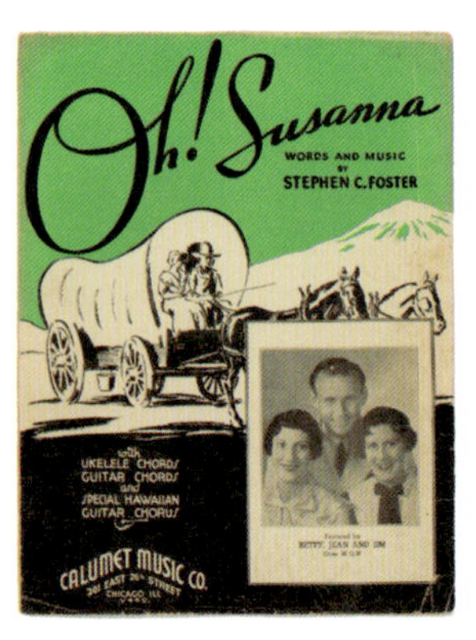

Oh! Susanna
WORDS AND MUSIC
BY
STEPHEN C. FOSTER
UKELELE CHORDS
GUITAR CHORDS
AND
SPECIAL HAWAIIAN
GUITAR CHORUS
BETTY JEAN AND JIM
CALUMET MUSIC CO.
CHICAGO ILLINOIS

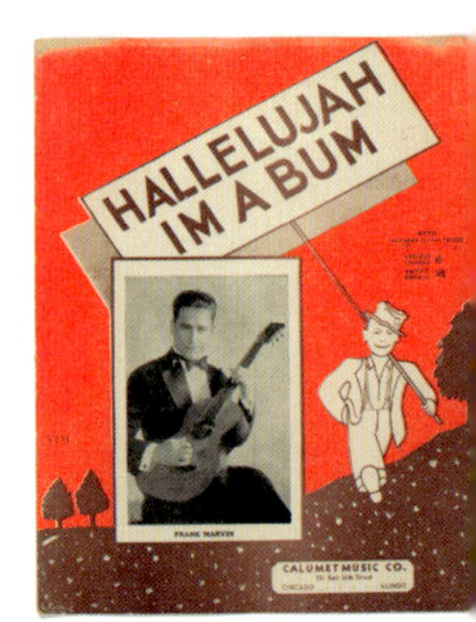

HALLELUJAH
I'M A BUM
FRANK MARVIN
CALUMET MUSIC CO.
CHICAGO ILLINOIS

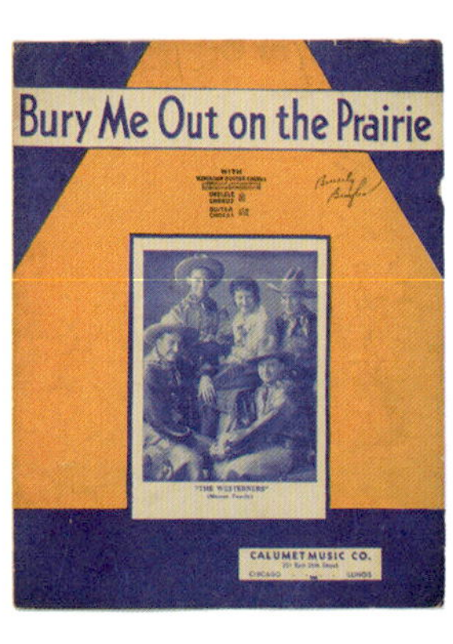

Bury Me Out on the Prairie
CALUMET MUSIC CO.
CHICAGO ILLINOIS

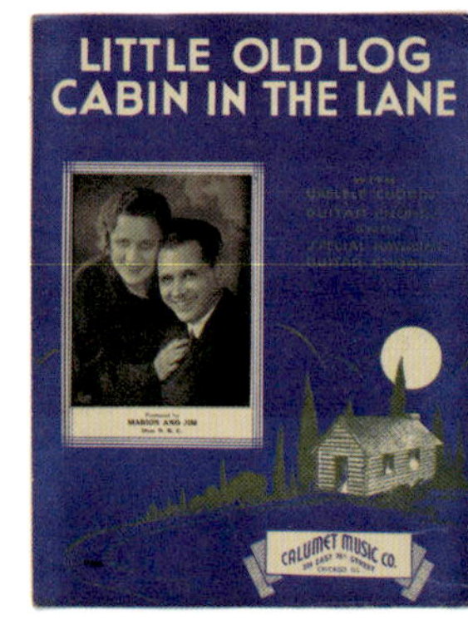

LITTLE OLD LOG
CABIN IN THE LANE
WITH
UKELELE CHORDS
GUITAR CHORDS
AND
SPECIAL HAWAIIAN
GUITAR CHORUS
MARION AND JIM
CALUMET MUSIC CO.
CHICAGO ILLINOIS

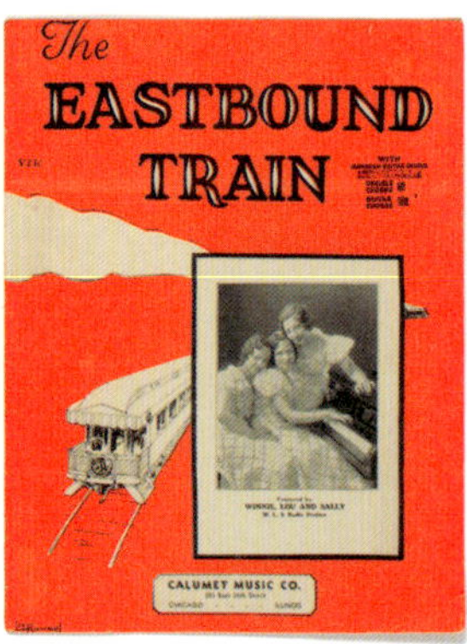

The
EASTBOUND
TRAIN
CALUMET MUSIC CO.
CHICAGO ILLINOIS

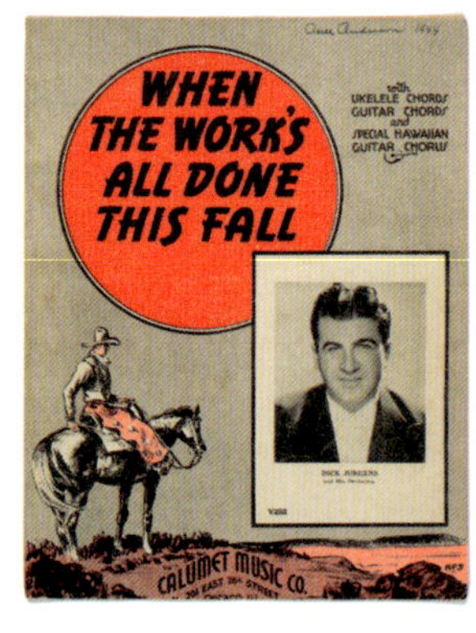

WHEN
THE WORK'S
ALL DONE
THIS FALL
WITH
UKELELE CHORDS
GUITAR CHORDS
AND
SPECIAL HAWAIIAN
GUITAR CHORUS
DICK JURGENS
and His Orchestra
CALUMET MUSIC CO.

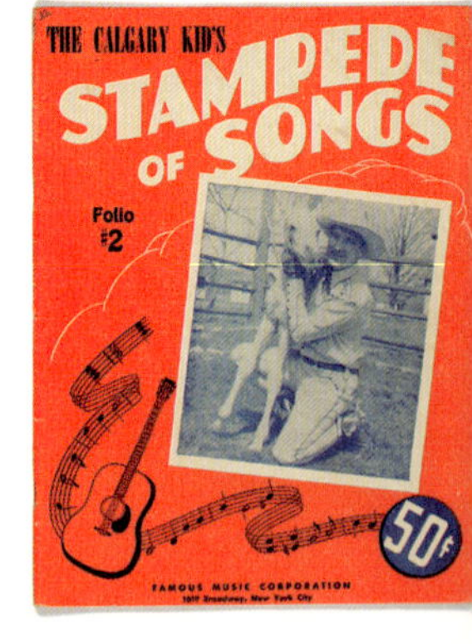

THE CALGARY KID'S
STAMPEDE
OF SONGS
Folio
#2
50¢
FAMOUS MUSIC CORPORATION
1619 Broadway, New York City

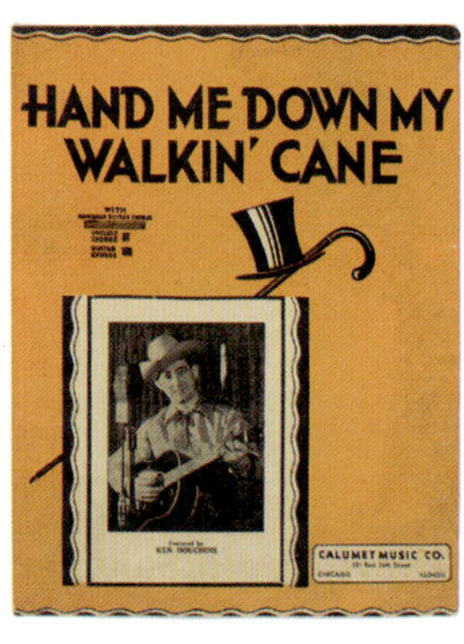

HAND ME DOWN MY
WALKIN' CANE
KEN MORGANS
CALUMET MUSIC CO.
CHICAGO ILLINOIS

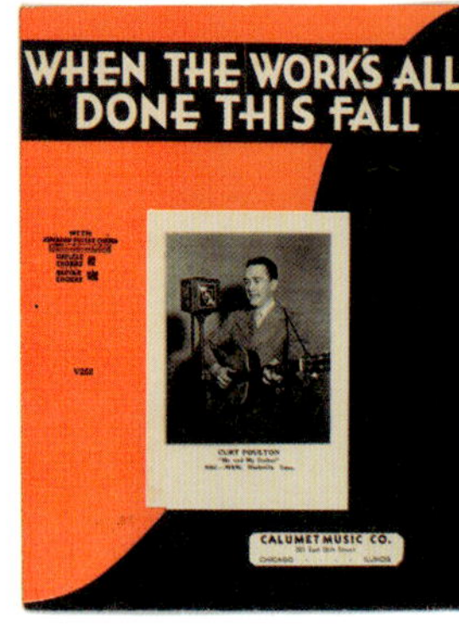

WHEN THE WORK'S ALL
DONE THIS FALL
CURT POULTON
CALUMET MUSIC CO.
CHICAGO ILLINOIS

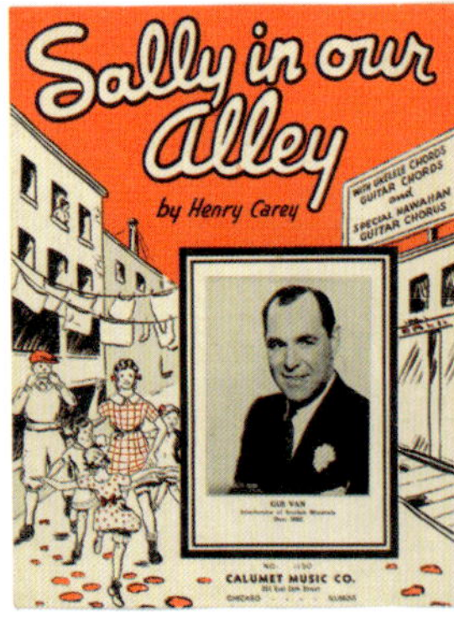

Sally in our
Alley
by Henry Carey
WITH UKELELE CHORDS
GUITAR CHORDS
AND
SPECIAL HAWAIIAN
GUITAR CHORUS
ELLE VALE
CALUMET MUSIC CO.
CHICAGO ILLINOIS

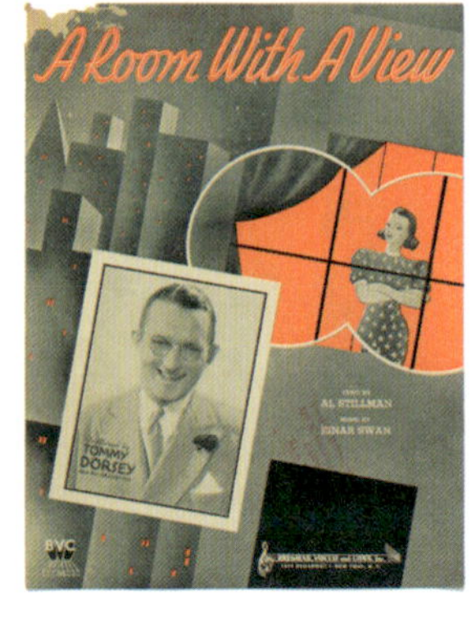

A Room With A View
WORDS by
AL STILLMAN
MUSIC by
EDGAR OMAN
TOMMY DORSEY

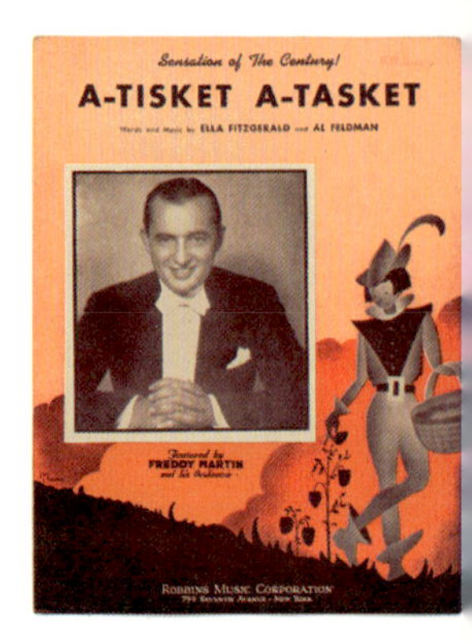

Sensation of The Century!
A-TISKET A-TASKET
Words and Music by ELLA FITZGERALD and AL FELDMAN
Featured by
FREDDY MARTIN
and his Orchestra
ROBBINS MUSIC CORPORATION
799 Seventh Avenue - New York

Johnny Otis Orch. . . . . *I Don't Care*, Savoy 775, 78, 1950
Johnny Otis Quintette . . . . *Double Crossing Blues*, Savoy 731, 78, 1950
Johnny White . . . . *Mean and Evil Blues* (Skeet's McDonald), Fortune 145, 78, 1950
"Lightnin' " Hopkins . . . . *New Worried Life Blues*, Sittin in with 649, 78, 1950
"Little" Jimmy Dickens . . . . *F-o-o-l-i-s-h Me* (McAlpin), Columbia 20962, 78, 1950
If It Ain't One Thing It's Another (Bryant), Columbia 20962, 78, 1950
Lowell Fulson . . . . *Low Society Blues* (Lloyd Glenn), Swing Time 226, 78, 1950
Blue Shadows (Lloyd Glenn), Swing Time 226, 78, 1950
Memphis Slim . . . . *Slim's Blues* (Chatman), Premium PR-860, 78, 1950
Havin' Fun (Sims), Premium PR-860, 78, 1950
Moon Mullican . . . . *Goodnight Irene* (Arranged by Mullican–Mann), King 886, 78, 1950
Mona Lisa (Livingston–Evans), King 886, 78, 1950
Roy Brown . . . . *New Rebecca*, DeLuxe 3304, 78, 1950
Hard Luck Blues, DeLuxe 3304, 78, 1950
Roy Milton . . . . *Short, Sweet and Snappy*, Specialty 414, 78, 1950
Where There Is No Love, Specialty 358, 78, 1950
Junior Jives, Specialty 358, 78, 1950
Ruth Brown . . . . *Teardrops from My Eyes* (Toombs), Atlantic 919, 78, 1950
Am I Making the Same Mistake Again? (Thomas), Atlantic 919, 78, 1950
Skeet's McDonald . . . . *The Tattoed Lady*, Fortune 145, 78, 1950
Spirit of Memphis Quartet . . . . *Blessed Are the Dead* (Arranged by Earl Malone), King 4340, 78, 1950
Days Passed and Gone (Arranged by Earl Malone), King 4340, 78, 1950
God's Got His Eyes on You (Jethroe Bledsoe), King 4440, 78, 1950
If You Make a Start to Heaven (Don't Turn Around) (Sammy Lewis), King 4440, 78, 1950
"T" Texas Tyler . . . . *The Old Country Church*, 4 Star 1403, 78, 1950
The Chuck Wagon Gang . . . . *Come Unto Me* (C. P. Jones), Columbia 20742, 78, 1950
I Am Bound to Travel On (Wright), Columbia 20742, 78, 1950
Willie Mae Ford Smith . . . . . . *Give Me Wings* (D. B. Hardy), Recorded Anthology of American Music Inc. 224, 45, 1950
Woody Guthrie . . . . *Dance Around*, Disc New York 5051, 78, 1950
Put Your Finger in the Air, Disc New York 5051, 78, 1950
Arthur "Guitar Boogie" Smith . . . . *Big Mountain Shuffle* (Smith), MGM 10945, 78, 1951
Chew Tabacco Rag (Briggs), MGM 10945, 78, 1951
Bill Monroe . . . . *The First Whippoorwill*, Decca 46386, 78, 1951
Christmas Time's A-Coming (Tex Logan), Decca 46386, 78, 1951
Billy Wright . . . . *Stacked Deck*, Savoy 781, 78, 1951
Brother Joe May . . . . *In That Day* (H. Dent), Specialty SP 815, 78, 1951
Precious Lord, Specialty SP 815, 78, 1951
Bull Moose Jackson . . . . *Sneaky Pete* (Sally Nix), King 4181, 78, 1951
Carl Smith . . . . *If Teardrops Were Pennies* (C. Butler), Columbia 20825, 78, 1951
Charles Brown . . . . *I'll Always Be in Love with You* (Green–Ruby–Stept), Aladdin 3091, 78, 1951
The Message (Clarence Landry), Aladdin 3091, 78, 1951
Clara Ward . . . . *When He Spoke*, Savoy 4026, 78, 1951
Oh My Lord, What a Time, Savoy 4026, 78, 1951
Clovers . . . . *One Mint Julep* (Toombs), Atlantic 963, 78, 1951
Hank Williams . . . . *Never Again (Will I Knock on Your Door)*, MGM 10352, 78, 1951
Lovesick Blues, MGM 10352, 78, 1951
Cold, Cold Heart, MGM 10904, 78, 1951
Dear John (Ritter–Gass), MGM 10904, 78, 1951
Howlin' Wolf . . . . *"Moanin' at Midnight"* (Carl Germany), Chess 1479, 78, 1951
"How Many More Years" (Carl Germany), Chess 1479, 78, 1951
James and Martha Carson . . . . *I'll Fly Away*, Capitol 1415, 78, 1951
Johnnie Ray . . . . *Cry* (Kohlman), Okeh 6840, 78, 1951
Lefty Frizzell . . . . *Always Late (with Your Kisses)* (Frizzell–B. Crawford), Columbia 20837, 78, 1951
Mom and Dad's Waltz, Columbia 20837, 78, 1951
Travellin' Blues (Rodgers), Columbia 20842, 78, 1951
Blue Yodel No. 6 (Rodgers), Columbia 20842, 78, 1951
Les Paul . . . . *Walkin' and Whistlin' Blues*, Capitol 1451, 78, 1951
Les Paul and Mary Ford . . . . *How High the Moon* (Morgan Lewis–Nancy Hamilton), Capitol 1451, 78, 1951
Lester Flatt & Earl Scruggs . . . . *Somehow Tonight* (Scruggs), Columbia 20830, 78, 1951
Jimmie Brown, the Newsboy (Carter Family), Columbia 20830, 78, 1951
Little Esther . . . . *Lookin' for a Man (to Satisfy My Soul)* (Latricia Walker), Federal 12036, 78, 1951
"Little" Jimmy Dickens . . . . *The Galvanized Washing Tub* (C. Clark–Turner), Columbia 20835, 78, 1951
The Sign on the Highway (McLeod), Columbia 20835, 78, 1951

Opposite: Sheet music and song books 1932-1945.

Louvin Brothers . . . . *They've Got the Church Outnumbered*, MGM 10988, 78, 1951
Weapon of Prayer, MGM 10988, 78, 1951
Maddox Bros. & Rose . . . . *If We Never Meet Again*, 4 Star 2S-6-(b), 78, 1951
The Land Where We'll Never Grow Old, 4 Star 2S-6-(a), 78, 1951
Muddy Waters . . . . *Long Distance Call* (Marshall–Paul), Chess 1452, 78, 1951
Too Young to Know, Chess 1452, 78, 1951
"Peppermint" Harris . . . .*I Got Loaded*, Aladdin 3097, 78, 1951
Red Foley . . . . . *Sugarfoot Rag Square Dance* (Hank Garland–Margaret Mellott–George Vaughn), Decca 46349, 78, 1951
Sister Jessie Mae Renfro . . . . *A Wonderful Savior*, Peacock 1571, 78, 1951
Rock of Ages, Hide Thou Me, Peacock 1571, 78, 1951
A Wonderful Savior, Peacock 1571, 78, 1951
Sonny Thompson . . . . *Mellow Blues—Part 1* (Thompson–Glover), King 4488, 78, 1951
Mellow Blues—Part 2 (Thompson–Glover), King 4488, 78, 1951
Treniers . . . . *Go! Go! Go!* (D. Hill–Gilbeaux–Claude Trenier), Okeh 6804, 78, 1951
Plenty of Money (Claude Trenier–Cliff Trenier), Okeh 6804, 78, 1951
Wilf Carter (Montana Slim "The Yodeling Cowboy") . . . . . *My Oklahoma Rose* (Hayes–Symes), RCA Victor 20-4446, 78, 1951
I Wish There Were Only Three Days in the Year (Jimmy Rule), RCA Victor 20-4446, 78, 1951
Willard McDaniel . . . .*3 A.M. Boogie*, Specialty 415, 78, 1951
Blues on the Delta, Specialty 415, 78, 1951
Wynonie Harris . . . .*Confessin' the Blues* (Brown–McShann), King 4461, 78, 1951
Bloodshot Eyes (Penny–Hall), King 4461, 78, 1951
Amos Milburn . . . . *Boo Hoo* (Rudolph Toombs), Aladdin 3159, 78, 1952
Rock, Rock, Rock ("Peppermint" Harris), Aladdin 3159, 78, 1952
Bill Haley . . . . *Rock the Joint* (Crafton–Keene–Bagby), Essex 303, 78, 1952
Carl Smith . . . . *Softly and Tenderly* (W. Thompson), Columbia 20986, 78, 1952
Amazing Grace (Newton–Walker), Columbia 20986, 78, 1952

Opposite and following fifteen overleaf pages: Allen Ruppersberg, "Pages" from NO TIME LEFT TO START AGAIN, 2012.
Below: Detail of *Prairie Lullaby* (Billy Hill), 1933.

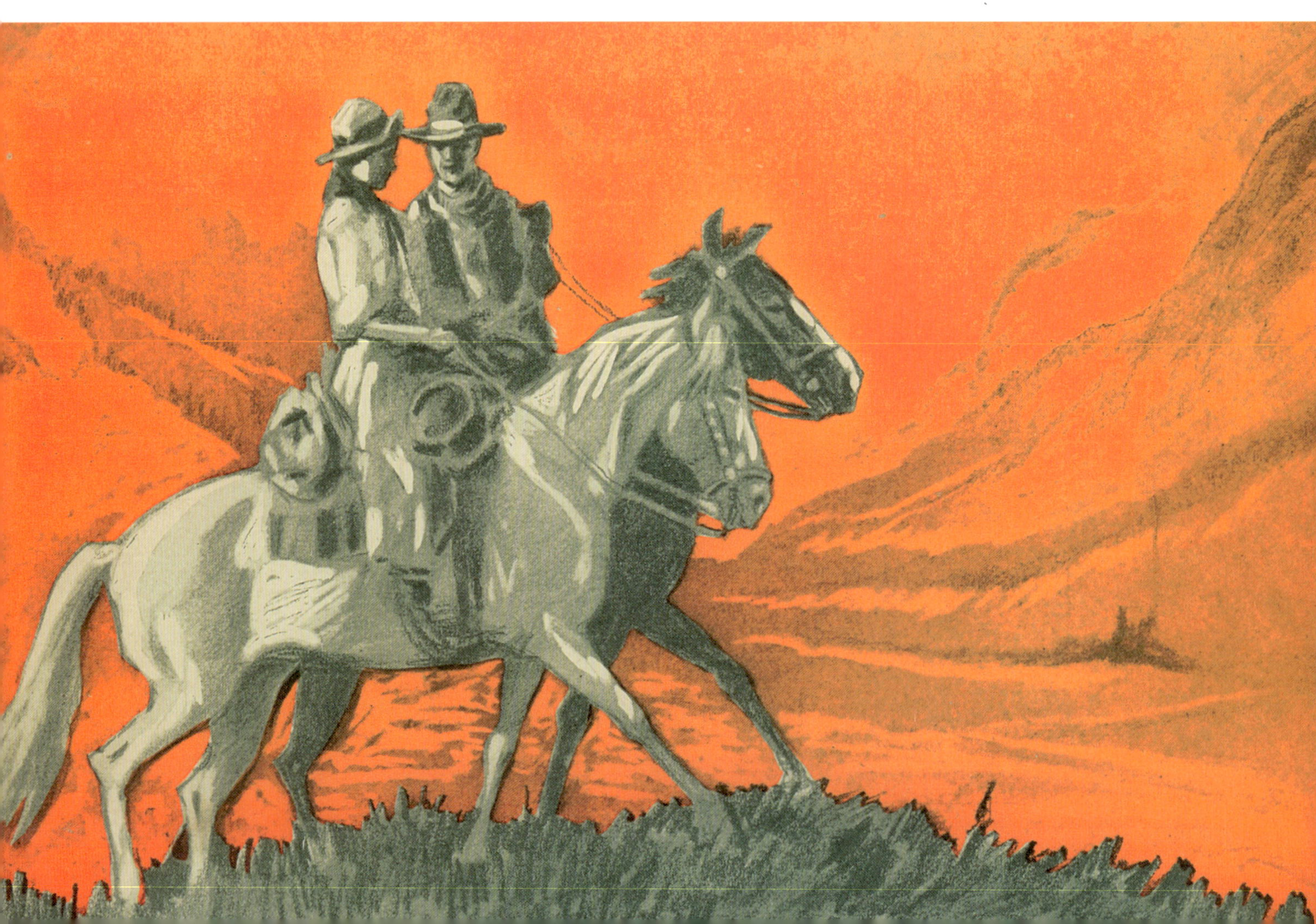

SECTION FIVE

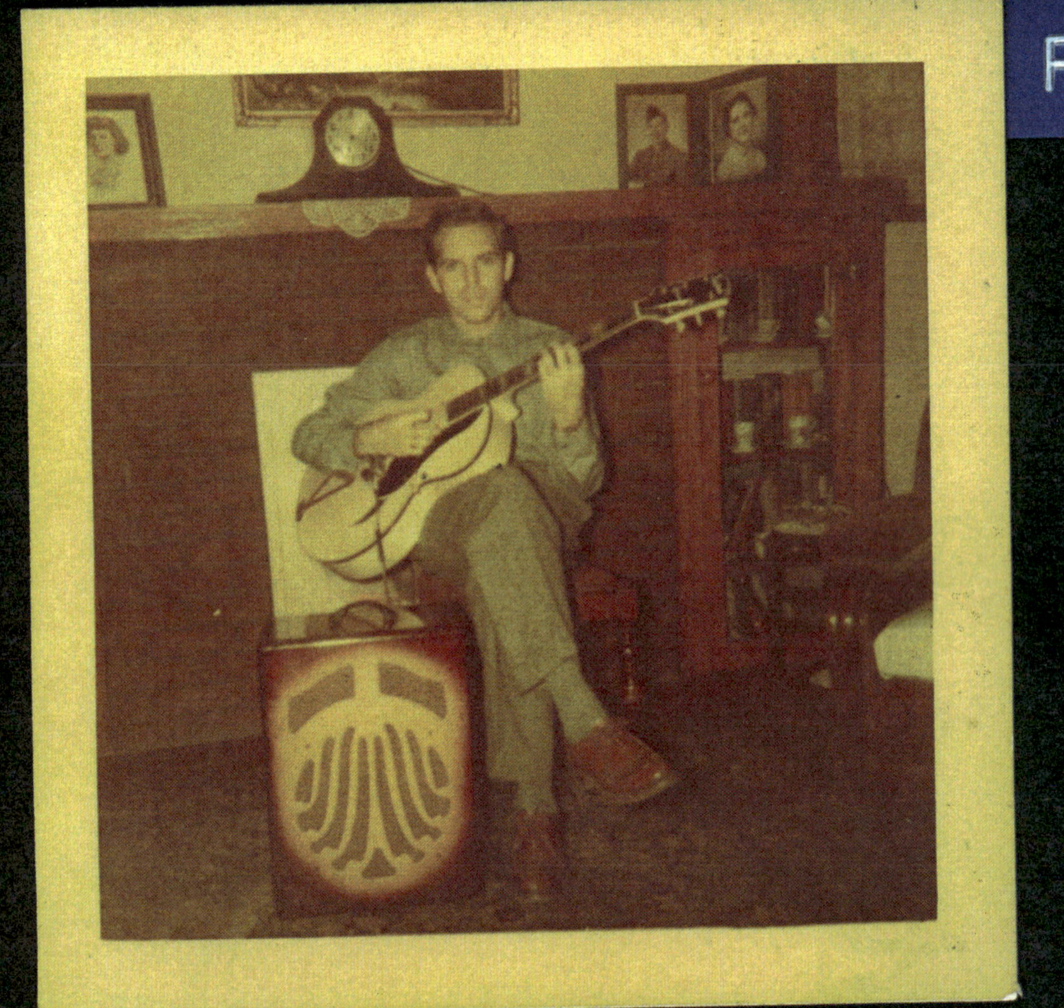

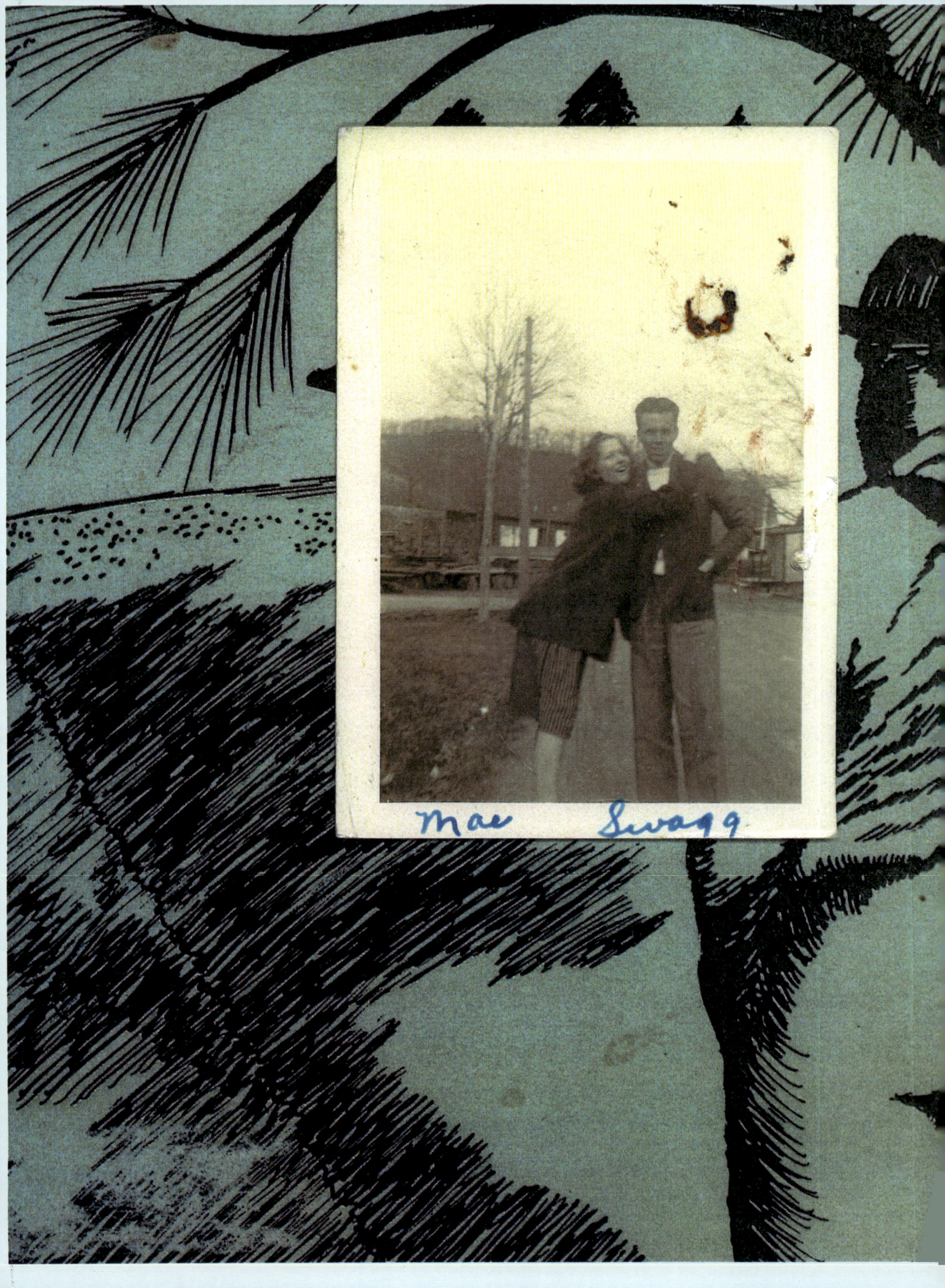

Mae   Swagg

your batteries are fresh
for flash pictures.

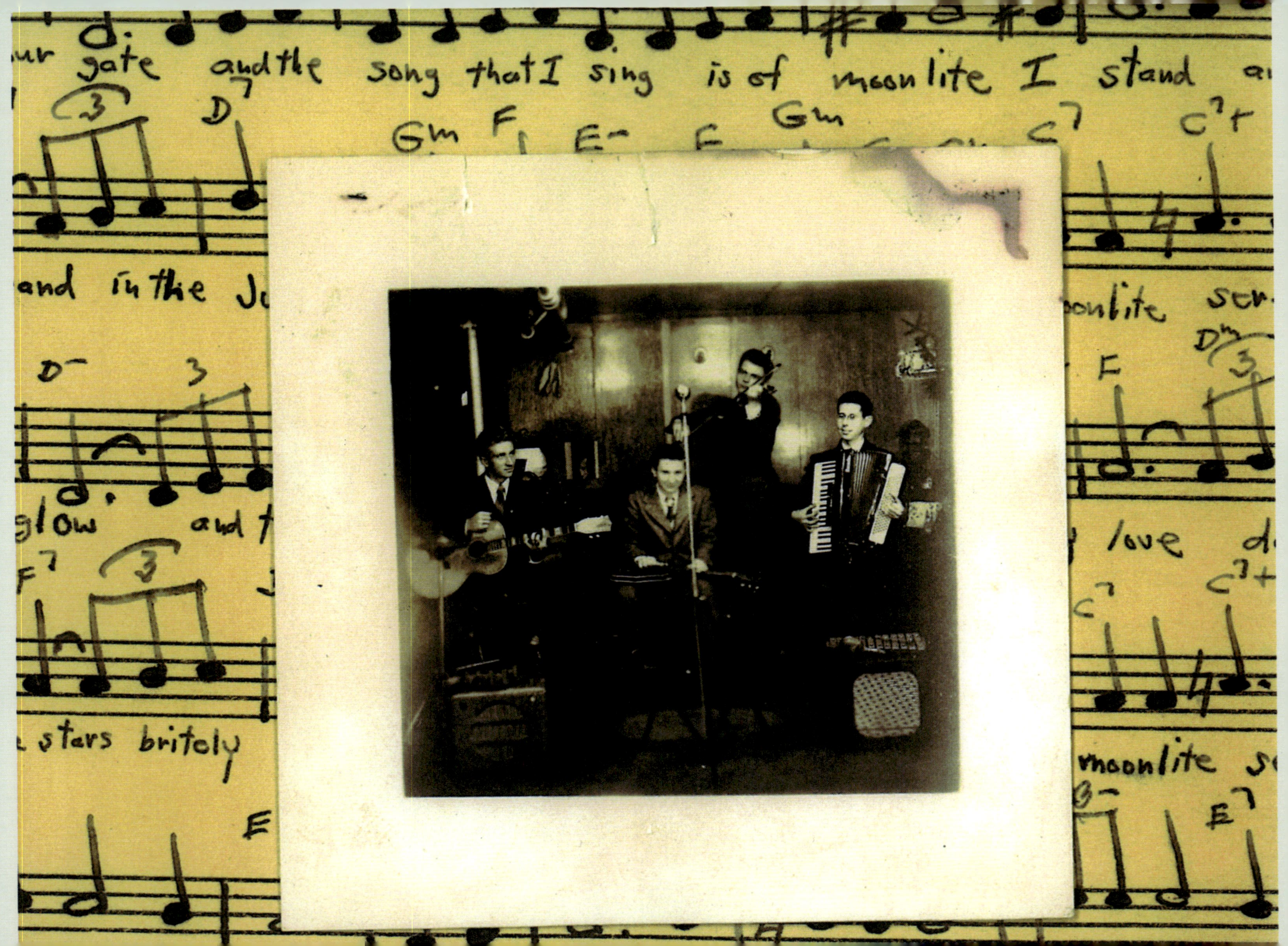
ur gate   and the   song that I sing   is of   moonlite I stand   a
D7   Gm F   E-   F   Gm   C7   C7+
and in the Ju   moonlite ser.
D-   3   E   Dm
glow   and t   love   d
F7   3   C7   C7+
e stars britoly   moonlite se
E   g-   E7

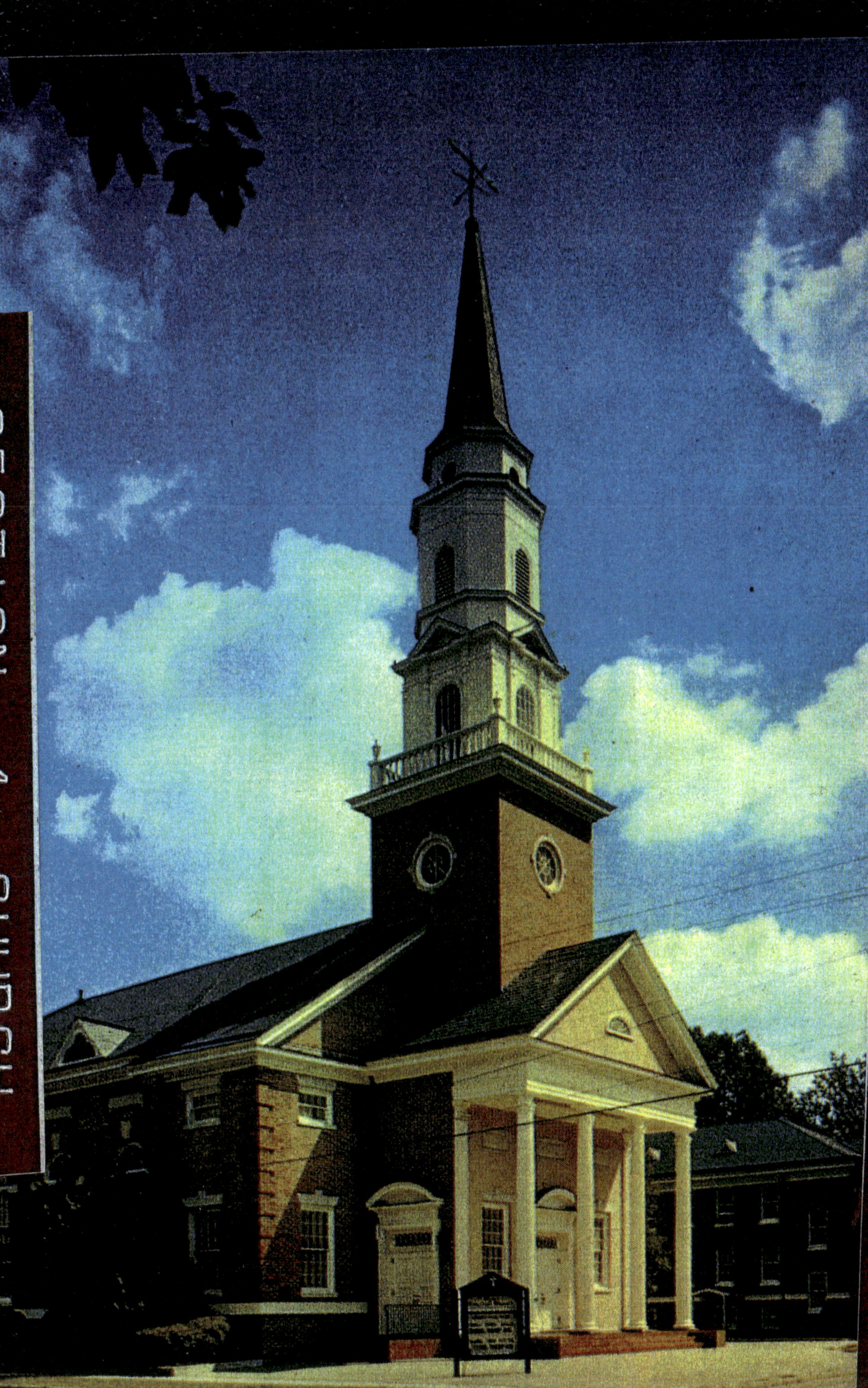

SECTION 4: CHURCH
NO TIME LEFT TO START AGAIN

POEMS

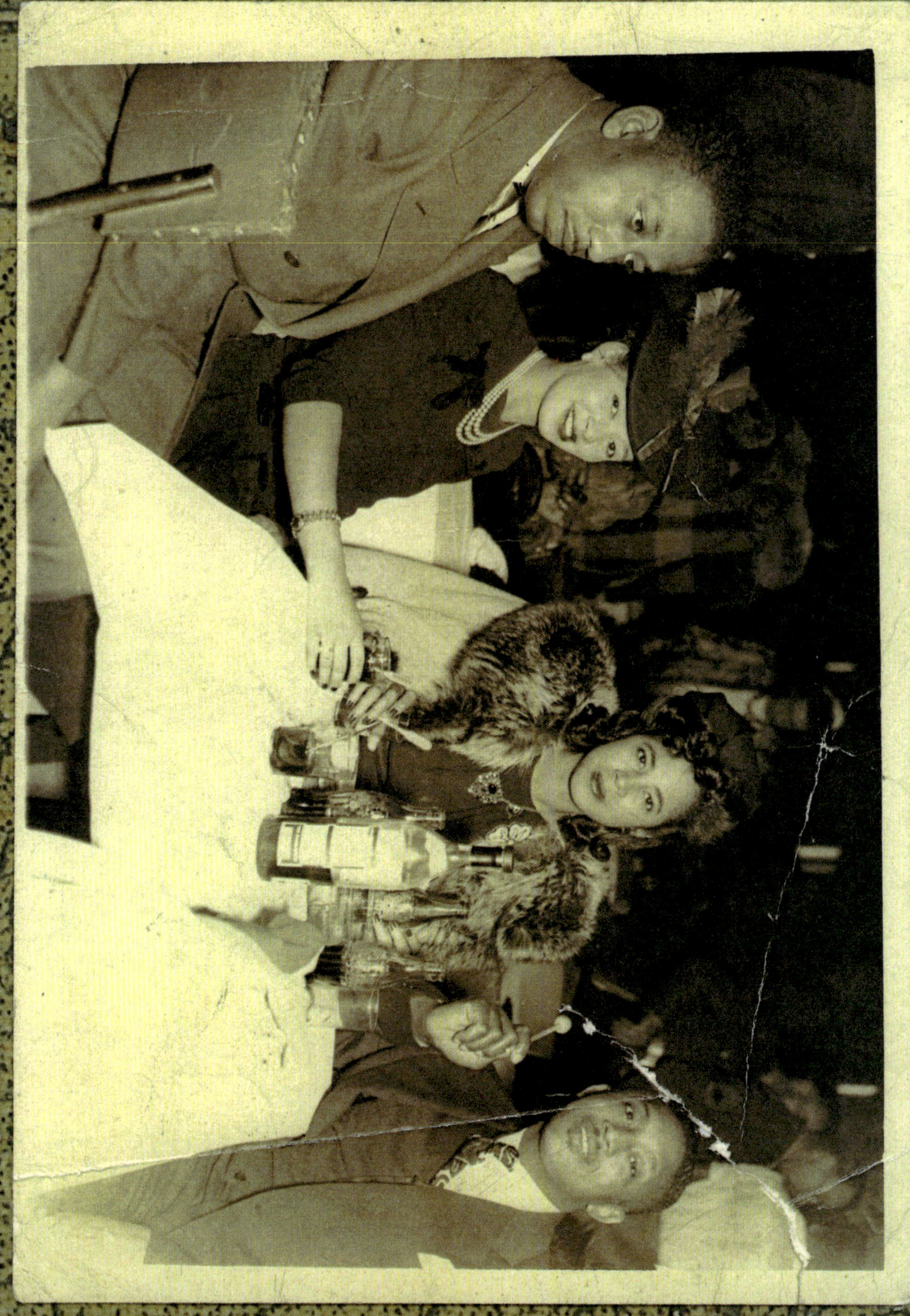

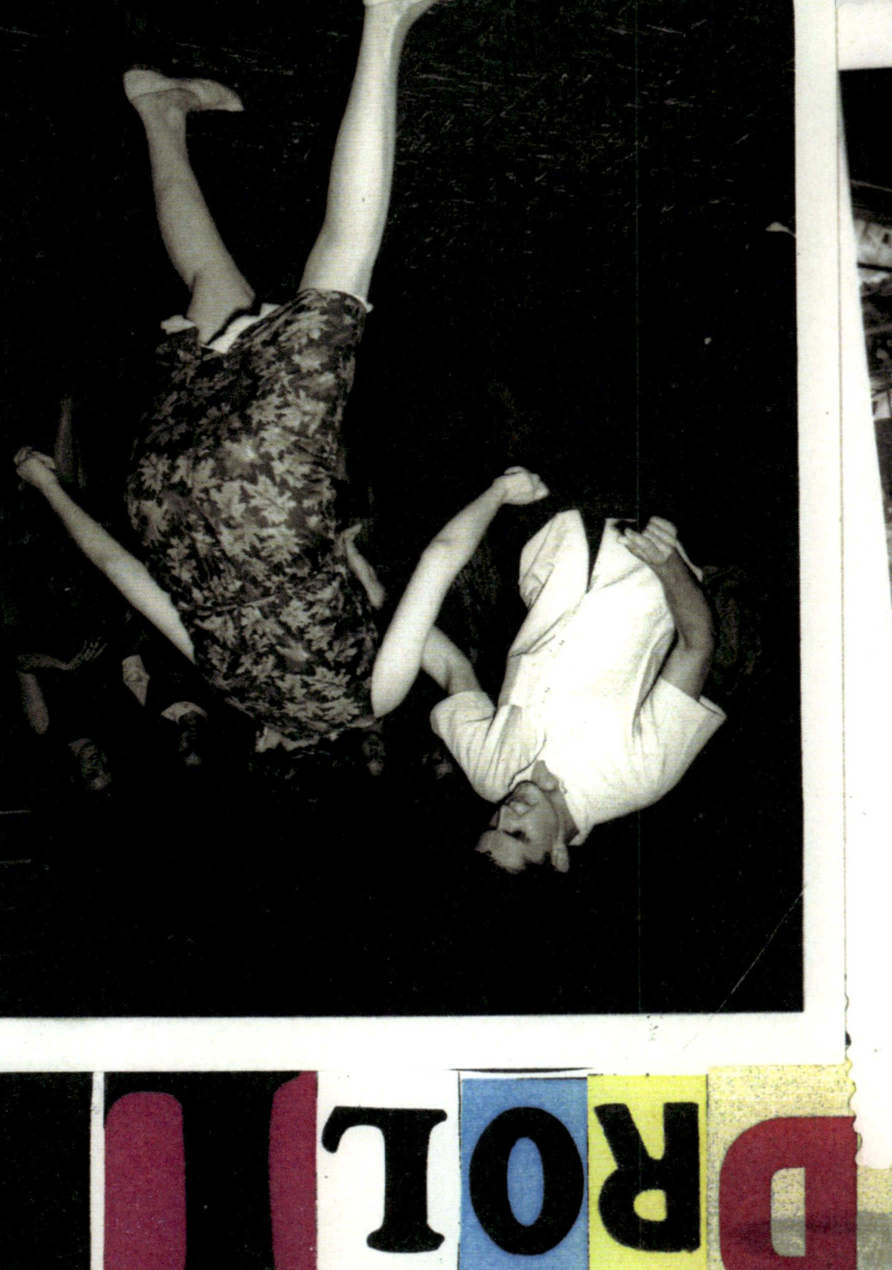
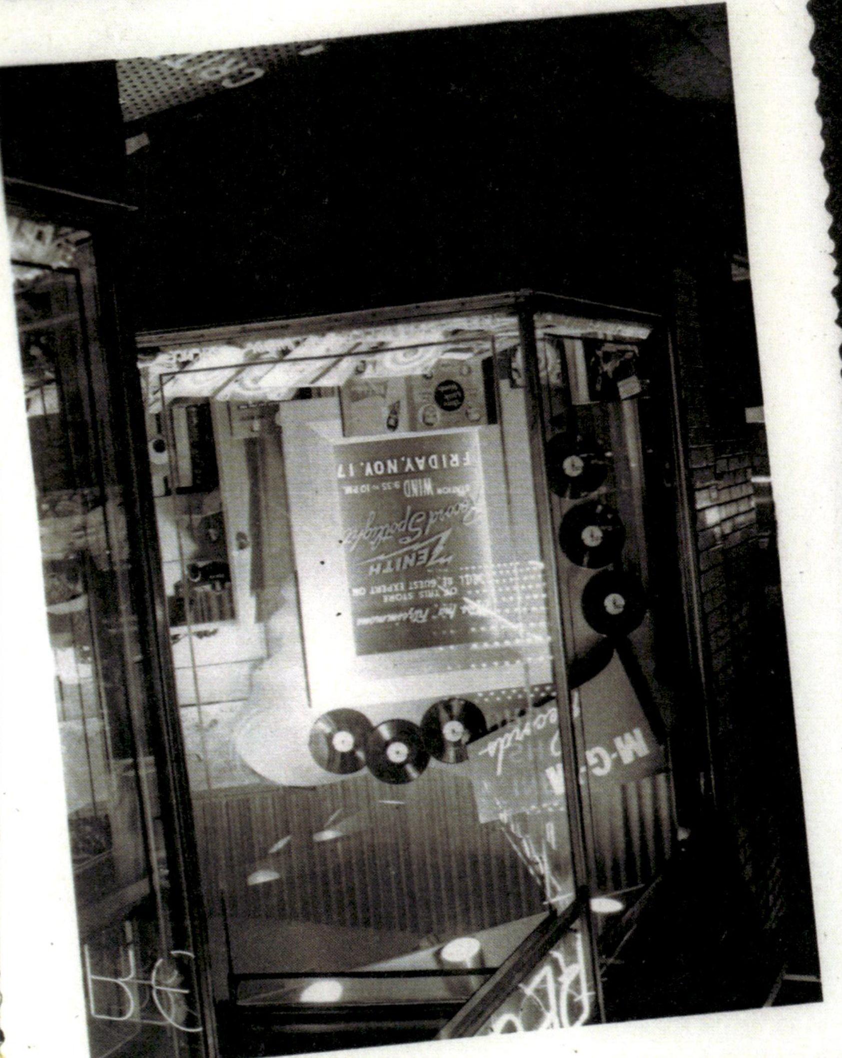

ROCK AND ROLL

NO TIME LEFT TO START AGAIN

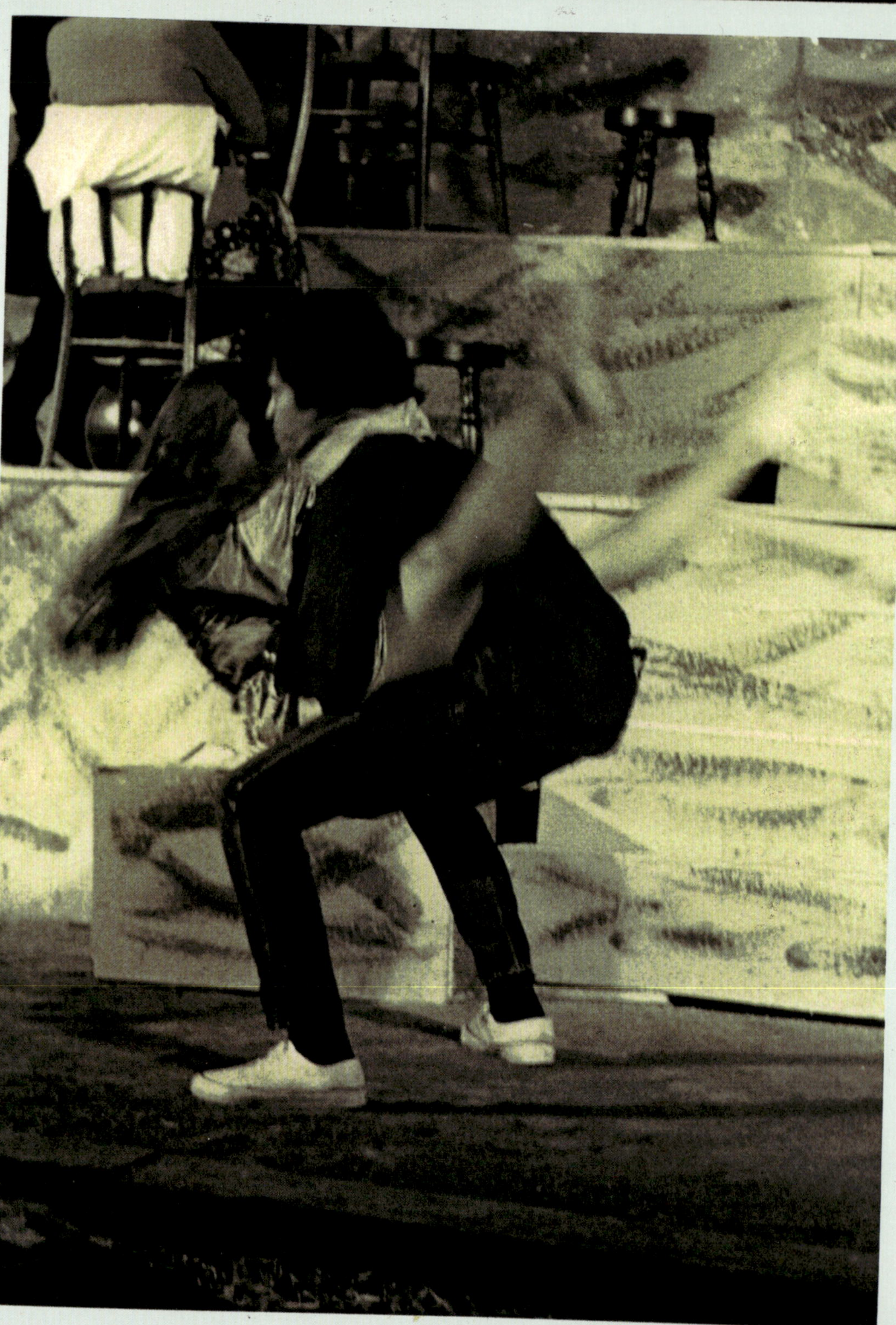

ROCK AND ROLL

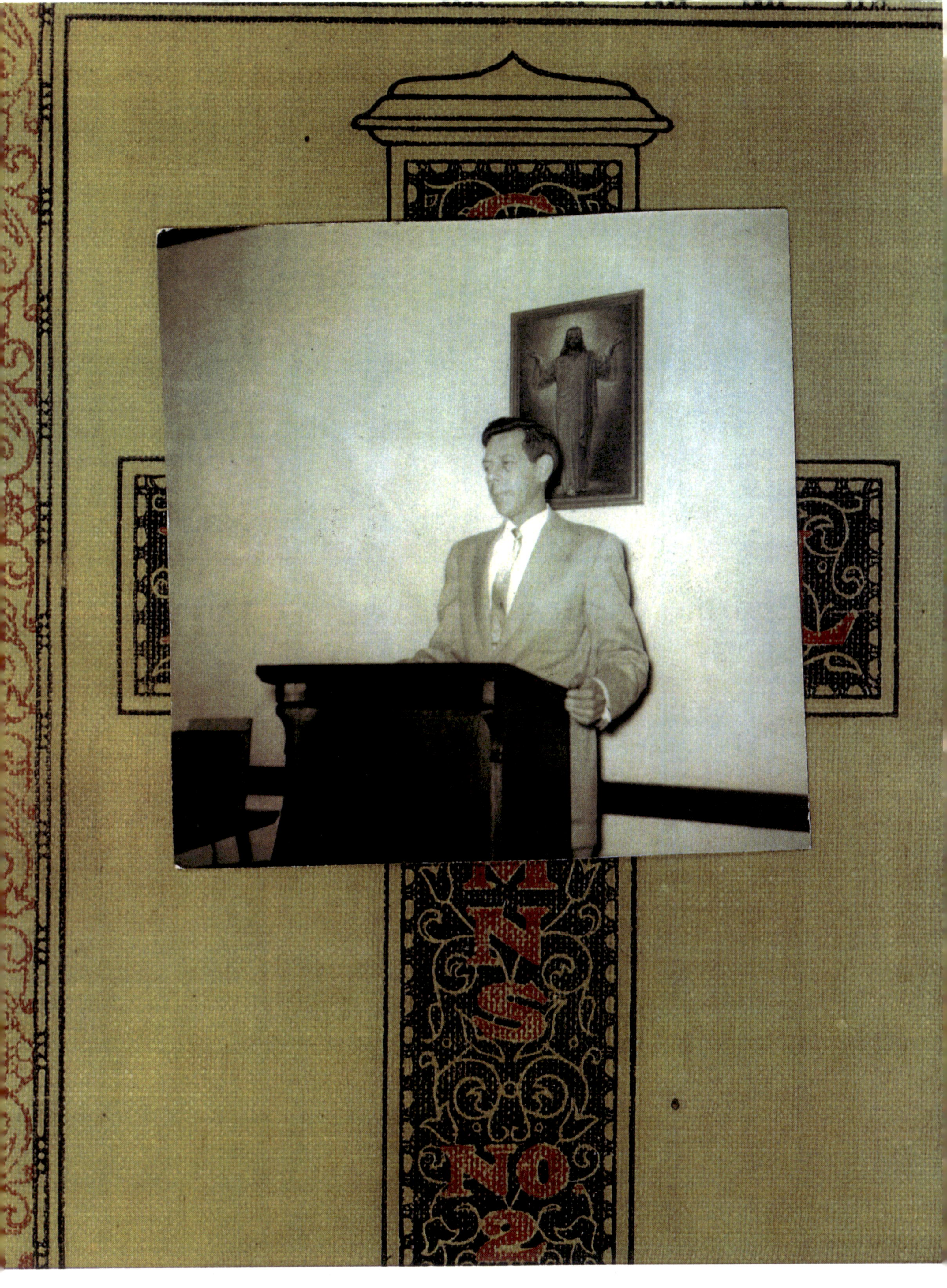

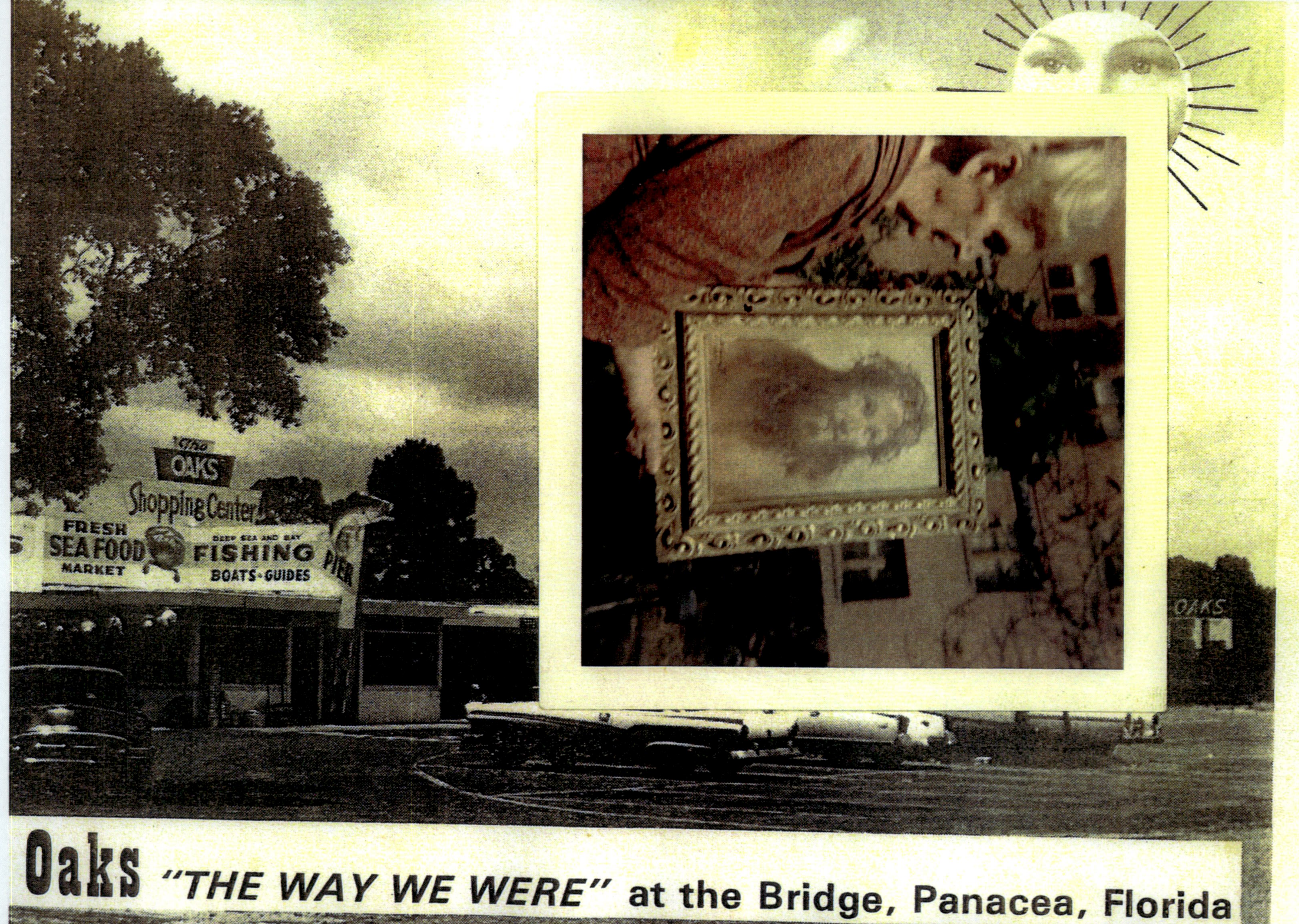

Oaks "THE WAY WE WERE" at the Bridge, Panacea, Florida

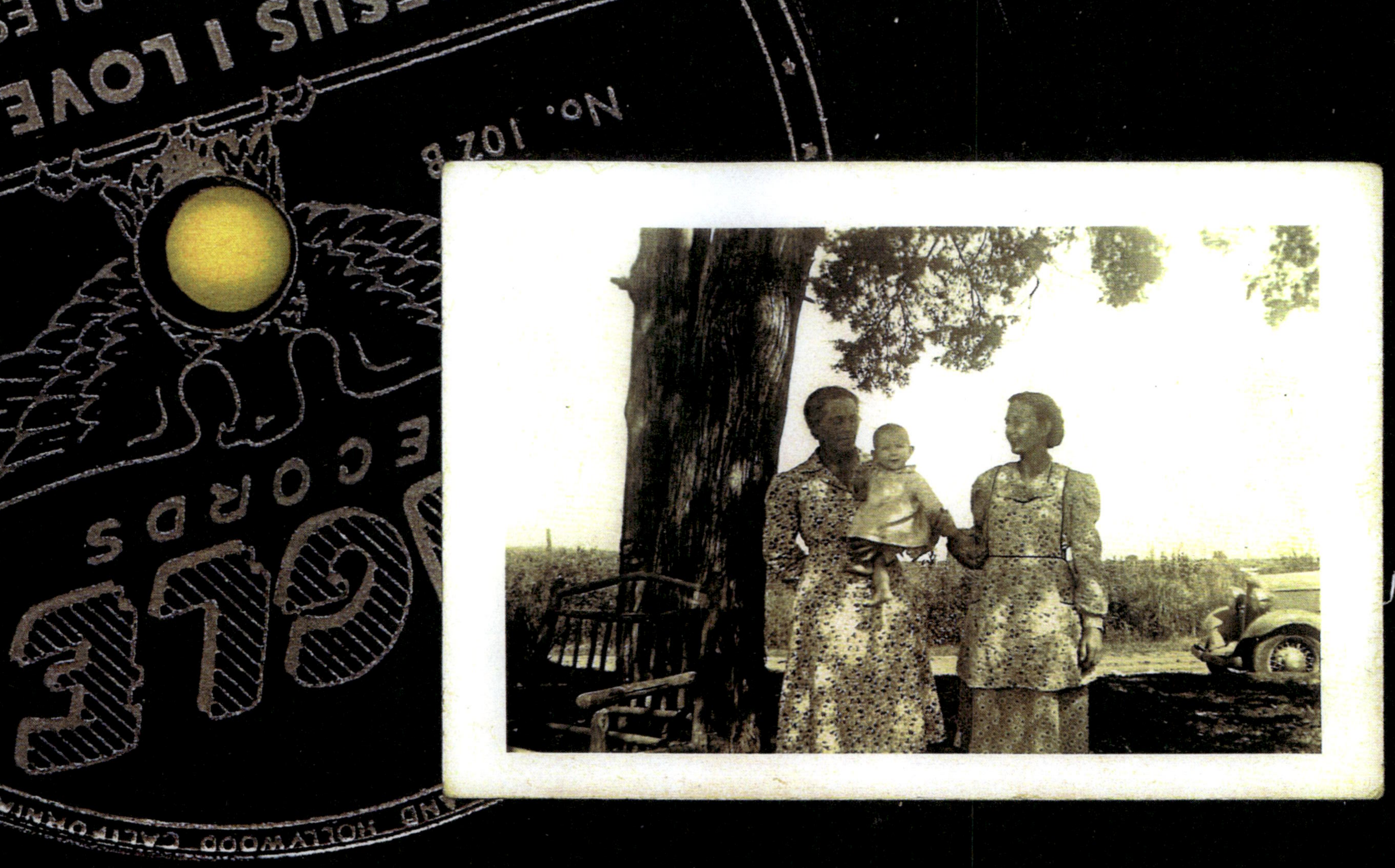
JESUS I LOVE
EAGLE RECORDS
HOLLYWOOD CALIFORNIA
No. 102B

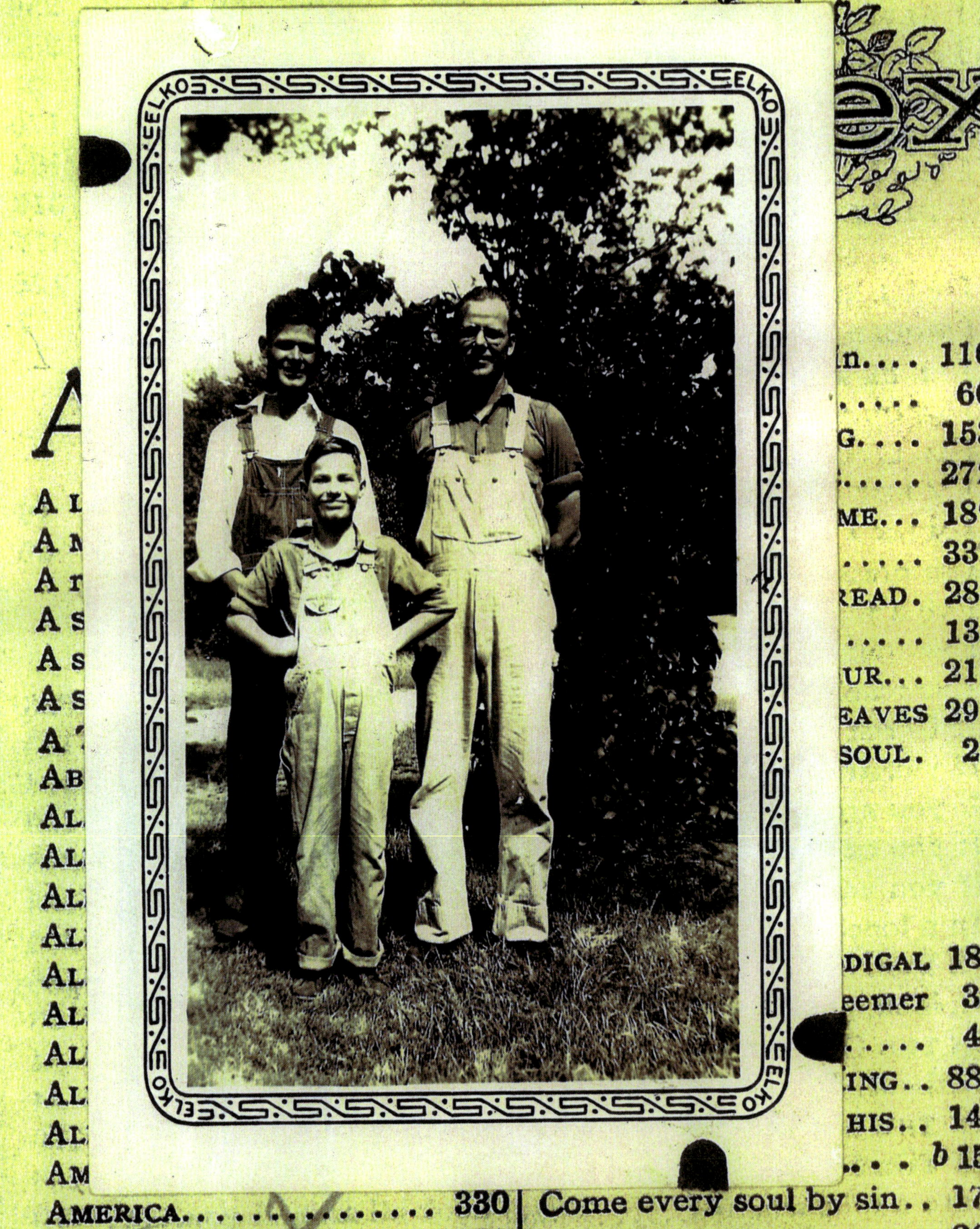

n Black, Silvertone 2705, 78, 1925

Lambkin   8, 192

From H   Colum

Ole Wag   a 3567

ee-Long   1925

ilin' on t   1925

Coon, V

essage,

o-Night   1925

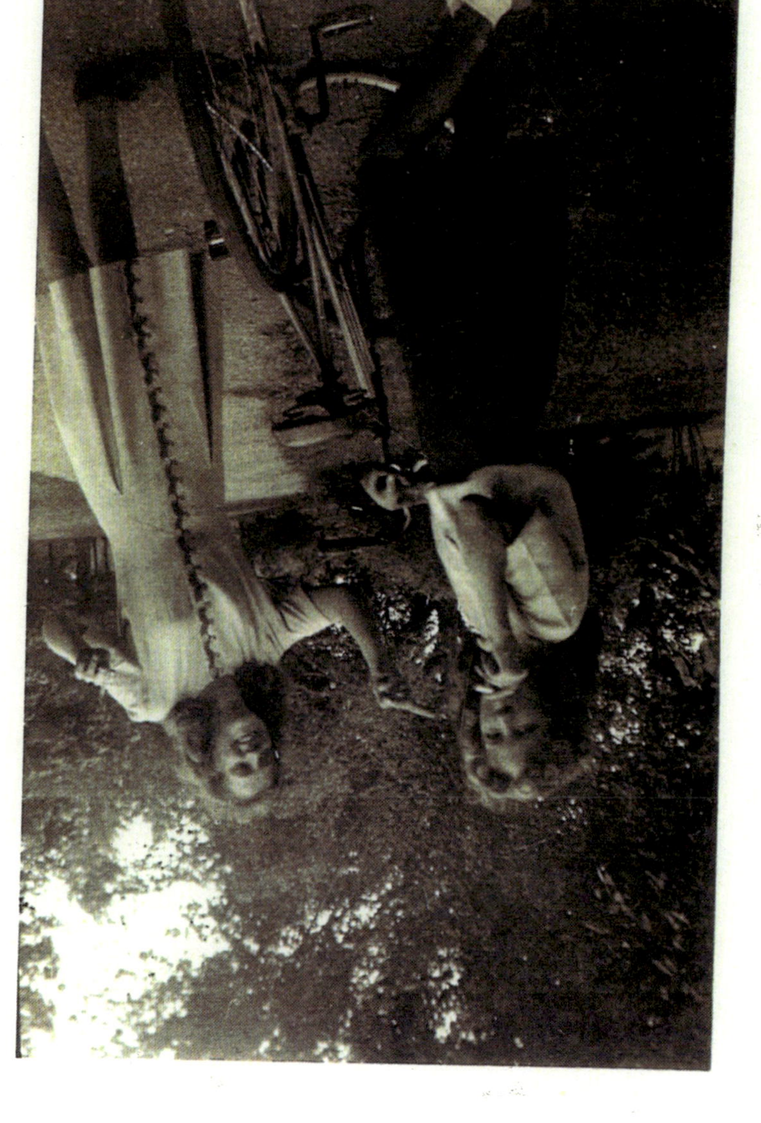

, Columbia 3567, 78, 1926

Of My Way (Carson Robison), Perfect 14615

loyd Collins (P.C. Brockman), Perfect 14615

452
9 1
DO NOT WRITE ABOVE
110
alists
SPACE
08
SSARY
c

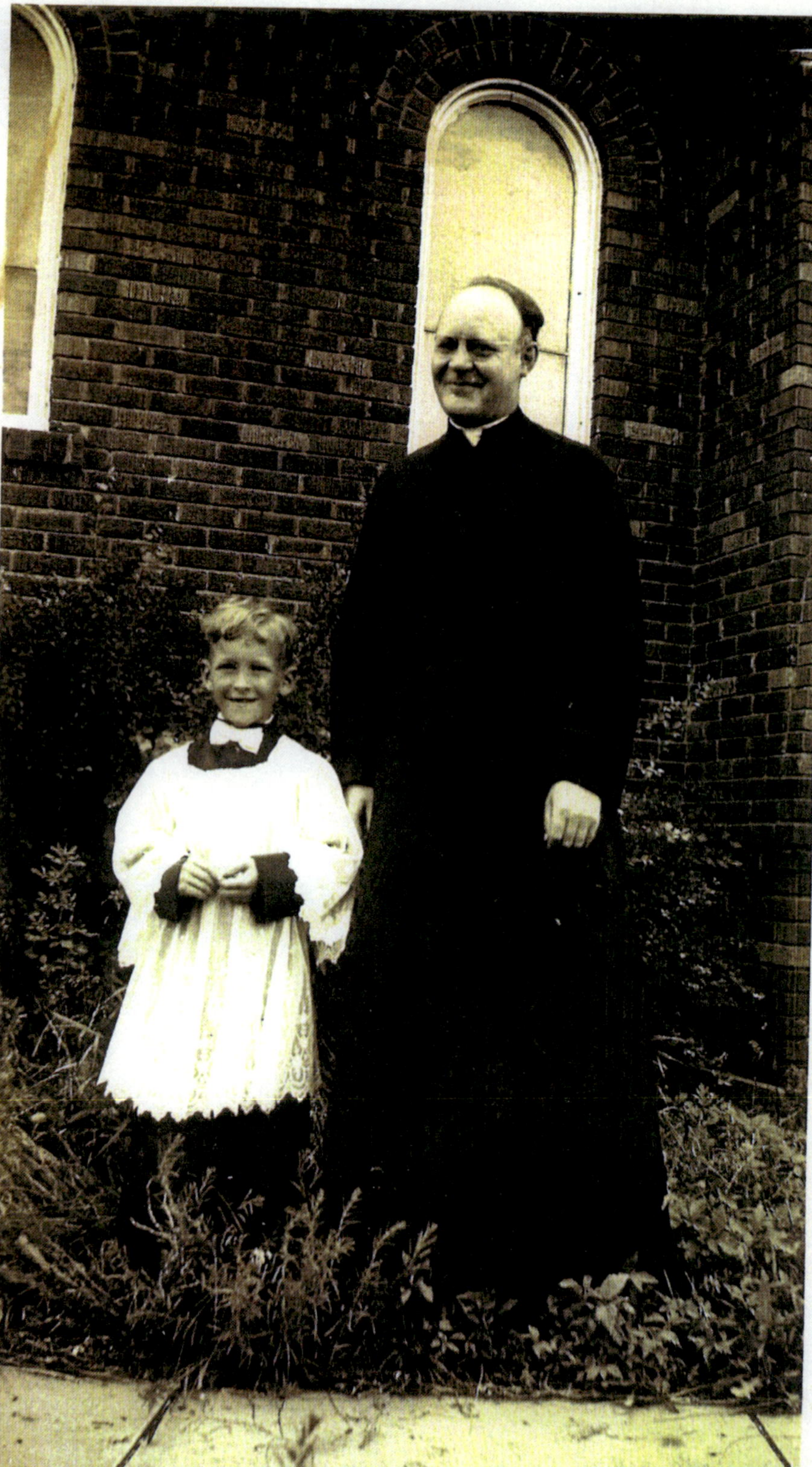

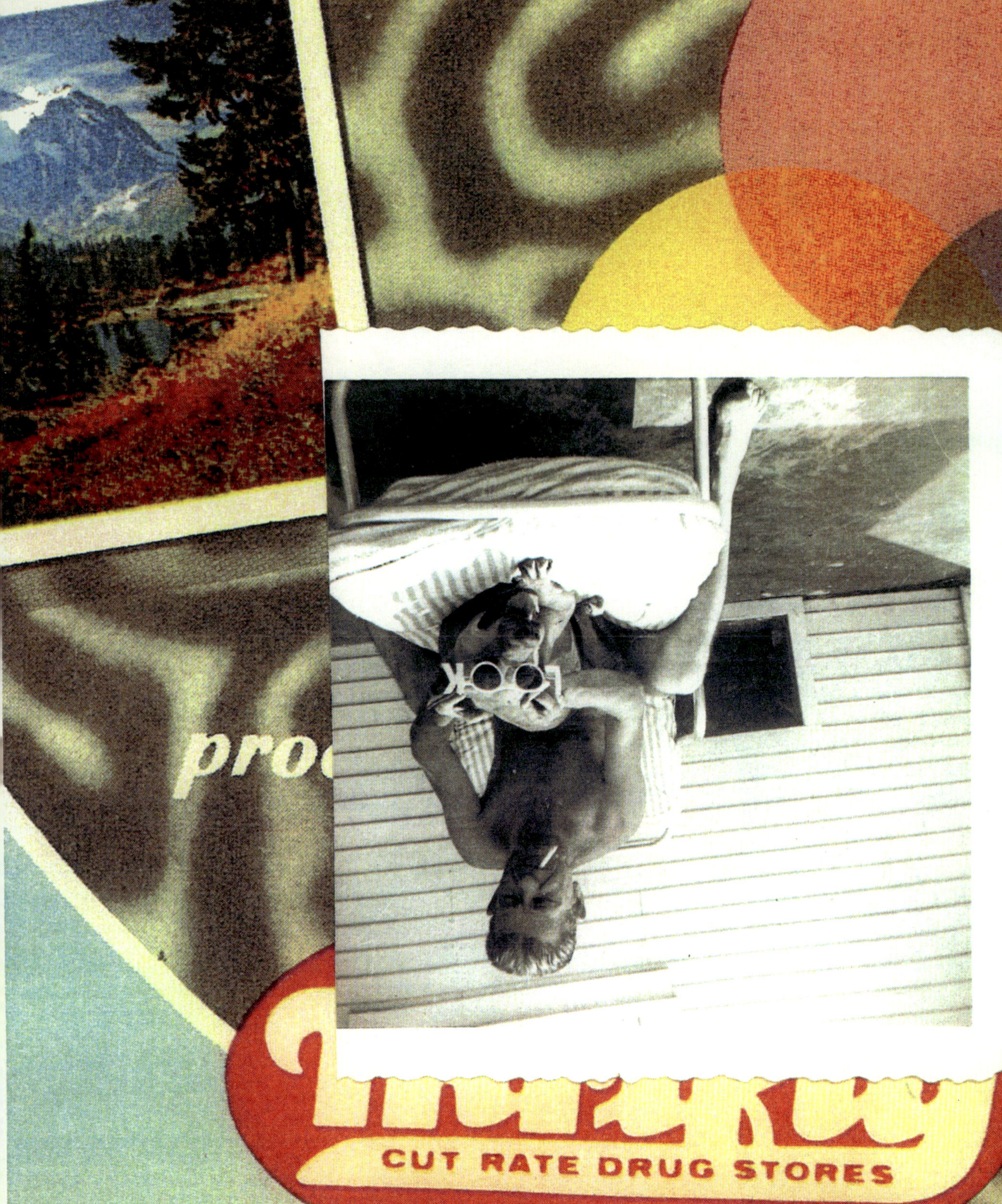
are your COLOR PR
proo
CUT RATE DRUG STORES

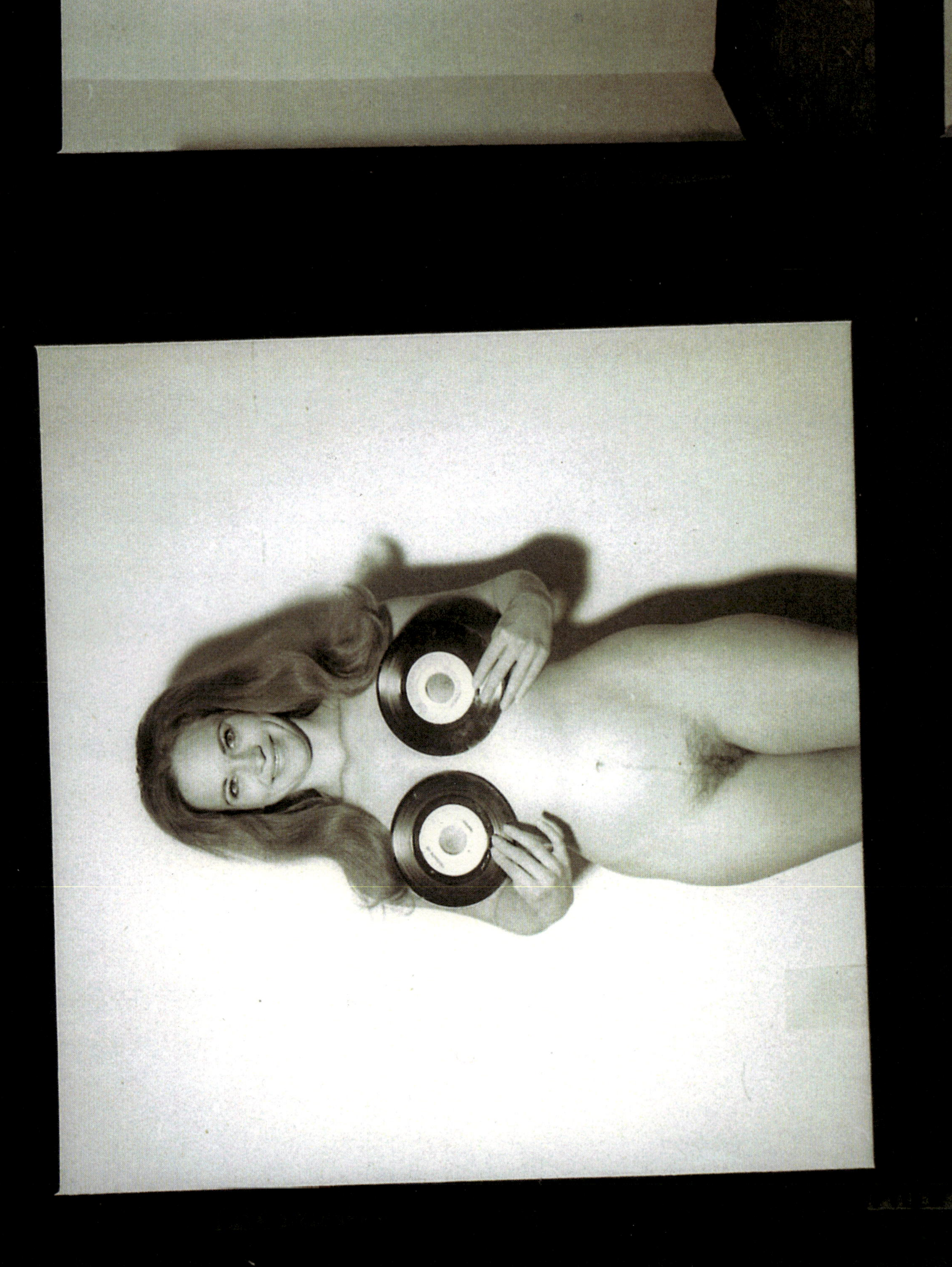

Clovers . . . . *Middle of the Night* (Nugetre), Atlantic 963, 78, 1952
Hey, Miss Fannie (Nugetre), Atlantic 977, 78, 1952
I Played the Fool (D. Alexis), Atlantic 977, 78, 1952
Count Basie Sextet . . . . *Stan Shorthair*, Clef 89102, 45, 1952
Daisy Mae and Old Brother Charlie. . . . . *Cotton Lisle Stockings and a Two Dollar Dress*
(Composed by D. M. Arnett), Columbia 20935, 78, 1952
Dave Landers. . . . .*Draw Up the Papers, Lawyer* (Shand–Matthews), MGM 10682, 78, 1952
Edna Galmon Cook . . . . *Nobody to Depend On*, Republic 7019, 78, 1952
Walk Through the Valley, Republic 7019, 78, 1952
Ella Mae Morse . . . . *Jump Back Honey* (Hadda Brooks), Capitol 2276, 78, 1952
Greyhound (Rudolph Toombs), Capitol 2276, 78, 1952
Faron Young . . . . *Foolish Pride* (Hal Smith), Capitol 2133, 78, 1952
Hank Williams . . . .*I Could Never Be Ashamed of You*, MGM 11366, 78, 1952
I'll Never Get Out of This World Alive (Williams–Rose), MGM 11366, 78, 1952
Your Cheatin' Heart, MGM 11416, 78, 1952
Howling Wolf . . . . *Morning at Midnight*, RPM 333, 78, 1952
Riding in the Moonlight, RPM 333, 78, 1952
Jerry Jericho . . . .*(Are You Washed in) The Blood of the Lamb*, 4 Star 2S-6-(a), 78, 1952
Pass Me Not (Oh Gentle Savior), 4 Star 2S-6-(b), 78, 1952
Jimmie Logsdon. . . . . *I Wanna Be Mama'd*, Decca 28502, 78, 1952
Jimmie Osborne . . . .*Mama Don't Agree*, King 1117, 78, 1952
Jimmy Witherspoon. . . . .*The Wind Is Blowin* (Witherspoon–Taub), Modern 857, 78, 1952
Would My Baby Make a Change (Witherspoon–Taub), Modern 857, 78, 1952
Joe Turner. . . . . *Poor Lover's Blues*, Atlantic 970, 78, 1952
Lefty Frizzell . . . . *I Know You're Lonesome While Waiting for Me*, Columbia 20997, 78, 1952
Forever (and Always) (Frizzell–Lyle), Columbia 20997, 78, 1952

Oposite and preceding fifteen overleaf pages: Allen Ruppersberg, "Pages" from NO TIME LEFT TO START AGAIN, 2012.
Below: Detail of *Tumbling Tumbleweeds* (Sons of the Pioneers), 1934.

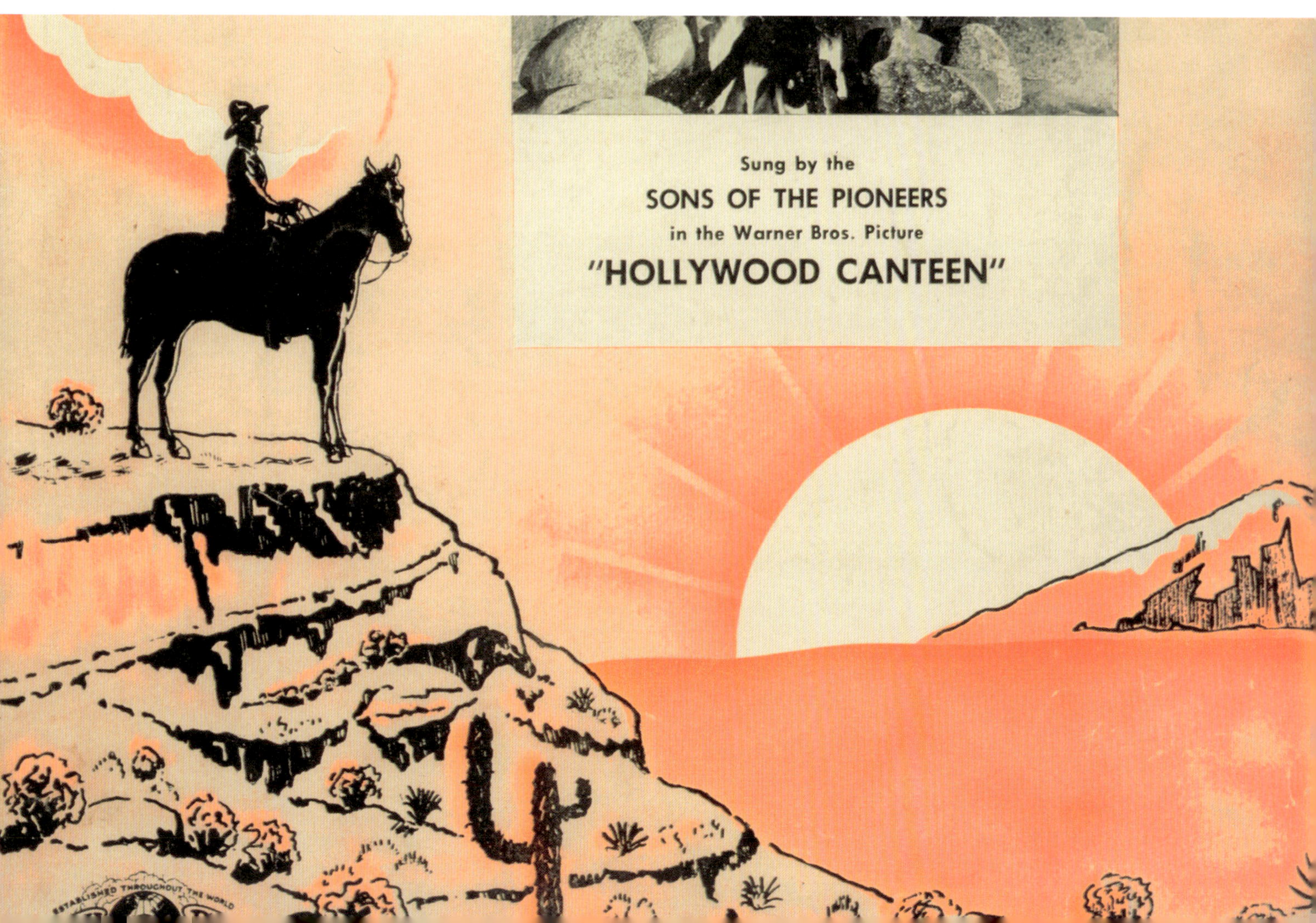

Little Willie Littlefield . . . . *K. C. Loving* (Stoller–Leiber), Federal 12110, 78, 1952
Pleading at Midnight, Federal 12110, 78, 1952
Lloyd Price . . . .*Lawdy Miss Clawdy*, Specialty 428, 78, 1952
Mailman Blues, Specialty 428, 78, 1952
Memphis Slim . . . . *No Mail Blues* (Peter Chapman), Mercury 8266, 78, 1952
Gonna Need My Help Some Day (Peter Chapman), Mercury 8266, 78, 1952
Ray Price . . . . *I Lost the Only Love I Knew* (Williams–Helms), Columbia 21025, 78, 1952
Rev. G. W. Killens . . . . *Great God Almighty* (Unrehearsed Hymn), Hollywood 196, 78, 1952
I Love the Lord (Unrehearsed Hymn), Hollywood 196, 78, 1952
Ruth Brown . . . .*5-10-15 Hours* (Toombs), Atlantic 962, 78, 1952
Be Anything (But Be Mine) (Gordon), Atlantic 962, 78, 1952
Slim Whitman . . . . *Indian Love Call* (Harbach–Hammerstein–Friml), Imperial 8156, 78, 1952
Sons of the Pioneers . . . . *Tumbling Tumbleweeds* (Bob Nolan), RCA Victor 48-0005, 45, 1952
Cool Water (Bob Nolan), RCA Victor 48-0005, 45, 1952
Soul Stirrers . . . . *It Won't Be Very Long* (R. Crain), Specialty SP 824, 78, 1952
How Far Am I from Canaan? (Brewster), Specialty SP 824, 78, 1952
Stewart Family . . . . *Sinner Read the Bible*, 4 Star 2s-9-(a), 78, 1952
Tattler's Wagon (Beavers), 4 Star 2s-9-(b), 78, 1952
T-Bone Walker . . . .*Street Walking Woman* (J. White), Imperial 5202, 78, 1952
Blues Is a Woman (F. Cadrez), Imperial 5202, 78, 1952
Varetta Dillard . . . .*A Letter in Blues* (A. M. Brunner), Savoy 847, 78, 1952
Wynonie Harris . . . . *Adam Come and Get Your Rib* (Weismantel–Glover), King 4565, 78, 1952
Drinking Blues (Henry Glover), King 4565, 78, 1952
Amos Milburn . . . . *One Scotch, One Bourbon, One Beer* (Rudolph Toombs), Aladdin 3197, 78, 1953
What Can I Do?, Aladdin 3197, 78, 1953
Bill Haley . . . .*Farewell—So Long—Good-Bye*, Essex 332, 78, 1953
Billy Eckstine . . . .*St. Louis Blues*—Part I (Handy), MGM 11573, 78, 1953
St. Louis Blues—Part II (Handy), MGM 11573, 78, 1953
Charlie Gore and Louis Innis . . . . *(You Ain't Nothin' But a Female) Hound Dog* (Otis–Innis–Mann), King 1212, 78, 1953
Mexican Joe (Mitchell Torok), King 1212, 78, 1953
Crows . . . . *Gee* (Davis–Watkins), Rama RR-5, 78, 1953
I Love You So (Watkins–Davis), Rama RR-5, 78, 1953
Edna Gallmon Cooke . . . . *He's So Good* (Cooke), Republic 7040, 78, 1953
Amen (Jarrett), Republic 7040, 78, 1953
Ella Mae Morse . . . . Have Mercy Baby (Marks–Ward), Capitol EAP 2-513, 45, 1953
How Can You Leave a Man Like This (Baker–Gerald), Capitol EAP 2-513, 45, 1953
Fats Domino . . . .*Please Don't Leave Me*, Imperial 5240, 78, 1953
The Girl I Love, Imperial 5240, 78, 1953
Going to the River (D. Bartholomew–A. Domino), Imperial 5231, 78, 1953
Mardi Gras in New Orleans (D. Longhair), Imperial 5231, 78, 1953
You Said You Love Me (D. Bartholomew–A. Domino), Imperial 5251, 78, 1953
Rose Mary (D. Bartholomew–A. Domino), Imperial 5251, 78, 1953
Hank Snow . . . .*Jimmie the Kid* (Jimmie Rodgers–Bob Neville), RCA Victor 47-5220, 45, 1953
Hawkshaw Hawkins . . . . *The Life Story of Hank Williams* (Hawkins–Innis), King 1174, 78, 1953
Jean Shephard . . . .*I'd Rather Die Young (Than Grow Old with You)* (Smith–Vaughn–Wood), Capitol 2502, 78, 1953
Jimmy Coe . . . .*After Hour Joint* (Cole–Walker–Palmer–Wickcliffe), States S-118, 78, 1953
Baby I'm Gone (Cole–Walker–Palmer–Wickcliffe), States S-118, 78, 1953
Joe Houston . . . . *Sabre-Jet*, Bayou 004, 78, 1953
Moody, Bayou 004, 78, 1953
Joe Turner . . . . Honey Hush (Brown), Atlantic 1073, 78, 1953
Crawdad Hole (Brown), Atlantic 1073, 78, 1953
Honey Hush (Brown), Atlantic 1073, 45, 1953
Johnny Ace . . . . The Clock (J. Mattis), Duke 112, 78, 1953
Aces Wild, Duke 112, 78, 1953
Johnny Bond . . . *The Ninety and Nine* (Composed by Clephane–Sankey Arranged by J. Bond), Columbia 21113, 78, 1953
Peace, Be Still! (Composed by M. A. Baker–H. R. Palmer Arranged by J. Bond), Columbia 21113, 78, 1953
Lefty Frizzell . . . .*The Darkest Moment (Is Just Before the Light of Day)*, Columbia 21194, 78, 1953
Run 'Em Off (O. Wheeler–T. Lee), Columbia 21194, 78, 1953
Little Walter . . . .*Off the Wall* (W. Jacobs), Checker 770, 78, 1953
Tell Me Mama (W. Jacobs), Checker 770, 78, 1953
I Hate to See You Go (W. Jacobs), Checker 825, 78, 1953
Too Late (W. Dixon), Checker 825, 78, 1953
Lula Reed . . . . *Watch Dog* (Henry Glover), King 4688, 78, 1953

Opposite: Song books 1934-1946.

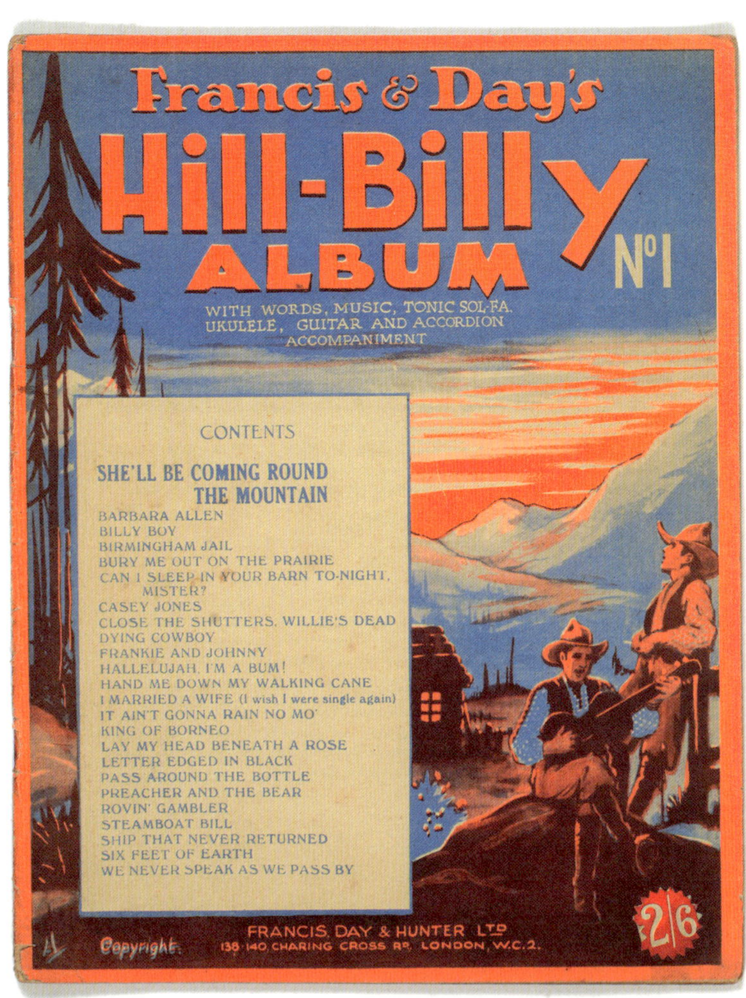

Francis & Day's
Hill-Billy
ALBUM
Nº1
WITH WORDS, MUSIC, TONIC SOL-FA,
UKULELE, GUITAR AND ACCORDION
ACCOMPANIMENT
CONTENTS
SHE'LL BE COMING ROUND THE MOUNTAIN
BARBARA ALLEN
BILLY BOY
BIRMINGHAM JAIL
BURY ME OUT ON THE PRAIRIE
CAN I SLEEP IN YOUR BARN TO-NIGHT, MISTER?
CASEY JONES
CLOSE THE SHUTTERS, WILLIE'S DEAD
DYING COWBOY
FRANKIE AND JOHNNY
HALLELUJAH, I'M A BUM!
HAND ME DOWN MY WALKING CANE
I MARRIED A WIFE (I wish I were single again)
IT AIN'T GONNA RAIN NO MO'
KING OF BORNEO
LAY MY HEAD BENEATH A ROSE
LETTER EDGED IN BLACK
PASS AROUND THE BOTTLE
PREACHER AND THE BEAR
ROVIN' GAMBLER
STEAMBOAT BILL
SHIP THAT NEVER RETURNED
SIX FEET OF EARTH
WE NEVER SPEAK AS WE PASS BY
Copyright
FRANCIS, DAY & HUNTER LTD
138-140, CHARING CROSS RD. LONDON, W.C.2.
2/6

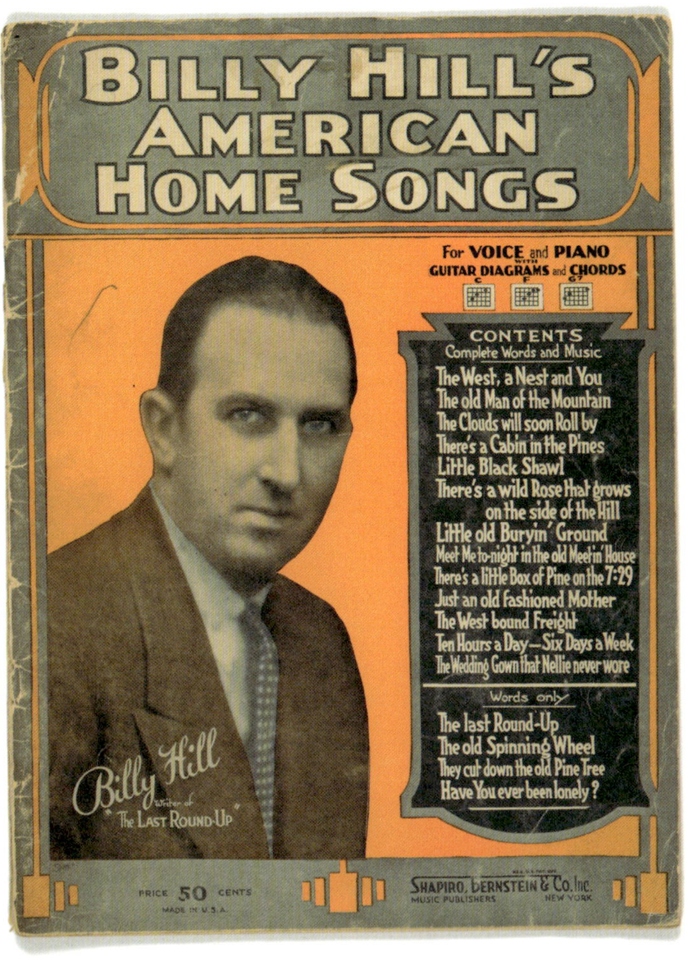

BILLY HILL'S
AMERICAN
HOME SONGS
For VOICE and PIANO
with GUITAR DIAGRAMS and CHORDS
CONTENTS
Complete Words and Music
The West, a Nest and You
The old Man of the Mountain
The Clouds will soon Roll by
There's a Cabin in the Pines
Little Black Shawl
There's a wild Rose that grows
on the side of the Hill
Little old Buryin' Ground
Meet Me to-night in the old Meet'in House
There's a little Box of Pine on the 7-29
Just an old fashioned Mother
The West bound Freight
Ten Hours a Day — Six Days a Week
The Wedding Gown that Nellie never wore
Words only
The last Round-Up
The old Spinning Wheel
They cut down the old Pine Tree
Have You ever been lonely?
Billy Hill
Writer of
"The Last Round-Up"
PRICE 50 CENTS
MADE IN U.S.A.
SHAPIRO, BERNSTEIN & Co. Inc.
MUSIC PUBLISHERS
NEW YORK

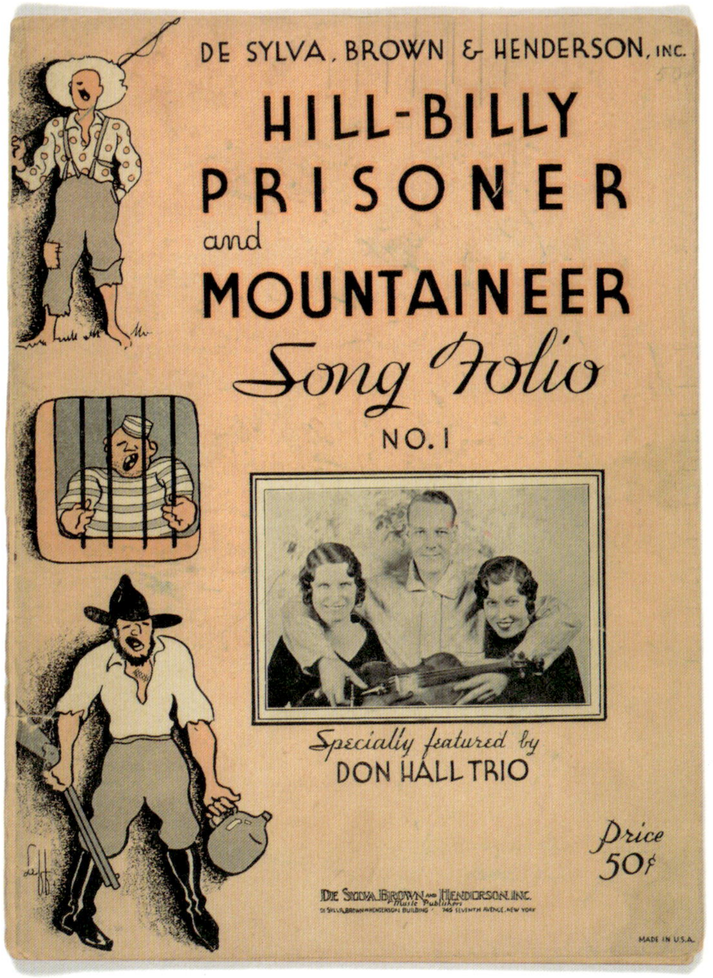

DE SYLVA, BROWN & HENDERSON, INC.
HILL-BILLY
PRISONER
and
MOUNTAINEER
Song Folio
NO. 1
Specially featured by
DON HALL TRIO
Price
50¢
DE SYLVA, BROWN AND HENDERSON, INC.
Music Publishers
745 ELEVENTH AVENUE, NEW YORK
MADE IN U.S.A.

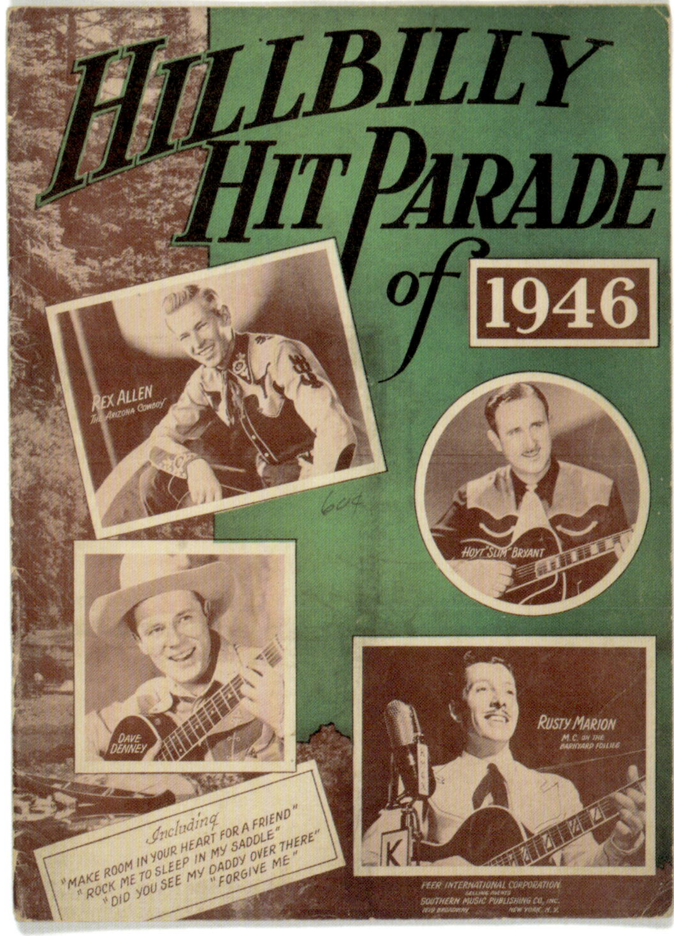

HILLBILLY
HIT PARADE
of 1946
REX ALLEN
The Arizona Cowboy
HOYT "SLIM" BRYANT
DAVE DENNEY
RUSTY MARION
M.C. of the
Barnyard Follies
Including
"MAKE ROOM IN YOUR HEART FOR A FRIEND"
"ROCK ME TO SLEEP IN MY SADDLE"
"DID YOU SEE MY DADDY OVER THERE"
"FORGIVE ME"
PEER INTERNATIONAL CORPORATION
SOUTHERN MUSIC PUBLISHING CO., INC.
NEW YORK, N. Y.

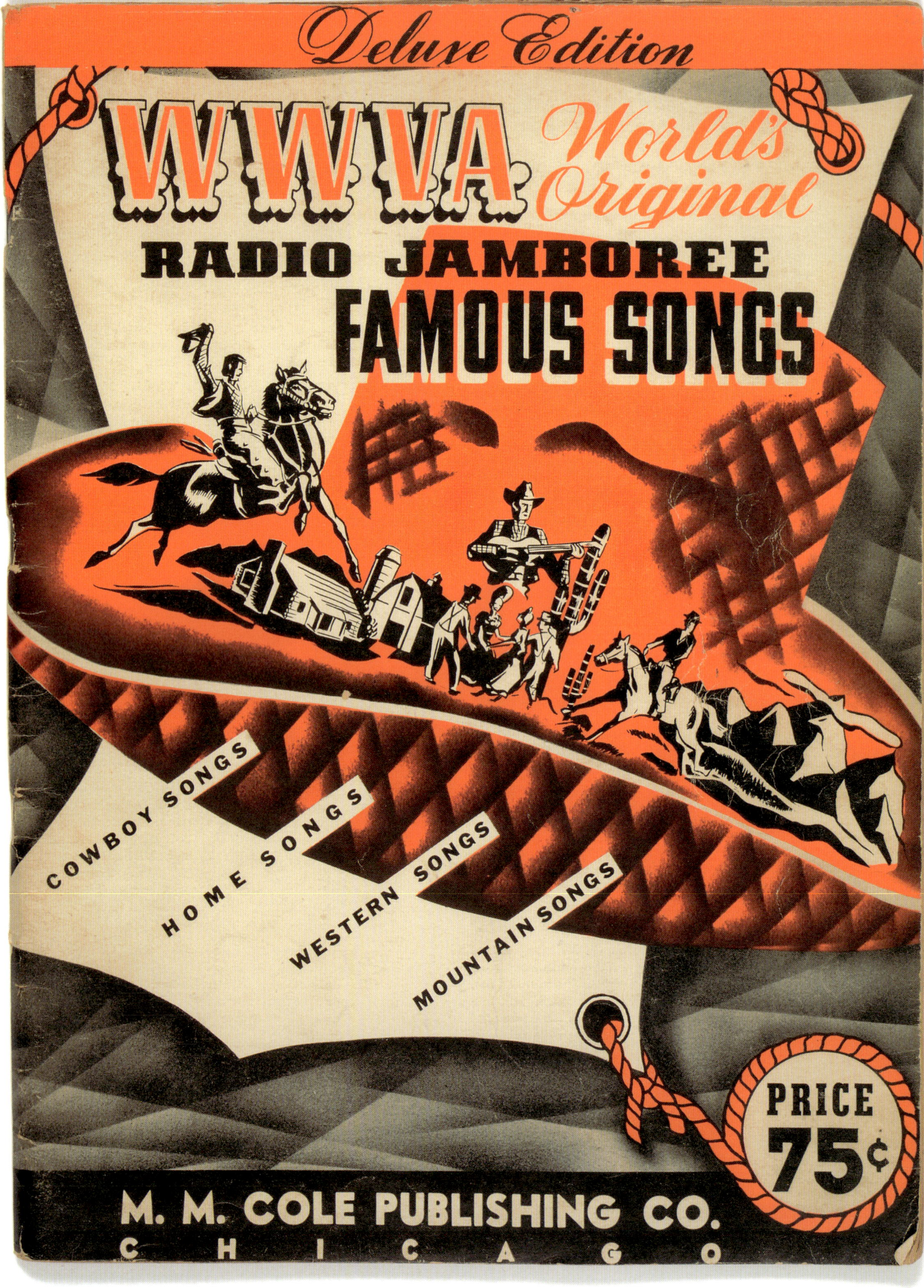

Deluxe Edition
WWVA World's Original
RADIO JAMBOREE
FAMOUS SONGS
COWBOY SONGS
HOME SONGS
WESTERN SONGS
MOUNTAIN SONGS
PRICE 75¢
M. M. COLE PUBLISHING CO.
CHICAGO

Lula Reed . . . . *Your Key Don't Fit It No More* (Evelyn–Glover), King 4688, 78, 1953

Margie Collie . . . . *His New War Bride* (Billy Wallace), Decca 28701, 78, 1953

Dim Lights, Thick Smoke (and Loud Loud Music) (Cousin Joe Maphis–Rose Lee–Max Fidler), Decca 28701, 78, 1953

Original Five Blind Boys of Alabama . . . . *I'll Fly Away*, Specialty XSP-850-45, 45, 1953

Precious Lord (T. A. Dorsey), Specialty XSP-850-45, 45, 1953

Oh Lord–Stand By Me (Every Day, Let Me Walk with Thee) (R. Martin), Specialty 842, 78, 1953

When I Lost My Mother (Something About the Lord Is Mighty Sweet) (J. Fields), Specialty 842, 78, 1953

Professor Alex Bradford . . . . *Too Close to Heaven*, Specialty 852, 78, 1953

I Don't Care What the World May Do, Specialty 852, 78, 1953

Ray Price . . . . *Don't Let the Stars Get in Your Eyes* (Willet), Columbia 21025, 78, 1953

Rose Maddox . . . . *These Wasted Years* (Composed by Bradshaw), Columbia 21155, 78, 1953

I'm a Little Red Caboose (Composed by Bradshaw, W. Evans), Columbia 21155, 78, 1953

Shirley and Lee . . . . *So in Love*, Aladdin 3192, 78, 1953

Shirley's Back, Aladdin 3192, 78, 1953

Spaniels . . . . *You Don't Move Me* (Gregory), Vee-Jay 107, 78, 1953

The Masters Family . . . . *They've Made a New Bible* (Composed by J. Masters), Columbia 21094-s, 78, 1953

Marching On to Glory (Composed by J. Masters), Columbia 21094-s, 78, 1953

The Orioles . . . . *Crying in the Chapel* (A. Glenn), Jubilee 5122, 78, 1953

Webb Pierce . . . . *There Stands the Glass* (Russ Hull–Mary Jean Shurt–A. Reisham), Decca 28834, 78, 1953

I'm Walking the Dog (A. Greshim), Decca 28834, 78, 1953

I'll Go On Alone (Marty Robinns), Decca 28534, 78, 1953

That's Me Without You (J. D. Miller), Decca 28534, 78, 1953

Willie Mabon . . . . *Worry Blues*, Chess 1531, 78, 1953

Willie Mae "Big Mama" Thornton . . . . *Hound Dog* (J. Leiber–M. Stoller–J. Otis), Peacock 1612, 78, 1953

Night Mare (J. Leiber–M. Stoller–J. Otis), Peacock 1612, 78, 1953

Cotton Picking Blues (D. Robey), Peacock 1621, 78, 1953

They Call Me Big Mama (Robey–Thornton), Peacock 1621, 78, 1953

5 Royales . . . . *Monkey Hips & Rice* (L. Pauling), Gusto GT4-2148, 45, 1954

B. B. King . . . . *You Upset Me Baby*, RPM 416, 78, 1954

Whole Lotta' Love (Davis–Josea), RPM 416, 78, 1954

Bill Doggett . . . . *Sweet Lorraine* (Burwell–Parish), King 4720, 78, 1954

Bill Haley . . . . *Dim, Dim the Lights (I Want Some Atmosphere)* (Beverly Ross–Julius Dixon), Decca 29317, 78, 1954

A. B. C. Boogie (Al Russel–Max Spickol), Decca 29204, 78, 1954

Shake, Rattle and Roll (C. Calhoun), Decca 29204, 78, 1954

Billy Graham London Crusade Choir . . . . *To God Be the Glory* (William Howard Doane–Fanny Jane Crosby), Recorded Anthology of American Music Inc. 224, LP, 1954

Christian Travelers . . . . *Oh What a Savior* (J. D. Mitchell), Peacock 1737, 78, 1954

Clyde McPhatter . . . . *What'cha Gonna Do* (Nugetre), Atlantic 1055, 78, 1954

Elmore James . . . . *Standing at the Crossroads* (Josea–Taub–Ling), Kent K 433x45, 45, 1954

Sunnyland (Josea–Taub–Ling), Kent K 433x45, 45, 1954

Fats Domino . . . . *Something's Wrong* (D. Bartholomew–A. Domino), Imperial 5262, 78, 1954

Don't Leave Me This Way (D. Bartholomew–A. Domino), Imperial 5262, 78, 1954

Little Walter . . . . *Mellow Down Easy* (W. Dixon), Checker 805, 78, 1954

Louis Jordan . . . . *Gal, You Need a Whippin'* (Cosy–Jordan), Aladdin 3279, 78, 1954

Medallions . . . . *Buick 59* (Vernon Green), Dootone 347, 78, 1954

The Letter (Vernon Green), Dootone 347, 78, 1954

Midnighters . . . . *Annie Had a Baby* (Clover–Mann), Federal 12195, 78, 1954

She's the One (Henry Ballard), Federal 12195, 78, 1954

Work with Me Annie (Henry Ballard), Federal 12169, 78, 1954

Until I Die (Henry Ballard), Federal 12169, 78, 1954

Percy Mayfield . . . . *You Don't Exist No More*, Specialty 499, 78, 1954

Ray Price . . . . *Oh Yes Darling!*, Columbia 21315, 78, 1954

If You Don't Somebody Else Will (Mathis–J. Lee–G. Hamilton), Columbia 21315, 78, 1954

Rose Maddox . . . . *Poor Little Heartbroken Rose* (Composed by Rollins–Robertson), Columbia 21253, 78, 1954

Marry Me Again (Composed by D. Rose–Maddox), Columbia 21253, 78, 1954

Roy Hamilton . . . . *You'll Never Walk Alone* (Hammerstein II–Rodgers), Epic 9015, 78, 1954

Royals . . . . *Until I Die* (Henry Ballard), Federal 12169, 78, 1954

Work with Me Annie (Henry Ballard), Federal 12169, 78, 1954

Ruth Brown . . . . *Oh What a Dream* (Willis), Atlantic 1036, 78, 1954

Please Don't Freeze (Chase), Atlantic 1036, 78, 1954

Somebody Touched Me (Nugetre), Atlantic 1044, 78, 1954

Stuart Hamblen . . . . *This Ole House*, RCA Victor 20-5739, 78, 1954

Opposite: *WWVA World's Original Radio Jamboreee Famous Songs*, 1942.

The Chords . . . . *Sh–Boom* (Keyes–Feaster–McRae–Edwards), Cat 104, 78, 1954
Little Maiden (Keyes–Feaster–McRae–Edwards), Cat 104, 78, 1954
The Orioles . . . .*Don't Go to Strangers* (Evans–Mann–Kent), Jubilee 5137, 78, 1954
Secret Love (Webester–Fain), Jubilee 5137, 78, 1954
The Penguins. . . . . *Earth Angel (Will You Be Mine)* (Curtis Williams), DooTone 348, 78, 1954
Tommy Collins. . . . . *High on a Hilltop*, Capitol 2701, 78, 1954
You Better Not Do That, Capitol 2701, 78, 1954
5 Royales. . . . . *School Girl* (L. Pauling), Gusto GT4-2148, 45, 1955
Bill Haley. . . . . *Birth of the Boogie* (Bill Haley–Billy Williamson–Johnny Grande), Decca 29418, 78, 1955
Rock–A–Beatin' Boogie, Decca 29713, 78, 1955
Burn That Candle (Winfield Scott), Decca 29713, 78, 1955
Bo Diddley. . . . . *Bo Diddley* (E. McDaniels), Checker 814, 78, 1955
I'm a Man (E. McDaniels), Checker 814, 78, 1955
Boyd Bennett. *My Boy—Flat Top* (John F. Young, Jr.), King 1494, 78, 1955
Banjo Rock and Roll (Allen–Ayers), King 1494, 78, 1955
Chuck Berry . . . .*Maybellene*, Chess 1604, 78, 1955
Chuck Miller . . . . *The House of Blue Lights* (Don Raye–Freddie Slack), Mercury 70627, 78, 1955
Eddie Dean . . . .*I Dreamed of a Hill-Billy Heaven* (Eddie Dean–Karen Anthony), Sage and Sand 180, 78, 1955
Faron Young . . . . *All Right*, Capitol F3169, 45, 1955
Go Back You Fool (Don Robertson–Hal Blair), Capitol F3169, 45, 1955
Fats Domino . . . . *All By Myself* (Domino–Bartholomew), Imperial 5357, 78, 1955
Troubles of My Own (Domino–Bartholomew), Imperial 5357, 78, 1955
Ain't It a Shame (Domino–Bartholomew), Imperial 5348, 78, 1955
La-La (Domino–Bartholomew), Imperial 5348, 78, 1955
Ferlin Husky . . . . *Don't Blame the Children* (John Lair), Capitol F3183, 45, 1955
George Beverly Shea . . . . *The Ninety Nine and Nine* (Ira D. Sankey–Elizabeth C. Cephane),
Recorded Anthology of American Music Inc. 224, LP, 1955
Joe Turner. . . . . *Boogie Woogie Country Girl* (Pomus–Ashby), Atlantic 1088, 78, 1955
Corrine Corrine (Willams–Chatman–Parrish), Atlantic 1088, 78, 1955
Larry Waters . . . . *Full Grown Woman* (Gallo–Fowler), DIG 108, 78, 1955
Don't Tell Me That You Love Me (Gallo–Waters), DIG D-108, 78, 1955
Little Richard. . . . . *I'm Just a Lonely Guy* (Lo Bostrie–Blackwell), Specialty 561, 78, 1955
Tutti-Frutti (Lo Bostrie–Penniman), Specialty 561, 78, 1955
Little Walter. . . . .*My Babe* (Dixon), Checker 811 , 78, 1955
Little Willie John . . . . *Need Your Love So Bad*, King 4841, 78, 1955
Home at Last (Rudy Toombs), King 4841, 78, 1955
Lowell Fulson . . . .*The Original Lonesome Christmas—Part 1* (L. Glenn), Hollywood 1022, 78, 1955
The Original Lonesome Christmas—Part 2 (L. Glenn), Hollywood 1022, 78, 1955
Mahalia Jackson . . . .*A Dusty Old Halo* (Bob Merrill), Columbia 40411, 78, 1955
The Treasures of Love (Gilkyson), Columbia 40411, 78, 1955
Mickey "Guitar" Baker . . . . *Rock with a Sock*, Rainbow 299, 78, 1955
Moonglows. . . . . *Lover, Love Me* (Fuqua), Chess 1611, 78, 1955
Professor Alex Bradford . . . .*Oh Lord—Save Me*, Specialty SP-879, 78, 1955
He'll Wash You Whiter Than Snow (C. Martin), Specialty SP-879, 78, 1955
Ravens. *The Bells of San Raquel* (Rivera–Woods–Utera–Menendez), Jubilee 5203, 78, 1955
Green Eyes (Barcelata–Wise–Leeds), Jubilee 5203, 78, 1955
Robins. . . . .*If Teardrops Were Kisses* (Mike Stoller–Jerry Leiber), Spark 110, 78, 1955
Whadaya Want? (Mike Stoller–Jerry Leiber), Spark 110, 78, 1955
"Sonny Boy" Williamson. . . . . *All My Love in Vain*, Checker 824, 78, 1955
Don't Start Me Talkin', Checker 824, 78, 1955
Spaniels. . . . . *You Painted Pictures* (B. Roth), Vee-Jay 154, 78, 1955
Hey, Sister Lizzie, Vee-Jay 154, 78, 1955
"Tennessee" Ernie Ford . . . . *I Am a Pilgrim* (Merle Travis), Capitol F3135, 45, 1955
The Platters . . . . *The Great Pretender* (Buck Ram), Mercury 70753, 78, 1955
I'm Just a Dancing Partner (Crain–Weiner), Mercury 70753, 78, 1955
Treniers. . . . .*Get Out of the Car* (Claude Trenier–Cliff Trenier), Okeh 7050, 78, 1955
Webb Pierce. . . . . *I Don't Care* (Cindy Walker–Webb Pierce), Decca 9-29480, 45, 1955
Willie Dixon . . . .*Walking the Blues* (Dupree–Baer), Checker 822, 78, 1955
Wrens . . . . *Beggin' for Love* (Concepcion), Rama 65, 78, 1955
Come Back My Love (Bobby Mansfield), Rama 65, 78, 1955
Bill Doggett . . . . *"Honky Tonk" Part I* (Doggett–Shepard–Scott–Butler), Loreli L-001, 45, 1956
"Honky Tonk" Part II (Doggett–Shepard–Scott–Butler), Loreli L-001, 45, 1956
Cadets. . . . .*Stranded in the Jungle* (Johnson–Smith), Modern 994, 78, 1956

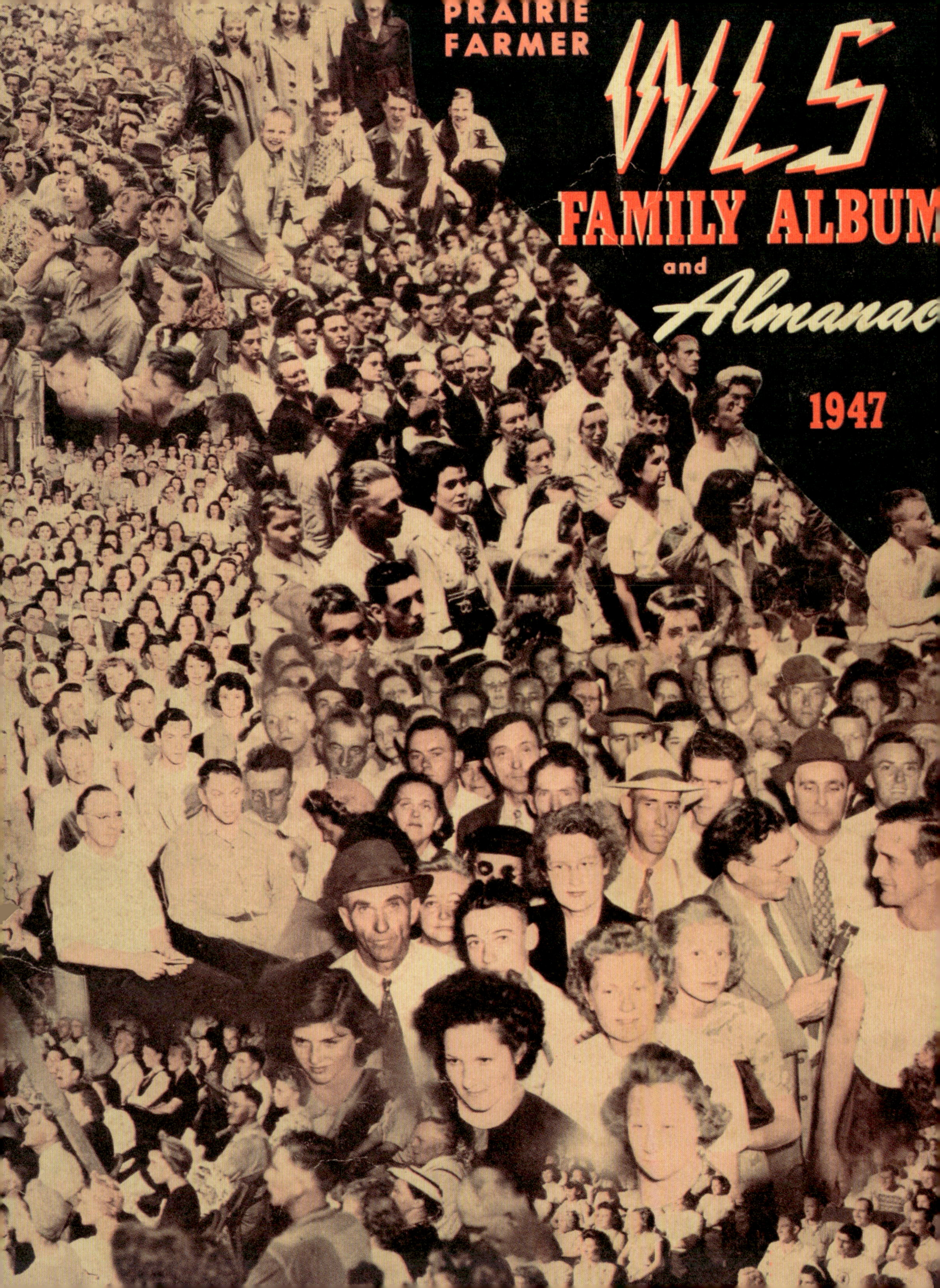

PRAIRIE FARMER
WLS
FAMILY ALBUM
and
Almanac
1947

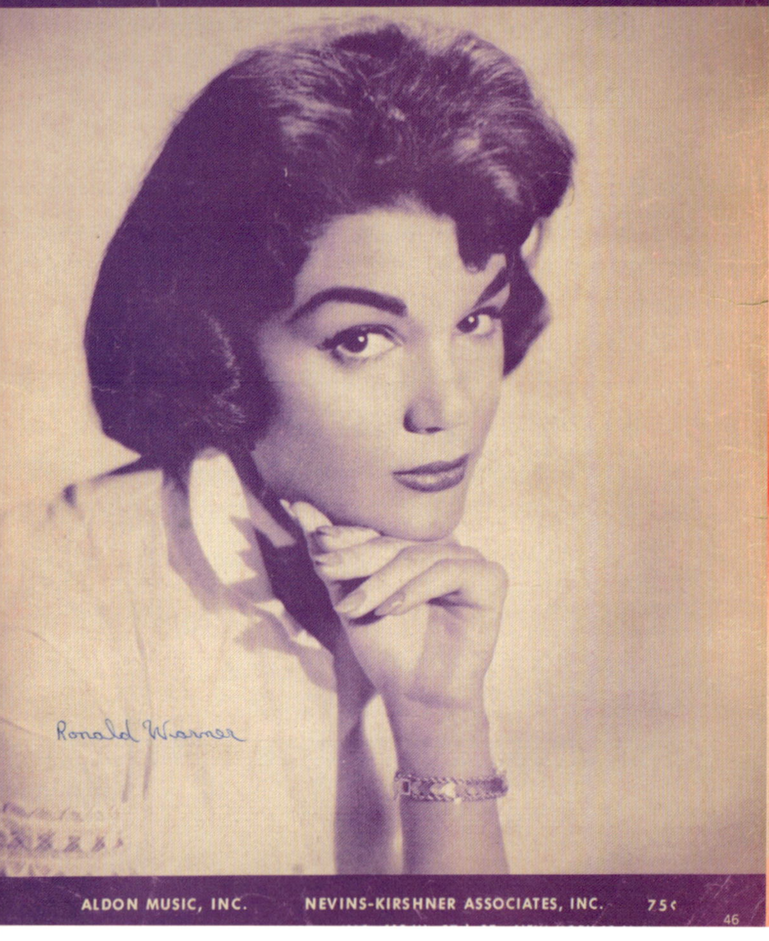

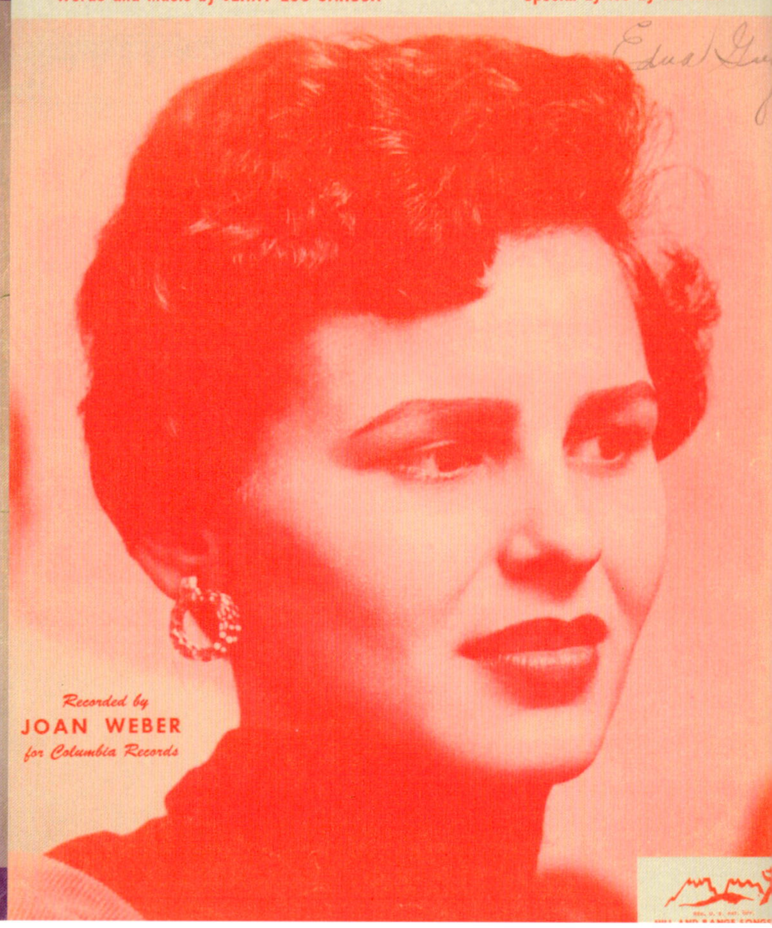

Chips	*Oh My Darlin'* (Johnson), Josie 45-803, 45, 1956	
	Rubber Biscuit (Johnson), Josie 45-803, 45, 1956	
Clyde McPhatter	*Without Love (There Is Nothing)* (Danny Small), Atlantic 1117, 78, 1956	
Elvis Presley	*I Was the One* (Schroeder–DeMetris–Blair–Peppers), RCA Victor 20-6420, 78, 1956	
	Heartbreak Hotel (Axton–Durden–Presley), RCA Victor 20-6420, 78, 1956	
	Don't Be Cruel (Otis Blackwell), RCA Victor 20-6604, 78, 1956	
	Hound Dog (Jerry Leiber–Mike Stoller), RCA Victor 20-6604, 78, 1956	
	Love Me Tender (Elvis Presley–Vera Maston), RCA Victor 47-6643, 45, 1956	
	Anyway You Want Me (That's How I Will Be) (Aaron Schroeder–Cliff Owen), RCA Victor 47-6643, 45, 1956	
Ernie Freeman Combo	*Jivin' Around—Part 1* (J Gray–M Akapoff), Cash 1017, 78, 1956	
	Jivin' Around—Part 2 (J Gray–M Akapoff), Cash 1017, 78, 1956	
Fats Domino	*My Blue Heaven* (G. Whiting & W. Donaldson), Imperial 5386, 78, 1956	
	I'm in Love Again (Domino–Bartholomew), Imperial 5386, 78, 1956	
	When My Dreamboat Comes Home (Friend–Franklin), Imperial 5396, 78, 1956	
	So-Long (Domino–Bartholomew), Imperial 5396, 78, 1956	
	Bo Weevil (Domino–Bartholomew), Imperial 5375, 78, 1956	
	Don't Blame It on Me (Domino–Bartholomew), Imperial 5375, 78, 1956	
	Blue Monday (Domino–Bartholomew), Imperial 5417, 78, 1956	
	What's the Reason I'm Not Pleasing You (Hatch, Tomlin, Poe & Grier), Imperial 5417, 78, 1956	
	Blueberry Hill (Lewis–Stock & Rose), Imperial X5407, 45, 1956	
	Tired of Crying, Imperial IMP 139, 45, 1956	
	You Said You Love Me (Domino–Bartholomew), Imperial IMP 139, 45, 1956	
	Rose Mary (Domino–Bartholomew), Imperial IMP 139, 45, 1956	
	All By Myself (Domino–Bartholomew), Imperial IMP 139, 45, 1956	
Gene Vincent	*Woman Love* (Jack Rhodes), Capitol 3450, 78, 1956	
	Be-Bop-A-Lula (Sheriff Tex Davis–Gene Vincent), Capitol 3450, 78, 1956	
George Hamilton IV	*A Rose and a Baby Ruth* (Johnny Dee), ABC Paramount 9765, 78, 1956	
	If You Don't Know, ABC Paramount 9765, 78, 1956	
Howlin' Wolf	*Smoke Stack Lightning* (Burnett), Chess 1618, 78, 1956	

Above: *Ev'rybody's Somebody's Fool* (Connie Francis), 1960, *Let Me Go, Lover!* (Joan Weber), 1954

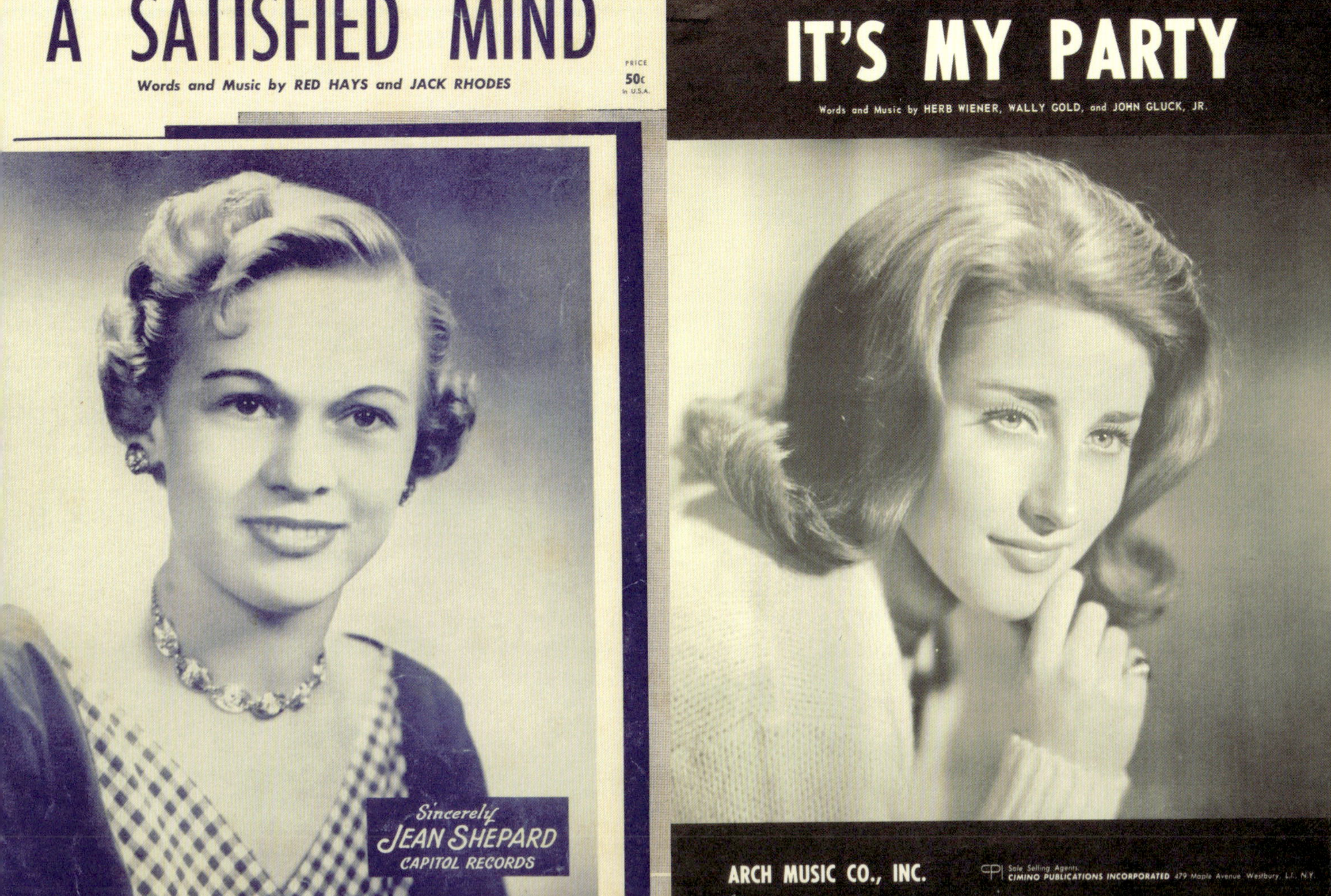

Howlin' Wolf. . . . . *You Can't Be Beat* (Burnett), Chess 1618, 78, 1956
Ivory Joe Hunter . . . . *Since I Met You Baby*, Atlantic 1111, 78, 1956
Joe Williams . . . . *As I Love You* (Livingston–Evans), Verve V-2004, 78, 1956
Kitty Wells . . . . *Searching (For Someone Like You)* (Pee Wee Madux), Decca 9-29956, 45, 1956
LaVerne Baker. . . . .*Jim Dandy* (Chase), Atlantic 1116, 78, 1956
Little Willie John . . . .*Letter From My Darling* (Singleton–McCoy), King 4935, 78, 1956
Louis Jordan . . . . *Big Bess* (McCrae–Thomas), Mercury 70993, 45, 1956
Louvin Brothers. . . . .*Where Will You Build*, Capitol 3467, 78, 1956
That's All He's Asking of Me, Capitol 3467, 78, 1956
Mahalia Jackson . . . .*Down By the Riverside*, Columbia 2552, LP, 1956
. . . . *You'll Never Walk Alone* (Hammerstein II–Rodgers), Columbia 2552, LP, 1956
Moonglows. . . . . *Over and Over Again* (B & A Weisman), Chess 1646, 78, 1956
I Knew From the Start (Moore–Subatsky), Chess 1646, 78, 1956
Muddy Waters . . . .*Don't Go No Farther* (Dixon), Chess 1630, 78, 1956
Diamonds at Your Feet (Morganfield), Chess 1630, 78, 1956
Penguins . . . . *My Troubles Are Not at An End* (Curtis Williams), Mercury 70799, 78, 1956
Porter Wagoner . . . . *How Can You Refuse Him Now* (Hank Williams), RCA Victor 47-6421, 45, 1956
What Would You Do? (If Jesus Came to Your House), RCA Victor 47-6421, 45, 1956
Pretenders. . . . . *Possessive Love* (Sunny Gale–Horace Linsley), Rama RR-198, 78, 1956
I've Got to Have You Baby (Jones–Goldner), Rama RR-198, 78, 1956
Ray Price . . . . *Wasted Words* (Gibson), Columbia 21562, 78, 1956
Sam Price . . . . *Tishomingo*, Savoy 45-1505, 45, 1956
Rib Joint (Price–David), Savoy 45-1505, 45, 1956
Shirley & Lee . . . . *Now That It's Over* (Leonard Lee), Aladdin 3338, 78, 1956
I Feel Good (Leonard Lee), Aladdin 3338, 78, 1956
Let the Good Times Roll (Leonard Lee), Aladdin 3325, 78, 1956
Do You Mean to Hurt Me So (Leonard Lee), Aladdin 3325, 78, 1956
Sister Rosetta Tharpe. *When They Ring the Golden Bell*, Mercury DJ-32x45, 45, 1956
Jericho, Mercury DJ-32x45, 45, 1956

Above: *A Satisfied Mind* (Jean Shepard), 1955, *It's My Party* (Lesley Gore), 1963

Smiley Lewis . . . . *Shame, Shame, Shame* (Ken Hopkins–Ruby Fisher), Imperial X5418, 45, 1956
No, No (D. Bartholemew–P. King), Imperial X5418, 45, 1956
Sonny James . . . . *Young Love* (Jack Morrow), Capitol 3602, 78, 1956
Sparkle Moore . . . . *Rock-A-Bop* (Barbara Morgan), Fraternity F-751, 45, 1956
Skull and Cross Bones (Barbara Morgan), Fraternity F-751, 45, 1956
B. B. King . . . . *Be Careful with a Fool* (King–Josea), RPM 494, 78, 1957
Quit My Baby (King–Ling), RPM 494, 45, 1957
Bill Doggett . . . . *Hot Ginger* (Doggett–Scott), King 45-5080, 45, 1957
Soft (Tiny Bradshaw), King 45-5080, 45, 1957
Bill Justis . . . . *Raunchy* (Justis–Manker), Phillips 3519, 78, 1957
Buddy Knox. . . . . *Party Doll* (Bowen–Knox), Roulette 4002, 78, 1957
Callahan Brothers . . . . *Take the News to Mother*, Conqueror 8689, 78, 1957
Maple on the Hill, Conqueror 8689, 78, 1957
Channels. . . . . *Stay As You Are* (Lewis–Dolphin), Gone 5012, 45, 1957
That's My Desire (C. Loveday–H. Kressa), Gone 5012, 45, 1957
Chuck Berry . . . . *Blue Feeling*, Chess 1671, 45, 1957
Rock & Roll Music, Chess 1671, 45, 1957
Chuck Willis . . . . *C. C. Rider*, Atlantic 45-1130, 45, 1957
Ease the Pain (Chuck Willis–Walter Thomas), Atlantic 45-1130, 45, 1957
Coasters . . . . *Searchin'* (Leiber–Stoller), Atco 6087, 78, 1957
Young Blood (Leiber–Stoller–Pomus), Atco 6087, 78, 1957
Danny & the Juniors . . . . *Sometimes (When I'm All Alone)* (White), ABC Paramount 78-9871, 78, 1957
At the Hop (Singer–Medora–White), ABC Paramount 78-9871, 78, 1957
Dell-Vikings. . . . . *Whispering Bells* (F. Lowery–C. Quick), Dot 45-15592, 45, 1957
Diamonds . . . . *Little Darlin'* (M. Williams), Mercury 71060x45, 45, 1957
The Stroll (Otis–Lee), Mercury 71242, 45, 1957
Dicky Doo and the Don'ts . . . . *Did You Cry* (Grant–Doo), Swan 4001, 78, 1957
Click Clack (Lee–Grant–Doo), Swan 4001, 78, 1957
Elvis Presley . . . . *All Shook Up* (Otis Blackwell–Elvis Presley), RCA Victor 47-6870, 45, 1957
That's When Your Heartaches Begin (Raskin–Brown–Fisher), RCA Victor 47-6870, 45, 1957
Jailhouse Rock (Jerry Leiber–Mike Stoller), RCA Victor 47-7035, 45, 1957
Treat Me Nice (Jerry Leiber–Mike Stoller), RCA Victor 47-7035, 45, 1957
Don't Leave Me Now (A. Schroader–B. Weisman), RCA Victor EPA-4114, 45, 1957
(You're So Square) Baby I Don't Care (Jerry Leiber–Mike Stoller), RCA Victor EPA-4114, 45, 1957
Young and Beautiful (A. Silver–A. Schroeder), RCA Victor EPA-4114, 45, 1957
Is It So Strange (Faron Young), RCA Victor EPA-4041, 45, 1957
I Want to Be Free (Jerry Leiber–Mike Stoller), RCA Victor EPA-4114, 45, 1957
Fats Domino . . . . *I'm Walkin'* (A. Domino–D. Bartholomew), Imperial 5428, 78, 1957
Ferlin Husky . . . . *Gone* (Smokey Rogers), Capitol 3628, 78, 1957
Jerry Lee Lewis . . . . *Mean Woman Blues* (Claude DeMetrius), Sun EPA-107, 45, 1957
I'm Feeling Sorry (Jack Clement), Sun EPA-107, 45, 1957
Whole Lot of Shakin' Going On (D. Williams–S. David), Sun EPA-107, 45, 1957
Turn Around (Carl Perkins), Sun EPA-107, 45, 1957
Jimmy Bowen . . . . *Ever Lovin' Fingers* (Lenier–Bowen), Roulette 4001, 78, 1957
I'm Stickin' with You (Bowen–Knox), Roulette 4001, 78, 1957
Jimmy Reed. . . . . *The Sun Is Shining*, Vee-Jay 248, 78, 1957
Baby, What's On Your Mind?, Vee-Jay 248, 78, 1957
Jimmy Witherspoon. . . . . *All Right Miss Moore* (Jesse Stone), RCA Victor 47-7075, 45, 1957
Joe Turner. . . . . *Rock a While* (Billy Nightingale), Atlantic 45-1100, 45, 1957
Lipstick, Powder and Paint (Jesse Stone), Atlantic 45-1100, 45, 1957
Johnnie & Joe . . . . *Over the Mountain: Across the Sea* (Rex Garvin), Chess 1654, 78, 1957
King Bees . . . . *Can't You Understand*, KRC 302-45, 45, 1957
Kitty Wells and Webb Pierce . . . . *When I'm with You* (Jim Anglin), Decca 9-30489, 45, 1957
Larry Williams . . . . *Bony Moronie*, Specialty 615, 45, 1957
You Bug Me, Baby (Williams–Bono), Specialty 615, 45, 1957
Short Fat Fannie (L. Williams), Specialty 608, 78, 1957
LaVern Baker. . . . . *St. Louis Blues* (Handy), Atlantic 45-1163, 45, 1957
Lester Flatt & Earl Scruggs . . . . *Let Those Brown Eyes Smile at Me* (Nail), Columbia 4-40990, 45, 1957
Don't Let Your Deal Go Down (J. Organ–Certain–Stacey–W. Walker), Columbia 4-40990, 45, 1957
Little Richard. . . . . *Rip It Up* (Blackwell–Marascalco), Specialty 579, 78, 1957
Ready Teddy (Blackwell–Marascalco), Specialty 579, 78, 1957
Send Me Some Lovin' (Marascalco–Price), Specialty 598, 45, 1957
Lucille (Penniman–Collins), Specialty 598, 45, 1957

Opposite: *Country Song, Hit Parader, Rhythm and Blues, Rock and Roll, Folk and Country, Song Hits* magazines 1950-1968.

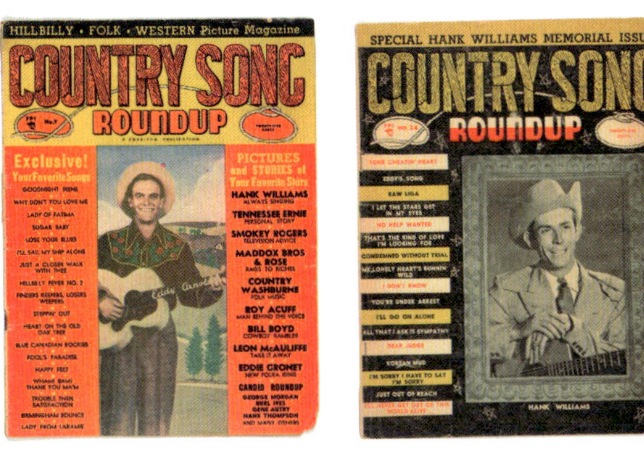
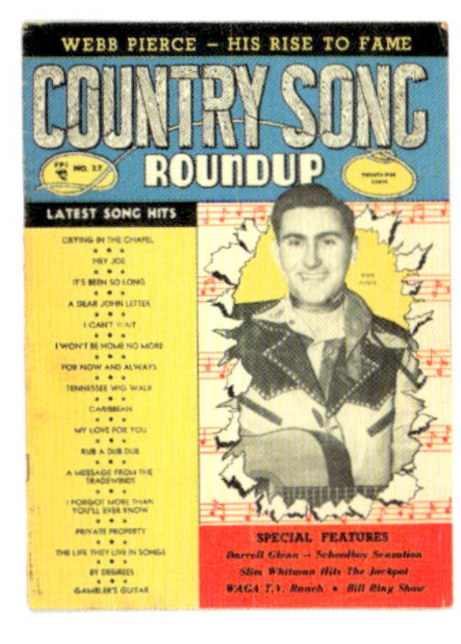
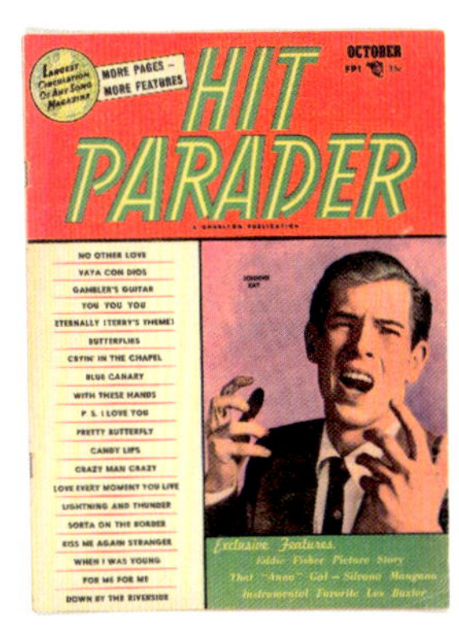
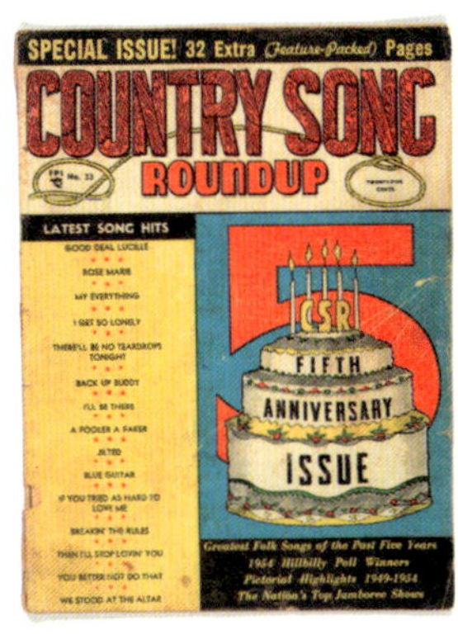
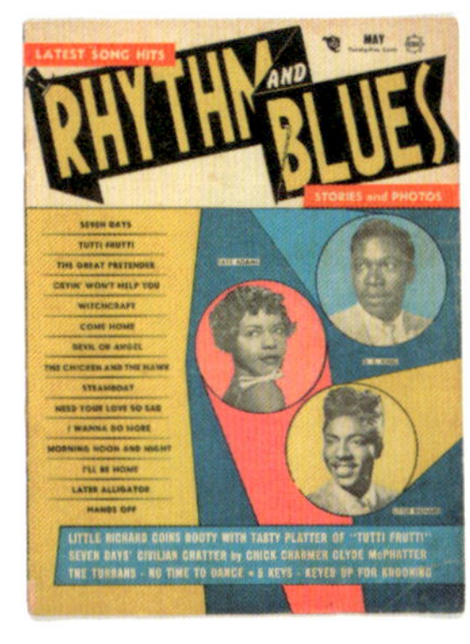
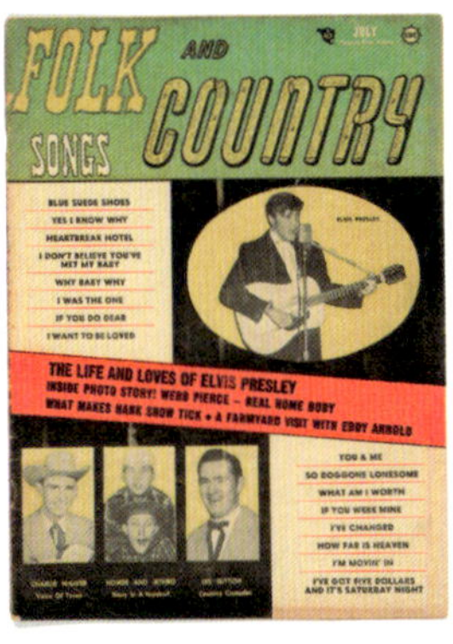
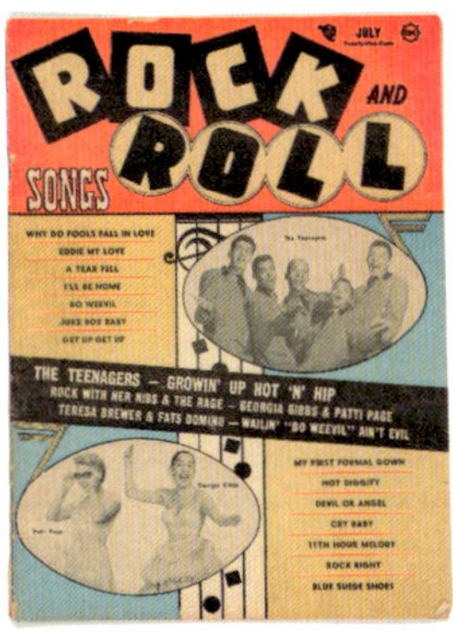
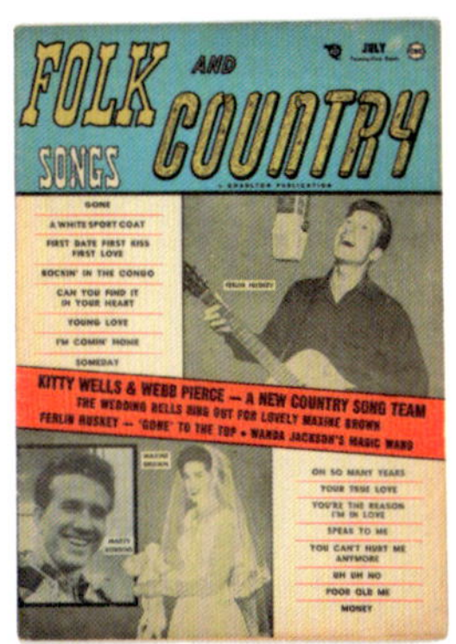
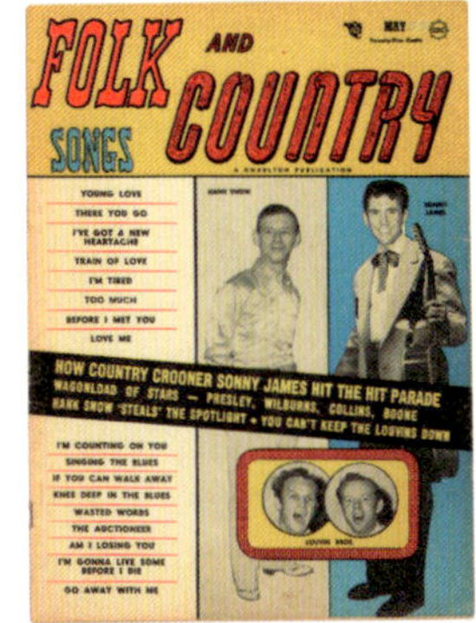
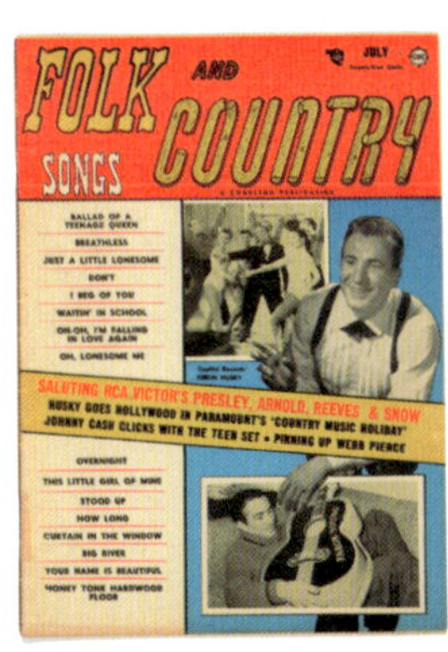
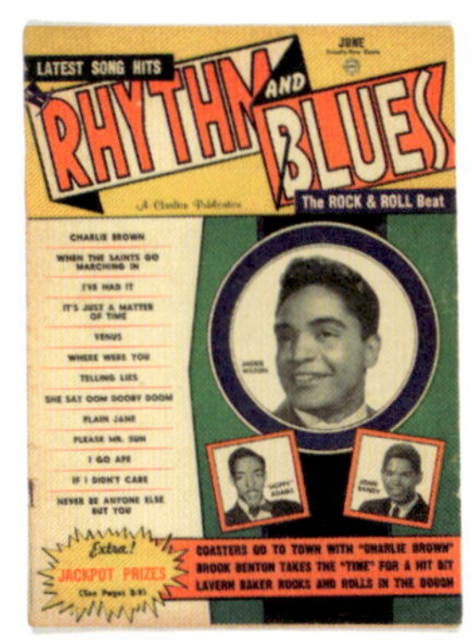
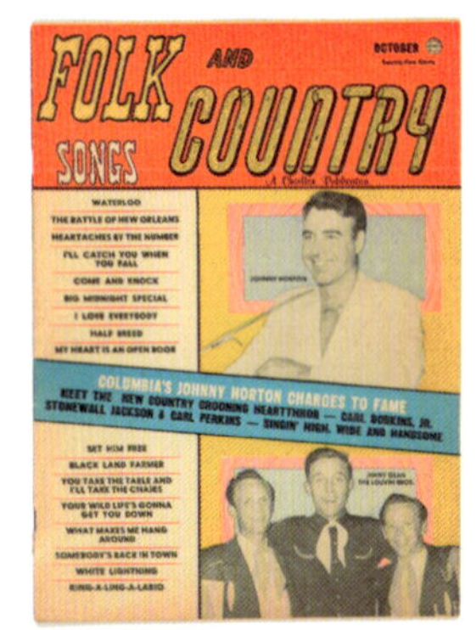
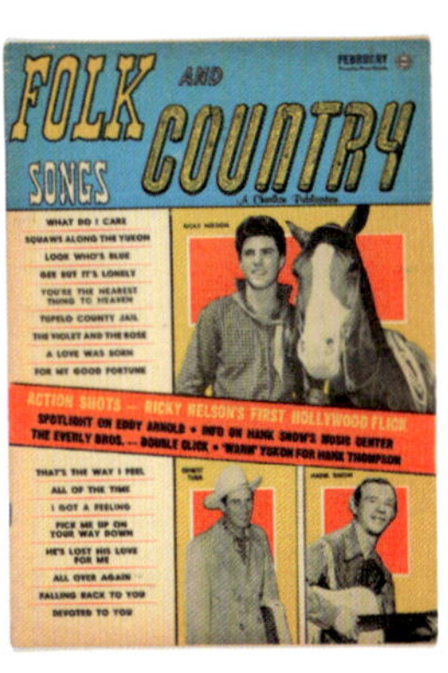
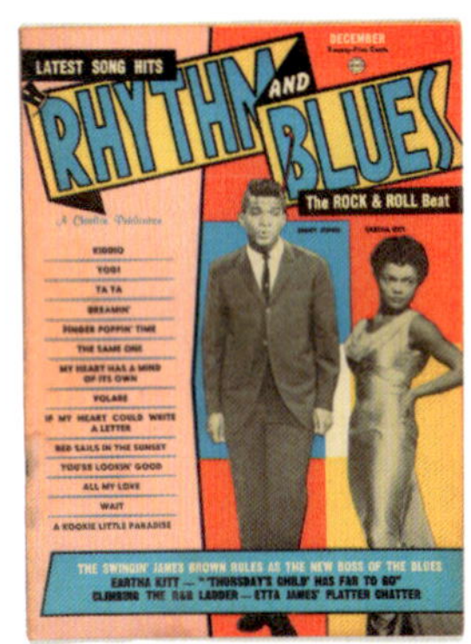
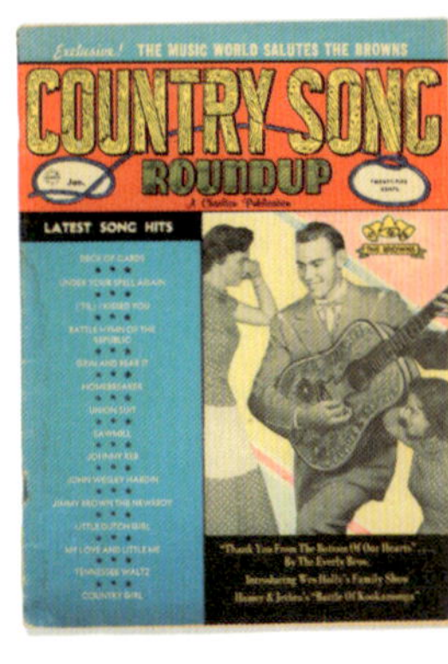
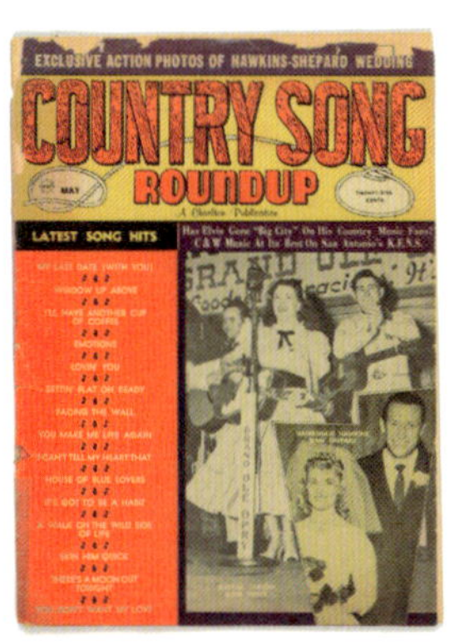
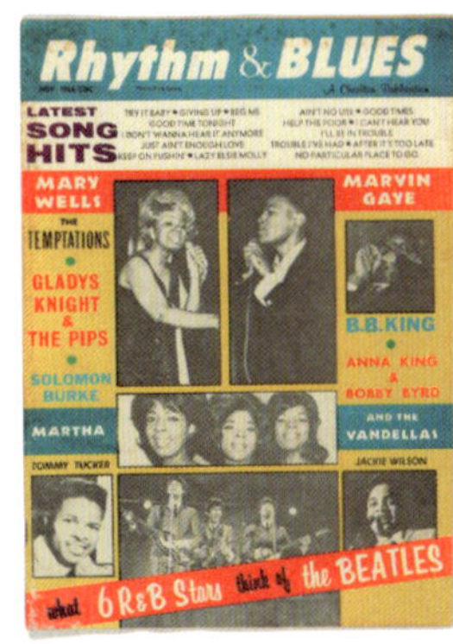
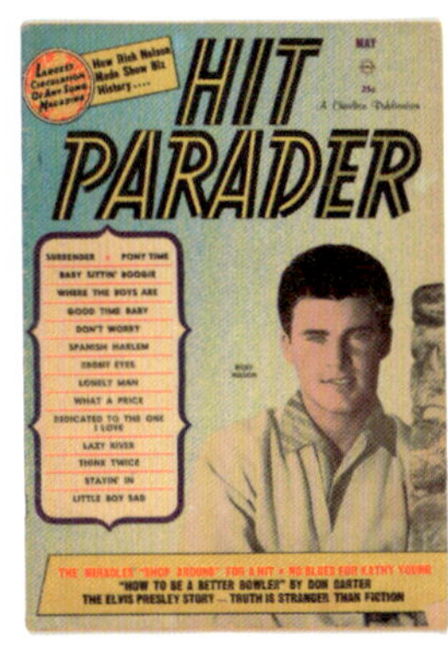
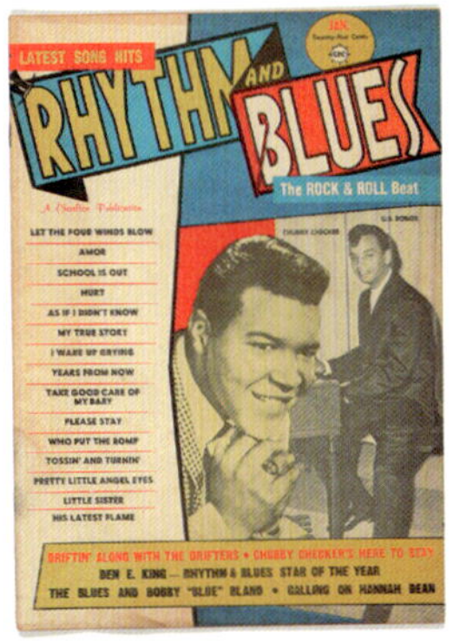
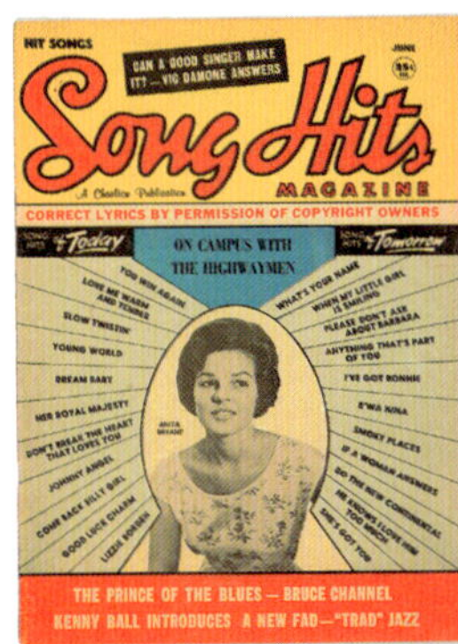
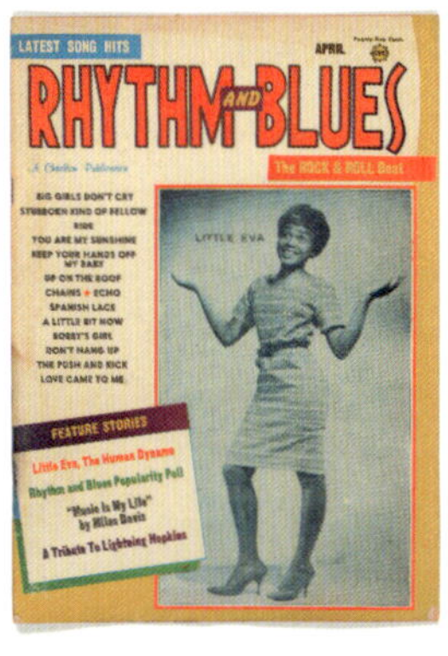
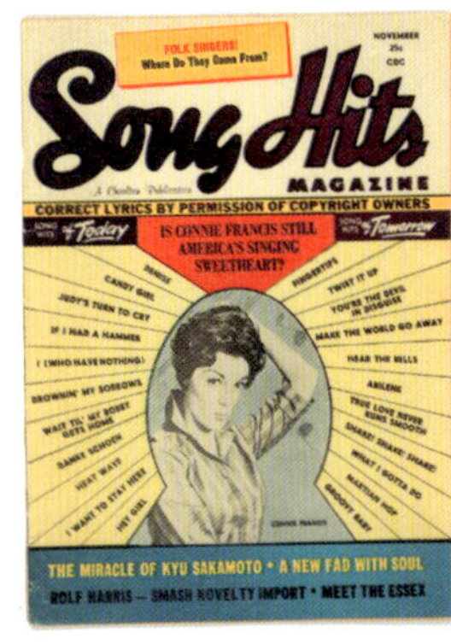
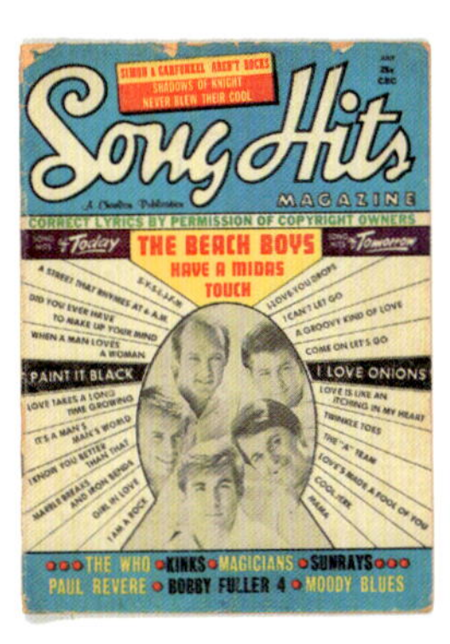
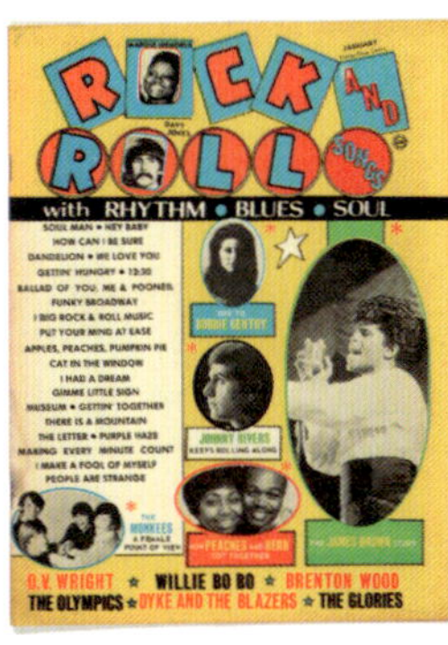

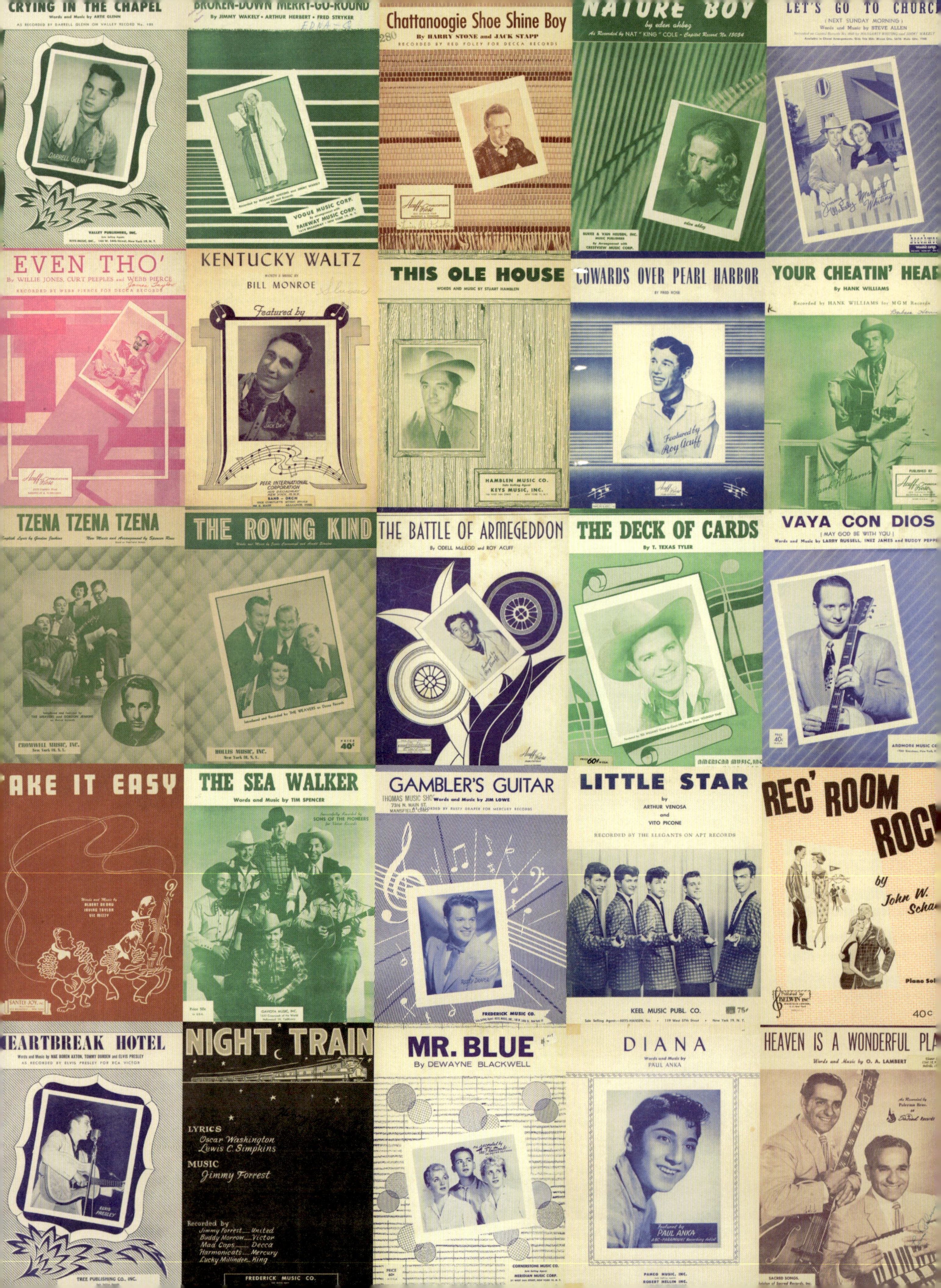

CRYING IN THE CHAPEL
Words and Music by ARTIE GLENN

BROKEN-DOWN MERRY-GO-ROUND
By JIMMY WAKELY • ARTHUR HERBERT • FRED STRYKER

Chattanoogie Shoe Shine Boy
By HARRY STONE and JACK STAPP

NATURE BOY
by eden ahbez
As Recorded by NAT "KING" COLE

LET'S GO TO CHURCH
(NEXT SUNDAY MORNING)
Words and Music by STEVE ALLEN

EVEN THO'
By WILLIE JONES, CURT PEEPLES and WEBB PIERCE

KENTUCKY WALTZ
BILL MONROE

THIS OLE HOUSE
Words and Music by STUART HAMBLEN

COWARDS OVER PEARL HARBOR
By FRED ROSE

YOUR CHEATIN' HEART
By HANK WILLIAMS

TZENA TZENA TZENA

THE ROVING KIND

THE BATTLE OF ARMEGEDDON
By ODELL McLEOD and ROY ACUFF

THE DECK OF CARDS
By T. TEXAS TYLER

VAYA CON DIOS
(MAY GOD BE WITH YOU)
Words and Music by LARRY RUSSELL, INEZ JAMES and BUDDY PEPPER

TAKE IT EASY

THE SEA WALKER
Words and Music by TIM SPENCER

GAMBLER'S GUITAR

LITTLE STAR
by ARTHUR VENOSA and VITO PICONE

REC' ROOM ROCK
by John W. Scha...
Piano Solo

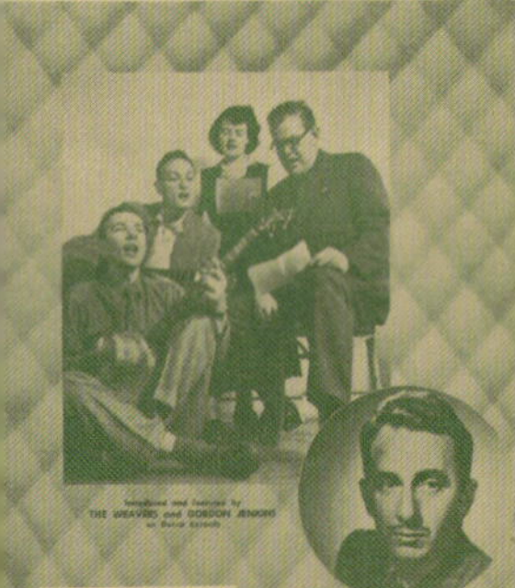
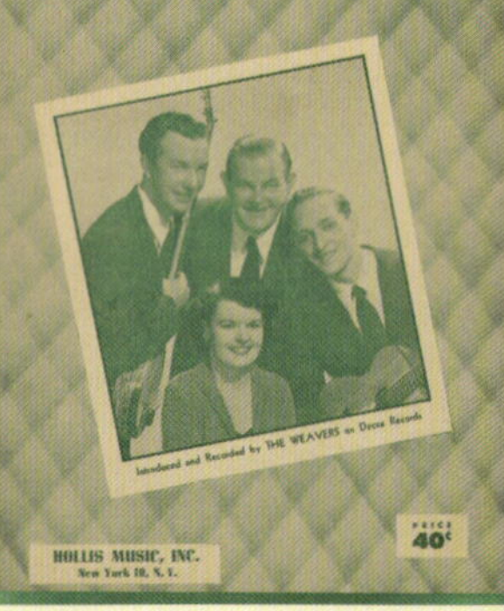
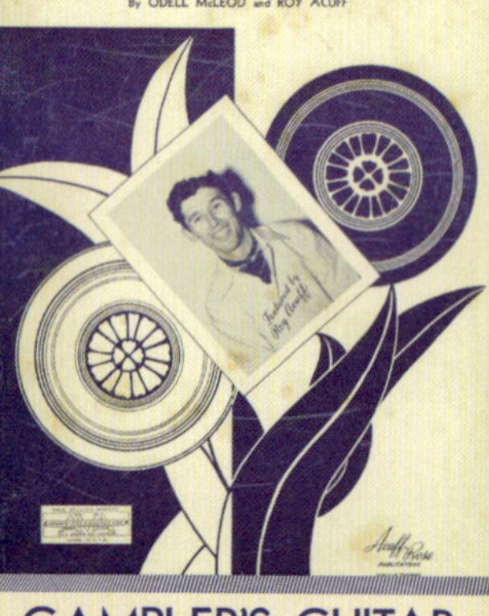
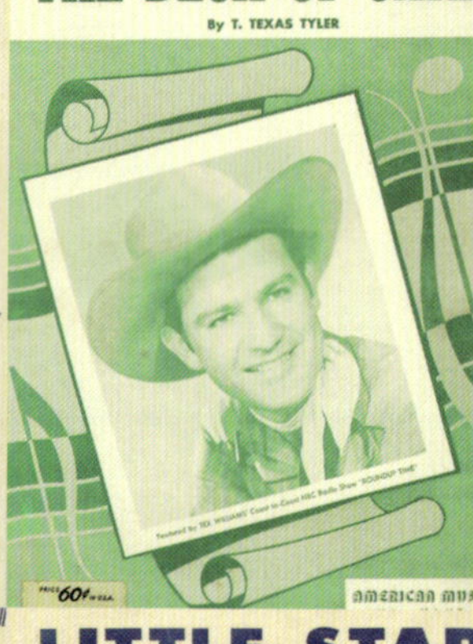
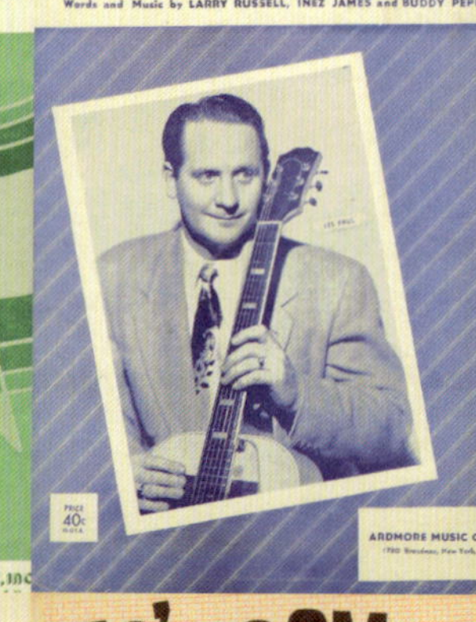
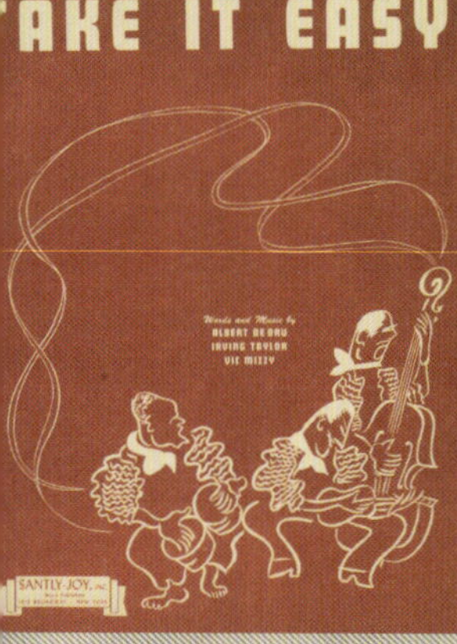
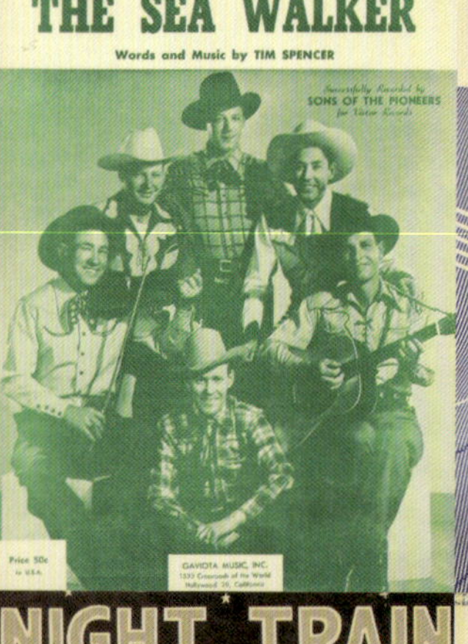
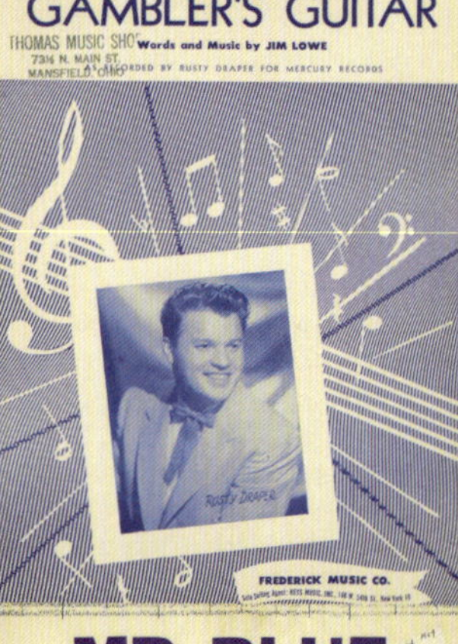
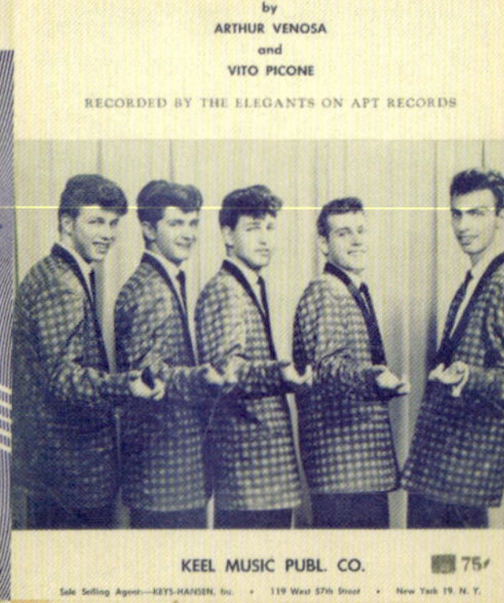
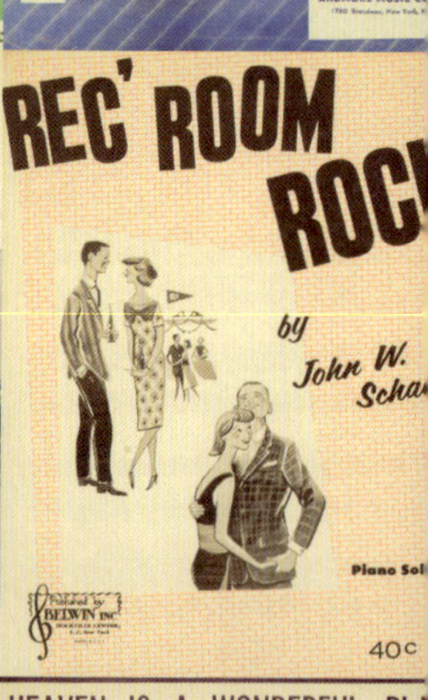

HEARTBREAK HOTEL
Words and Music by MAE BOREN AXTON, TOMMY DURDEN and ELVIS PRESLEY

NIGHT TRAIN
LYRICS Oscar Washington, Lewis C. Simpkins
MUSIC Jimmy Forrest

MR. BLUE
By DEWAYNE BLACKWELL

DIANA
Words and Music by PAUL ANKA

HEAVEN IS A WONDERFUL PLA...
Words and Music by O. A. LAMBERT

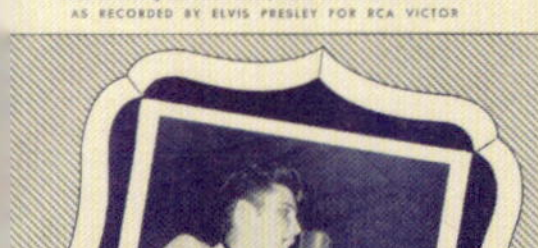
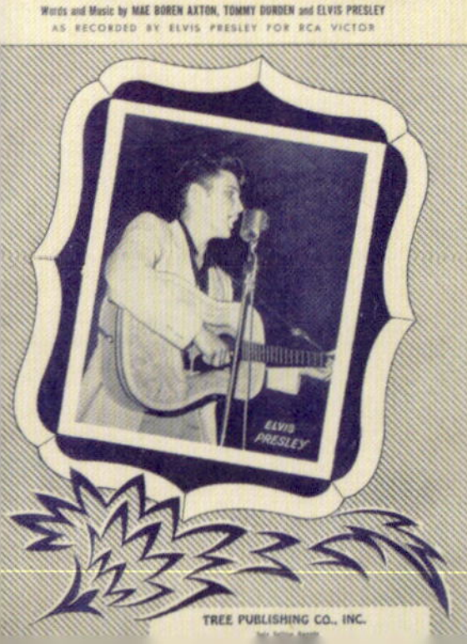
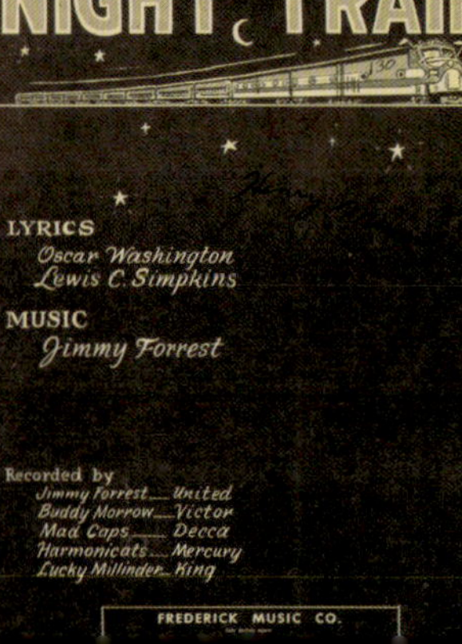
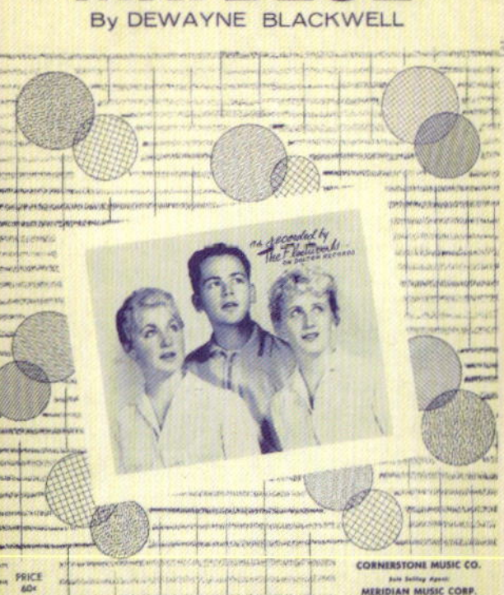
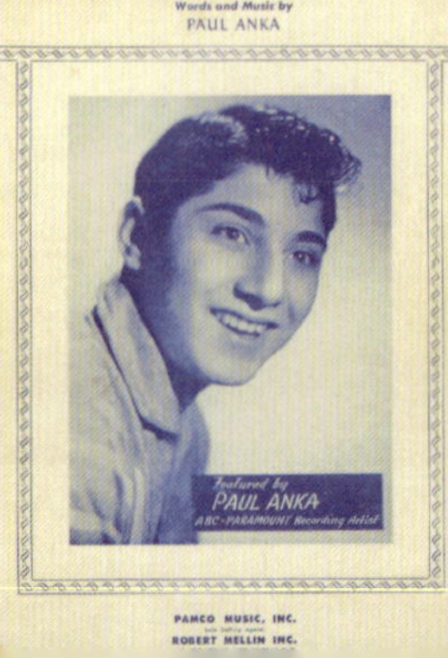
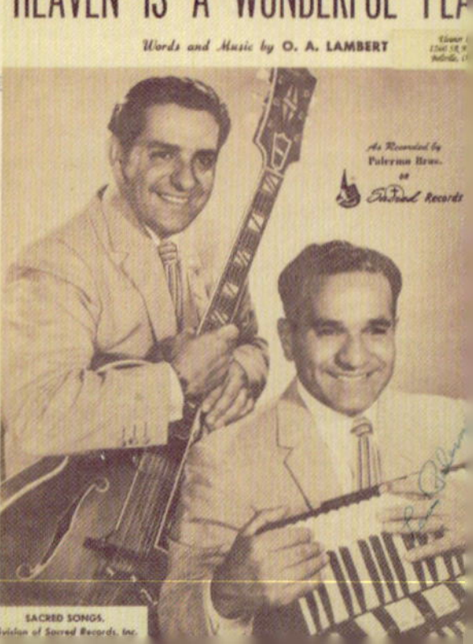

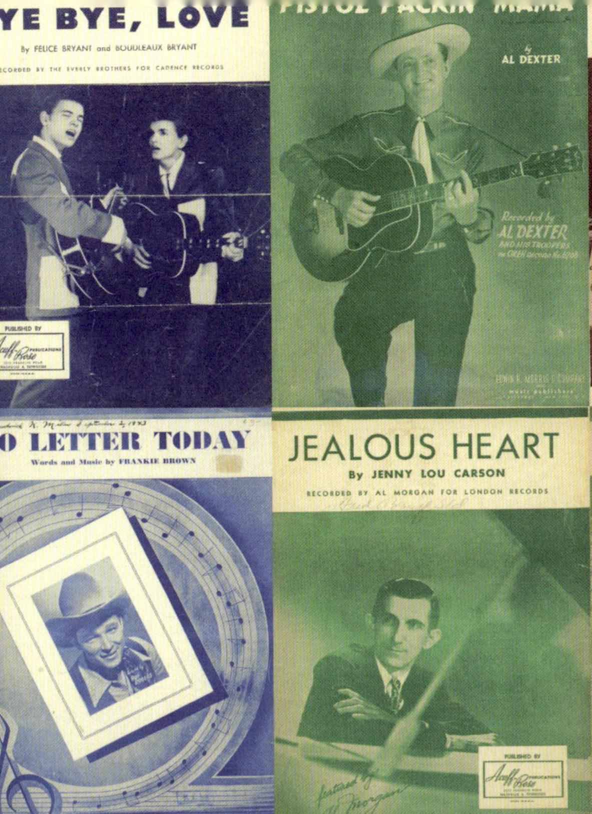
YE BYE, LOVE
By FELICE BRYANT and BOUDLEAUX BRYANT
PISTOL PACKIN' MAMA
By AL DEXTER
A MIGHTY PRETTY WALTZ
By AL HOFFMAN and NORMAN GIMBEL
LET'S GO TO CHURCH
(Next Sunday Morning)
Words and Music by STEVE ALLEN

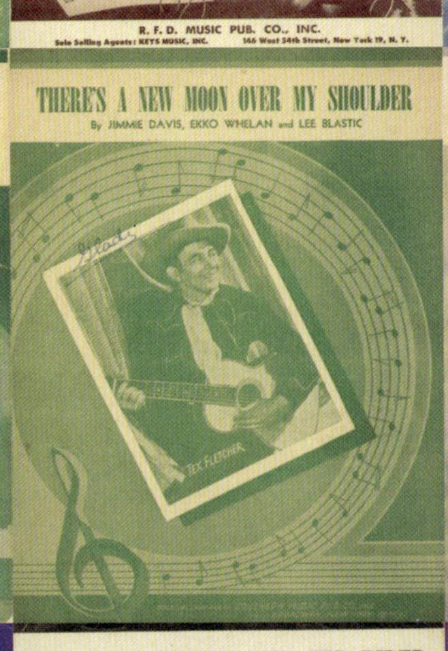
JINGLE-BELL ROCK
Words and Music by JOE BEAL and JIM BOOTHE
CORNELL MUSIC, INC.

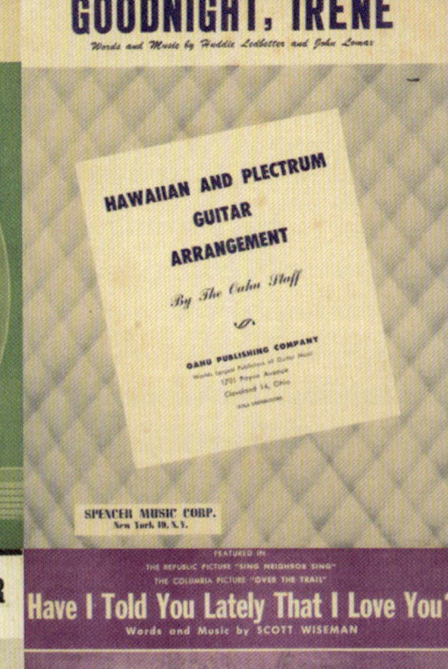
NO LETTER TODAY
Words and Music by FRANKIE BROWN

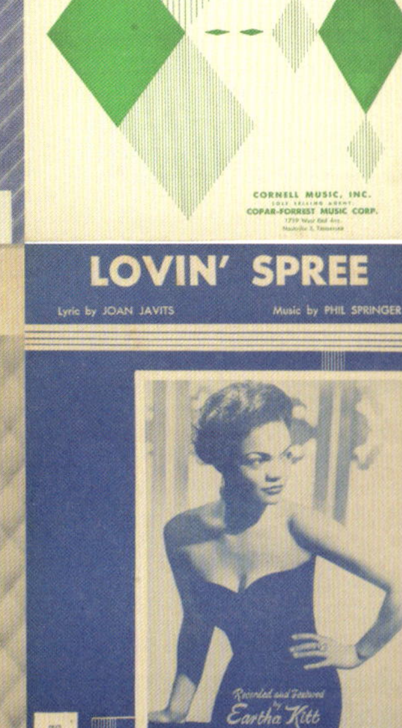
JEALOUS HEART
By JENNY LOU CARSON

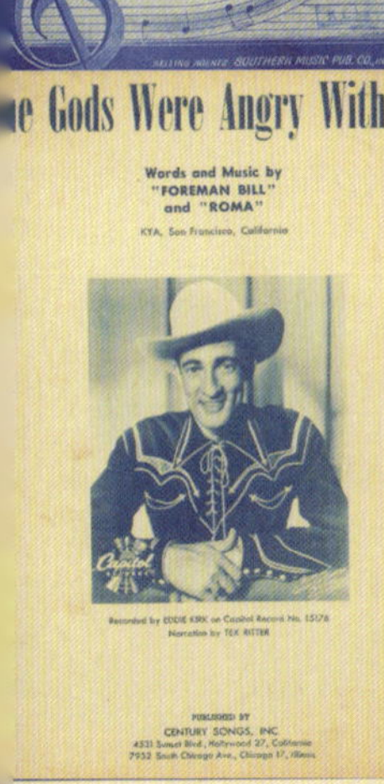
THERE'S A NEW MOON OVER MY SHOULDER
By JIMMIE DAVIS, EKKO WHELAN and LEE BLASTIC

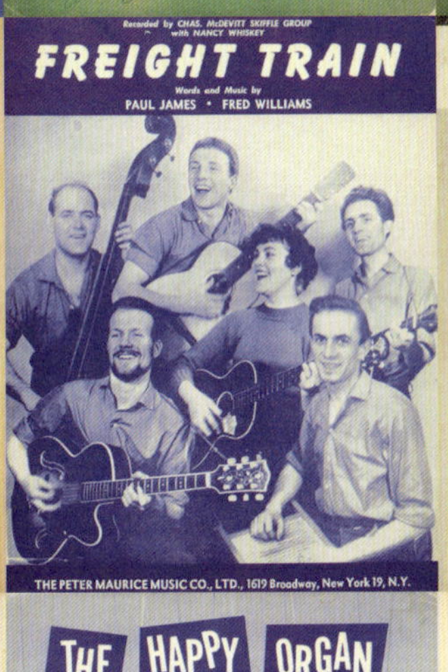
GOODNIGHT, IRENE
HAWAIIAN AND PLECTRUM GUITAR ARRANGEMENT

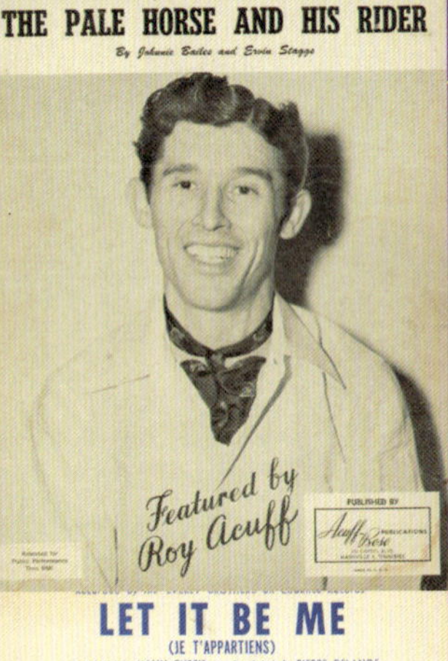
LOVIN' SPREE
Lyric by JOAN JAVITS   Music by PHIL SPRINGER
Eartha Kitt

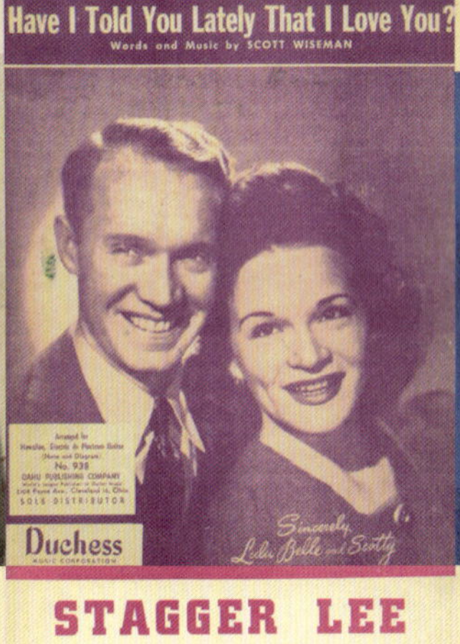
The Gods Were Angry With Me
Words and Music by "FOREMAN BILL" and "ROMA"

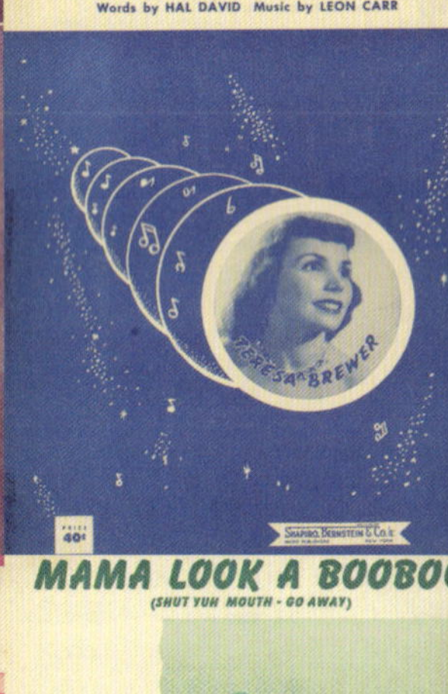
FREIGHT TRAIN
Words and Music by PAUL JAMES   FRED WILLIAMS
THE PETER MAURICE MUSIC CO., LTD., 1619 Broadway, New York 19, N.Y.

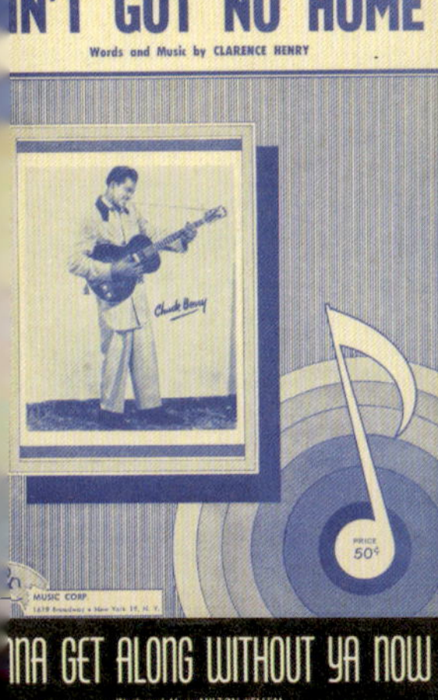
THE PALE HORSE AND HIS RIDER
By Johnnie Bailes and Ervin Staggs
Featured by Roy Acuff

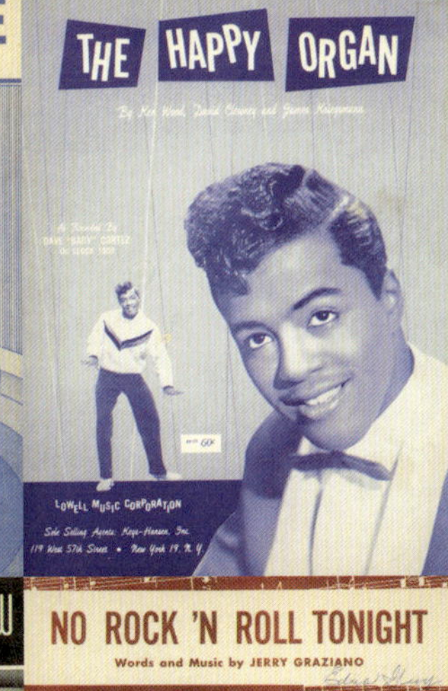
Have I Told You Lately That I Love You?
Words and Music by SCOTT WISEMAN
Duchess

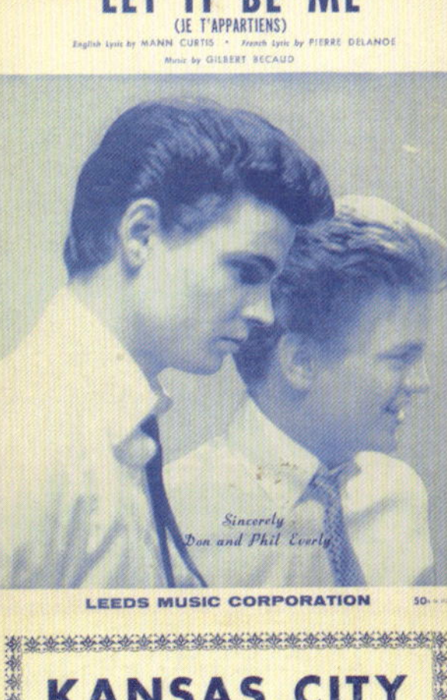
BELL BOTTOM BLUES
Words by HAL DAVID   Music by LEON CARR

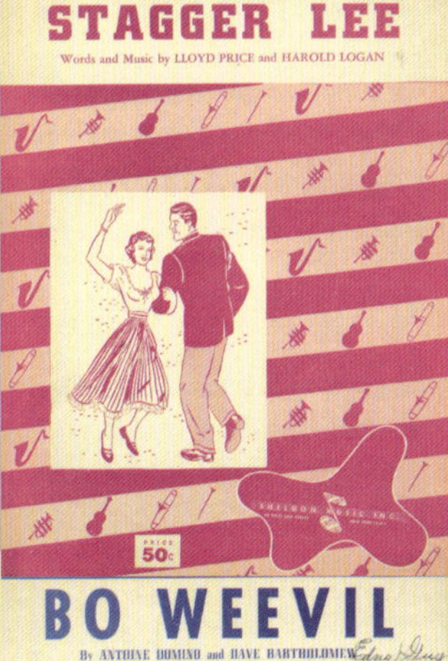
AIN'T GOT NO HOME
Words and Music by CLARENCE HENRY

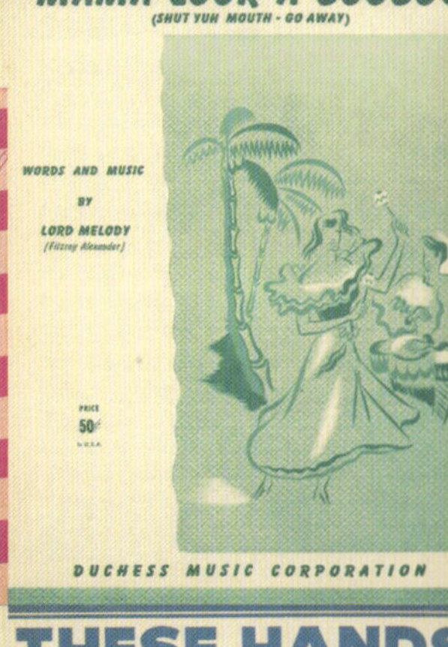
THE HAPPY ORGAN
LOWELL MUSIC CORPORATION

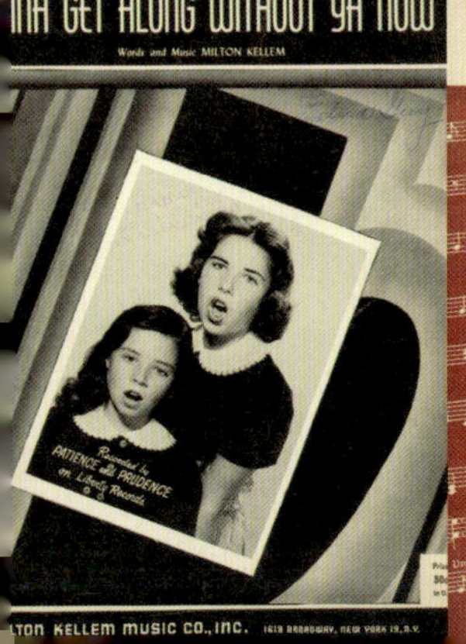
LET IT BE ME
(JE T'APPARTIENS)
English Lyric by MANN CURTIS   French Lyric by PIERRE DELANOE
Music by GILBERT BECAUD
LEEDS MUSIC CORPORATION

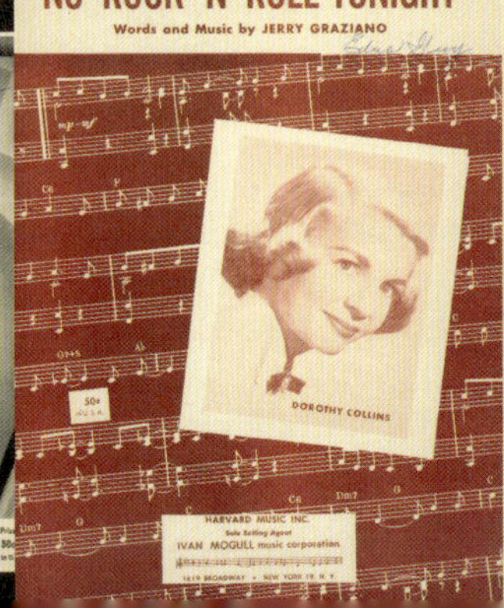
STAGGER LEE
Words and Music by LLOYD PRICE and HAROLD LOGAN

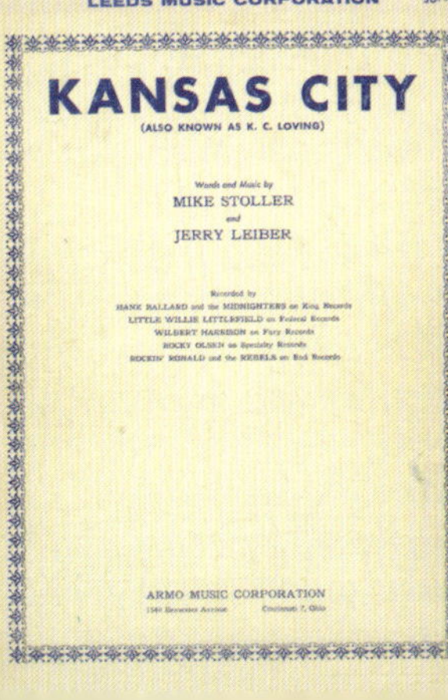
MAMA LOOK A BOOBOO
(SHUT YUH MOUTH - GO AWAY)
WORDS AND MUSIC BY LORD MELODY
DUCHESS MUSIC CORPORATION

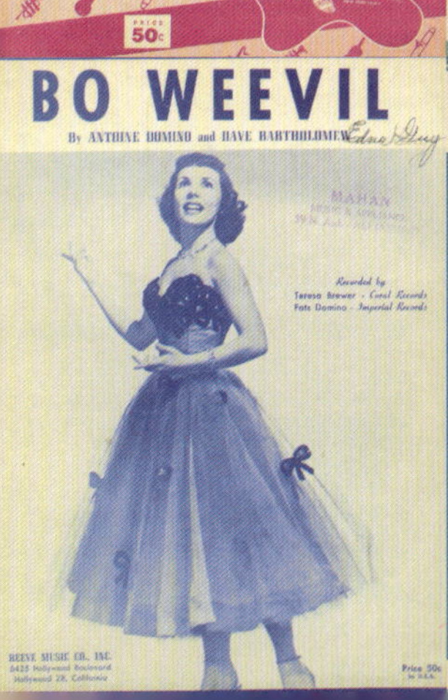
NO ROCK 'N ROLL TONIGHT
Words and Music by JERRY GRAZIANO
DOROTHY COLLINS

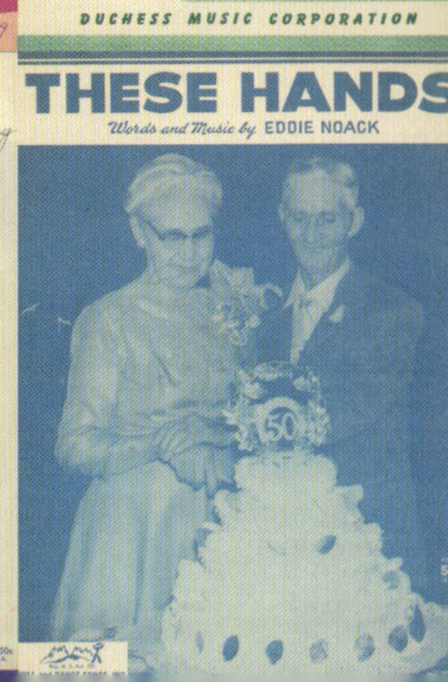
KANSAS CITY
(ALSO KNOWN AS K. C. LOVING)
Words and Music by MIKE STOLLER and JERRY LEIBER
ARMO MUSIC CORPORATION
BO WEEVIL
By ANTOINE DOMINO and DAVE BARTHOLOMEW
THESE HANDS
Words and Music by EDDIE NOACK

Lloyd Price. . . . . *Georgianna* (Price–Boskent), KRC 303-45, 45, 1957
Mickey & Sylvia . . . .*Dearest* (McDaniel–Polk–Gibson), Collectibles 4568, 45, 1957
                                       Love Is Strange (Ethel Smith), Collectibles 4568, 45, 1957
Paul Anka . . . . *Tell Me That You Love Me* (Anka, arranged and Conducted by Sid Feller), Columbia 4022, 78, 1957
          I Love You, Baby (Anka, arranged and Conducted by Don Costa), Columbia 4022, 78, 1957
Rev. C. L. Franklin. . . . . *I'm Going Through*—Part 1, Chess 1655, 78, 1957
                                   I'm Going Through—Part 2, Chess 1655, 45, 1957
Roberta Martin Singers . . . .*Nothing But a God*, Savoy 4087, 78, 1957
                             Sinner Man, Where You Gonna Run To, Savoy 4087, 78, 1957
Shirley & Lee . . . . *That's What I Wanna Do* (Leonard Lee), Aladdin 3362, 78, 1957
                           When I Saw You (Leonard Lee), Aladdin 3362, 78, 1957
Thurston Harris. . . . .*Little Bitty Pretty One* (R. Byrd), Aladdin 3398, 78, 1957
               I Hope You Won't Hold It Against Me (Ross and Ross), Aladdin 3398, 78, 1957
Webb Pierce and Kitty Wells . . . . *One Week Later* (Gary Walker), Decca 9-30489, 45, 1957
B. B. King . . . .*Please Accept My Love* (Garlow), Kent 315, 78, 1958
                            You've Been An Angel (King–Taub), Kent 315, 78, 1958
                          You Know I Go for You (Taub–Ling–King), Kent 301, 78, 1958
             Why Do Everything Happen to Me (Taub–King–Josea), Kent 301, 78, 1958
Big Bopper. . . . . *Chantilly Lace* (J. P. Richardson), Mercury 71343, 45, 1958
        Purple People Eater Meets Witch Doctor (Rick Johnson–J. P. Richardson), Mercury 71343, 45, 1958
Bill Doggett . . . . *Hold It* (Scott–Butler), King 45-5149, 45, 1958
Bobby Darin . . . .*Splish Splash* (Darin–Murray), Atco 45-6117, 45, 1958
Bumps Blackwell Orch. . . . .*MS & DB*, Keen 3-4010, 45, 1958
                                   Sumpin' Jumpin', Keen 3-4010, 45, 1958
Carl Belew . . . .*Everytime I'm Kissing You*, 4 Star 1721, 45, 1958
                24 Hour Night (R. Moore–C. Klemer–D. Wheeler), 4 Star 1721, 45, 1958
Champs. . . . .*Train to Nowhere* (Dave Burgess), Challenge 1016, 78, 1958
                         Turnpike (Dave Burgess), Challenge 59026, 45, 1958
                  Rockin' Mary (Dave Burgess–Dash Crofts), Challenge 59026, 45, 1958
Chuck Berry . . . . *Carol*, Chess 1700, 78, 1958
                                 Johnny B. Goode, Chess 1691, 45, 1958
                               Around & Around, Chess 1691, 45, 1958
                                  Hey Pedro, Chess 1700, 78, 1958
Chuck Willis . . . .*What Am I Living For* (Jay–Harris), Atlantic 1179, 45, 1958
                       Hang Up My Rock and Roll Shoes, Atlantic 1179, 45, 1958
Coasters . . . . *Three Cool Cats* (Lieber–Stoller), Atco 45-6132, 45, 1958
                         Charlie Brown (Lieber–Stoller), Atco 45-6132, 45, 1958
                         Takety Yak (Leiber–Stoller), Atco 45-6116, 45, 1958
                Zing! Went the Strings of My Heart (Hanley), Atco 45-6116, 45, 1958
Conway Twitty. . . . .*I'll Try* (Composed by Twitty–Nance), MGM K12677, 45, 1958
               It's Only Make Believe (Composed by Twitty–Nance), MGM K12677, 45, 1958
Cozy Cole. . . . . *Topsy I* (Battle–Durham), Love 5003, 45, 1958
                           Topsy II (Battle–Durham), Love 5003, 45, 1958
Elchords . . . . *Gee I'm in Love* (R. Moore–J. Jones), Good 545, 45, 1958
                      Peppermint Stick (R. Moore–J. Jones), Good 545, 45, 1958
Elegants . . . . *Little Star* (Venosa–Picone), Apt 45-25005, 45, 1958
        Getting Dizzy (Moschella–Romano–Picone–Venosa–Tardogna), Apt 45-25005, 45, 1958
Everly Brothers . . . . *All I Have to Do Is Dream* (Boudleaux Bryant), Cadence 1348, 45, 1958
                         Claudette (Boudleaux Bryant), Cadence 1348, 45, 1958
Fent* Robinson. . . . . *The Freeze* (D. Dean), Duke 190, 78, 1958
                      Mississippi Steamboat (Robey–Scott), Duke 191 , 78, 1958
Harvey . . . . *Ten Commandments of Love* (M. Paul), Chess 1705, 45, 1958
Huey "Piano" Smith . . . . *Don't You Know Yockomo* (Vincent–Smith), Ace 553, 45, 1958
Ivory Joe Hunter . . . . *Baby Baby Count on Me*, Atlantic 45-1173, 45, 1958
                             You're on My Mind, Atlantic 45-1173, 45, 1958
Jackie Wilson . . . .*Lonely Teardrops* (Berry Gordy Jr.–Tyran Carlo), Brunswick 55105, 45, 1958
Jody Reynolds . . . . *Endless Sleep* (Jody Reynolds–Dolores Nance), Demon FF-1507, 45, 1958
Joe Jones . . . . *The Prisoner's Song* (Guy Massey), Roulette 4087, 45, 1958
Kodoks . . . . *Oh Gee, Oh Gosh*, Fury 1015, 78, 1958
                                Make Believe World, Fury 1015, 78, 1958
LaVern Baker . . . .*I Cried a Tear* (Al Julia), Atlantic 45-2007, 45, 1958
                   Dix–A–Billy (Harris–Evans–Reardon), Atlantic 45-2007, 45, 1958

Preceding overleaf: Sheet music 1943-1959.
Opposite: *Country Song, Hit Parader, Rhythm and Blues* and *Rock and Roll* magazines, dates 1950-1963.

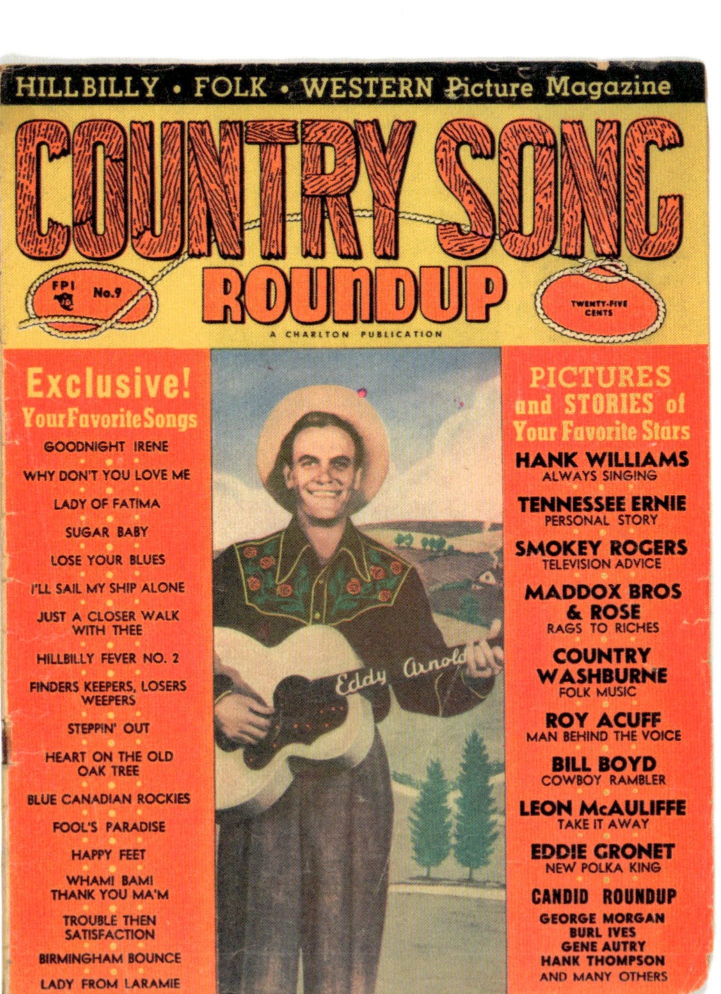

HILLBILLY · FOLK · WESTERN Picture Magazine
COUNTRY SONG
ROUNDUP
FPI No. 9
A CHARLTON PUBLICATION
TWENTY-FIVE CENTS
Exclusive!
Your Favorite Songs
GOODNIGHT IRENE
WHY DON'T YOU LOVE ME
LADY OF FATIMA
SUGAR BABY
LOSE YOUR BLUES
I'LL SAIL MY SHIP ALONE
JUST A CLOSER WALK WITH THEE
HILLBILLY FEVER NO. 2
FINDERS KEEPERS, LOSERS WEEPERS
STEPPIN' OUT
HEART ON THE OLD OAK TREE
BLUE CANADIAN ROCKIES
FOOL'S PARADISE
HAPPY FEET
WHAM! BAM! THANK YOU MA'M
TROUBLE THEN SATISFACTION
BIRMINGHAM BOUNCE
LADY FROM LARAMIE
PICTURES and STORIES of Your Favorite Stars
HANK WILLIAMS
ALWAYS SINGING
TENNESSEE ERNIE
PERSONAL STORY
SMOKEY ROGERS
TELEVISION ADVICE
MADDOX BROS & ROSE
RAGS TO RICHES
COUNTRY WASHBURNE
FOLK MUSIC
ROY ACUFF
MAN BEHIND THE VOICE
BILL BOYD
COWBOY RAMBLER
LEON McAULIFFE
TAKE IT AWAY
EDDIE GRONET
NEW POLKA KING
CANDID ROUNDUP
GEORGE MORGAN
BURL IVES
GENE AUTRY
HANK THOMPSON
AND MANY OTHERS
Eddy Arnold

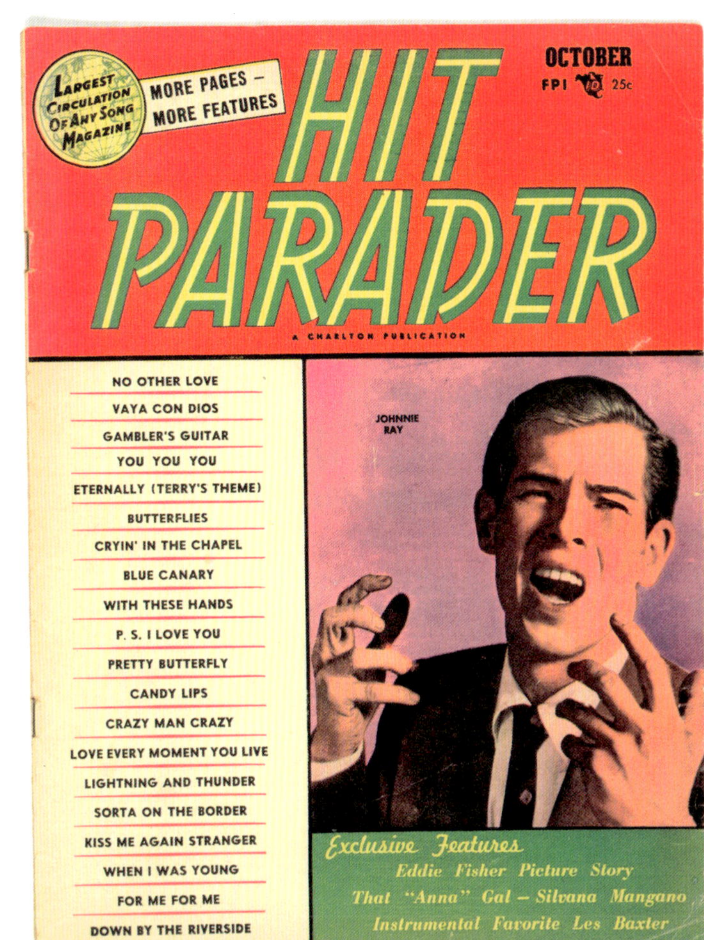

LARGEST CIRCULATION OF ANY SONG MAGAZINE
MORE PAGES — MORE FEATURES
OCTOBER
FPI 25c
HIT PARADER
A CHARLTON PUBLICATION
JOHNNIE RAY
NO OTHER LOVE
VAYA CON DIOS
GAMBLER'S GUITAR
YOU YOU YOU
ETERNALLY (TERRY'S THEME)
BUTTERFLIES
CRYIN' IN THE CHAPEL
BLUE CANARY
WITH THESE HANDS
P. S. I LOVE YOU
PRETTY BUTTERFLY
CANDY LIPS
CRAZY MAN CRAZY
LOVE EVERY MOMENT YOU LIVE
LIGHTNING AND THUNDER
SORTA ON THE BORDER
KISS ME AGAIN STRANGER
WHEN I WAS YOUNG
FOR ME FOR ME
DOWN BY THE RIVERSIDE
Exclusive Features
Eddie Fisher Picture Story
That "Anna" Gal - Silvana Mangano
Instrumental Favorite Les Baxter

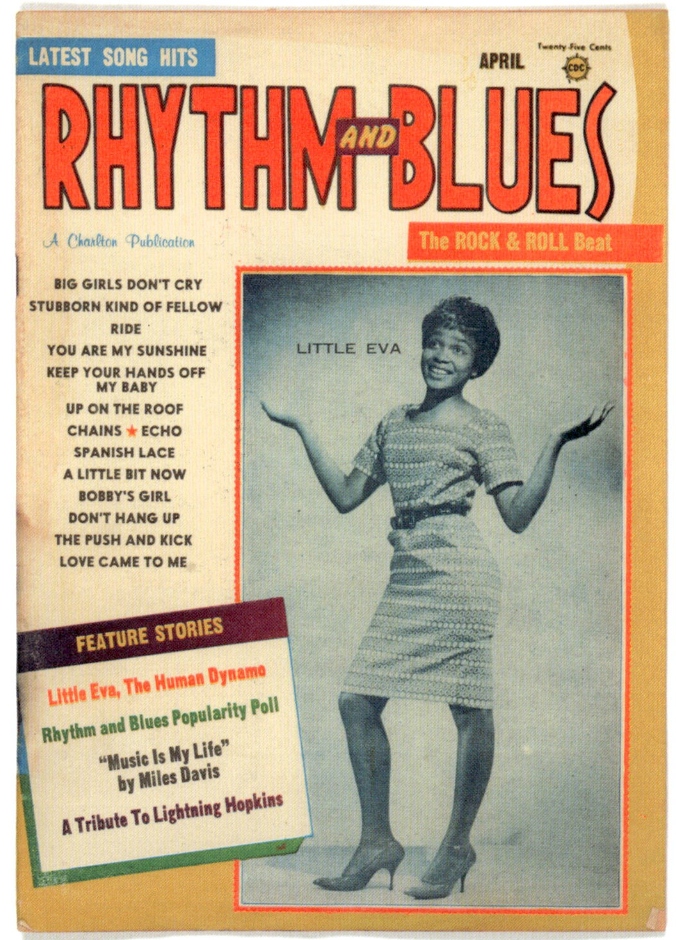

LATEST SONG HITS
APRIL
Twenty-Five Cents
RHYTHM AND BLUES
A Charlton Publication
The ROCK & ROLL Beat
BIG GIRLS DON'T CRY
STUBBORN KIND OF FELLOW
RIDE
YOU ARE MY SUNSHINE
KEEP YOUR HANDS OFF MY BABY
UP ON THE ROOF
CHAINS ★ ECHO
SPANISH LACE
A LITTLE BIT NOW
BOBBY'S GIRL
DON'T HANG UP
THE PUSH AND KICK
LOVE CAME TO ME
LITTLE EVA
FEATURE STORIES
Little Eva, The Human Dynamo
Rhythm and Blues Popularity Poll
"Music Is My Life"
by Miles Davis
A Tribute To Lightning Hopkins

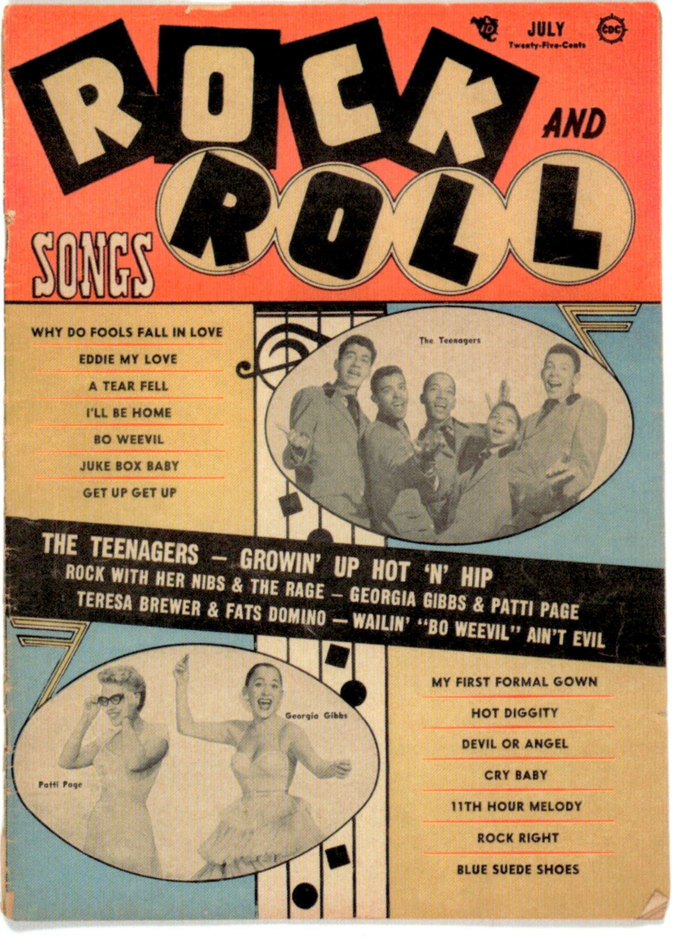

JULY
Twenty-Five-Cents
ROCK AND ROLL
SONGS
WHY DO FOOLS FALL IN LOVE
EDDIE MY LOVE
A TEAR FELL
I'LL BE HOME
BO WEEVIL
JUKE BOX BABY
GET UP GET UP
The Teenagers
THE TEENAGERS — GROWIN' UP HOT 'N' HIP
ROCK WITH HER NIBS & THE RAGE — GEORGIA GIBBS & PATTI PAGE
TERESA BREWER & FATS DOMINO — WAILIN' "BO WEEVIL" AIN'T EVIL
Patti Page
Georgia Gibbs
MY FIRST FORMAL GOWN
HOT DIGGITY
DEVIL OR ANGEL
CRY BABY
11TH HOUR MELODY
ROCK RIGHT
BLUE SUEDE SHOES

Little Anthony . . . . *Two People in the World* (Barrett–Wright), End E-1027, 45, 1958
Tears on My Pillow (Bradford–Lewis), End E-1027, 45, 1958
Little Richard. . . . . *Good Golly, Miss Molly* (Marascalco–Blackwell), Specialty 624, 78, 1958
Hey–Hey–Hey–Hey (R. Penniman), Specialty 624, 78, 1958
I'll Never Let You Go, Specialty 645, 45, 1958
Lloyd Price. . . . . *You Need Love* (Price–Logan), ABC Paramount 45-9972, 45, 1958
Stagger Lee (Archibald–Price–Logan), ABC Paramount 45-9972, 45, 1958
Monotones. . . . . *You Never Loved Me*, Argo 5290, 45, 1958
Book of Love, Argo 5290, 45, 1958
Ricky Nelson . . . .*Lonesome Town* (B. Knight), Imperial 45-IM-1720, 45, 1958
I Got a Feeling (B. Knight), Imperial IM-1720, 45, 1958
Roy Hamilton. . . . . *Pleadging My Love* (Robey–F. Washington), Epic 5-9294, 45, 1958
Sam Cooke . . . . *For Sentimental Reasons* (Silver–Heyman–Sherman), Keen 4-4002, 78, 1958
Desire Me (Bruce Culver), Keen 4-4002, 78, 1958
Blue Moon (Rodgers–Hart), Keen 3-2008, 45, 1958
Love You Most of All (B. Campbell), Keen 3-2008, 45, 1958
For Sentimental Reasons (Silver–Heyman–Sherman), Keen 4-4002, 45, 1958
Silhouettes . . . . *Get a Job*, Ember 1029, 78, 1958
I Am Lonely, Ember 1029, 78, 1958
Teddy Bears. . . . . *Don't You Worry My Little Pet* (Phillip Spector), Dore 45-503, 45, 1958
To Know Him, Is to Love Him (Phillip Spector), Dore 45-503, 45, 1958
Warren Storm . . . . *Mama Mama Mama (Look What Your Little Boy's Done)* (J. Miller), Nasco 45-6015, 45, 1958
Prisoner's Song (G. Massey), Nasco 45-6015, 45, 1958
Barrett Strong . . . . Oh I Apologize (W. Robinson & B. Gordy, Jr.), Anna 1111, 45, 1959
Money (That's What I Want) (J. Bradford & B. Gordy, Jr.), Anna 1111, 45, 1959
Bill Black's Combo. . . . .*Smokie—Part 1*, Hi 2018, 45, 1959
Smokie—Part 2, Hi 2018, 45, 1959
Bill Doggett . . . . *Rainbow Riot—Part 1* (Gibson–Carlington), King 45-5159, 45, 1959
Rainbow Riot—Part 2 (Gibson–Carlington), King 45-5159, 45, 1959
Billy Graham London Crusade Choir. . . . . *Just As I Am, Without One Plea (Woodworth)*
(Willaim B. Bradbury–Charlotte Elliott), Recorded Anthology of American Music Inc. 224, 45, 1959
Bobby Bland . . . .*I'll Take Care of You* (Brook Benton), Duke 314, 45, 1959
Chuck Berry . . . . *Little Queenie*, Chess 1722, 45, 1959
Almost Grown, Chess 1722, 45, 1959
Clyde McPhatter . . . .*Try Try Baby* (Ertegun–Wexler), Atlantic 2028, 78, 1959
Since You've Been Gone (Sedaka–Greenfield), Atlantic 2028, 78, 1959
There You Go (Ertegun–Wexler), Atlantic 2038, 45, 1959
Dave "Baby" Cortez . . . . *Love Me as I Love You* (Wood–Clowney), Clock 1009, 45, 1959
The Happy Organ (Wood–Clowney–Kriegsmann), Clock 1009, 45, 1959
Dee Clark . . . . *Just Keep It Up* (O. Blackwell), Abner 1026, 45, 1959
Drifters . . . . *Oh My Love* (Patterson–Lebish), Atlantic 45-2025, 45, 1959
There Goes My Baby (Nelson–Patterson–Treadwell), Atlantic 45-2025, 45, 1959
Duane Eddy. . . . . *Cannonball* (L. Hazlewood–D. Eddy), Jamie 1111, 45, 1959
Mason Dixon Lion (L. Hazlewood–D. Eddy), Jamie 1111, 45, 1959
Flamingos . . . . *I Only Have Eyes for You* (Harry Warren), End E-1046, 45, 1959
Gene & Eunice. . . . .*Go–On Kokomo* (E. Leny), Case 1001, 45, 1959
Poco–Loco (F. Wilson), Case 1001, 45, 1959
Jerry Fuller . . . . *Charlene* (L. Spring–C. Summers), Challenge 59057, 45, 1959
Jimmy Clanton . . . . *Just a Dream* (J. Clanton–C. Matassa), Ace 546, 45, 1959
Johnny Preston . . . . *Running Bear* (J. P. Richardson), Mercury 71474, 45, 1959
Little Junior Parker . . . .*Stranded* (D. Malone), Duke 309, 45, 1959
Lowell Fulson . . . . *That's Alright* (J. Lane), Checker 937, 45, 1959
It Took a Long Time, Checker 937, 45, 1959
Raiders . . . . *Hocus Pocus* (Smith–Goldsmith), Andex 3-4015, 45, 1959
Yoo Hoo (Lou Adler–Herb Alpert), Andex 3-4015, 45, 1959
Sammy Turner . . . . *Lavender-Blue* (Larry Morey–Eliot Daniel), Big Top 45-3016, 45, 1959
Sandy Nelson. . . . . *Teen Beat* (Nelson–Egnoian), Original Sound Record Co. OR-5, 45, 1959
Spacemen . . . . *The Lonely Jet Pilot* (B. Ross–J. Dixon), Alton A-254, 45, 1959
The Clouds (Julius Dixon), Alton A-254, 45, 1959
Swan Silvertones . . . .*Singin' in My Soul* (L. Johnson), Vee-Jay 894, 45, 1959
Sinking Sand (C. Jeter), Vee-Jay 894, 45, 1959
The Consolers . . . . *Every Christian Mother* (S. Pugh), Nashboro 646, 78, 1959
Help Me to Understand (S. Pugh), Nashboro 646, 78, 1959

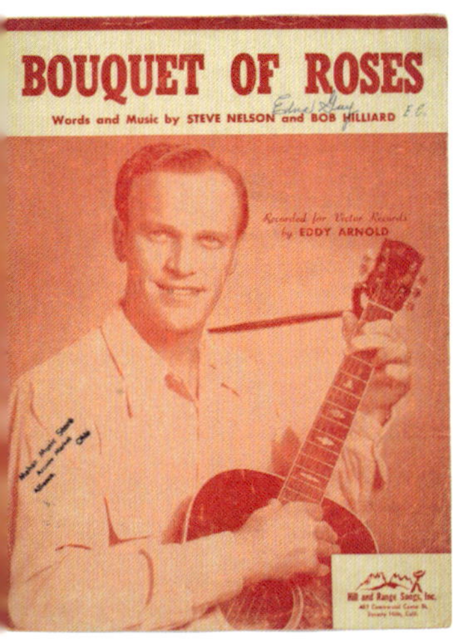
BOUQUET OF ROSES
Words and Music by STEVE NELSON and BOB HILLIARD
Recorded for Victor Records by EDDY ARNOLD
Hill and Range Songs, Inc.

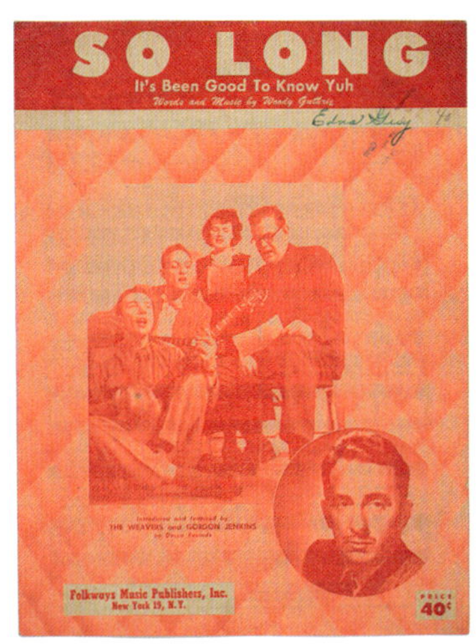
SO LONG
It's Been Good To Know Yuh
Words and Music by Woody Guthrie
Folkways Music Publishers, Inc.
New York 19, N.Y.
PRICE 40¢

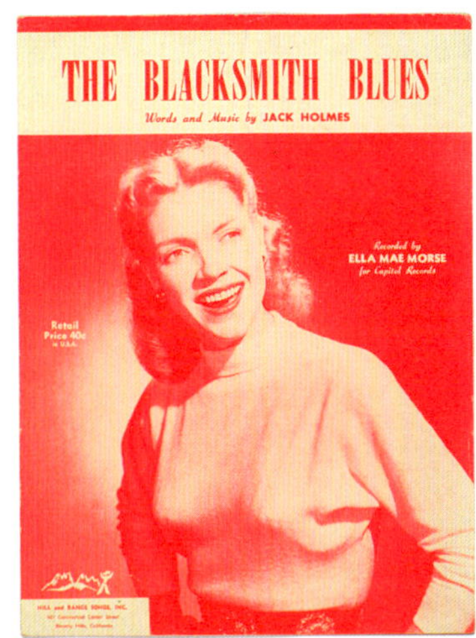
THE BLACKSMITH BLUES
Words and Music by JACK HOLMES
Recorded by ELLA MAE MORSE
for Capitol Records
Retail Price 60¢

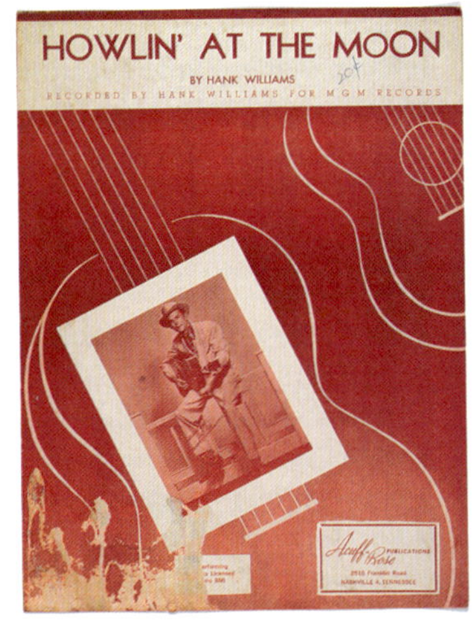
HOWLIN' AT THE MOON
RECORDED BY HANK WILLIAMS FOR M G M RECORDS
BY HANK WILLIAMS
Acuff-Rose Publications

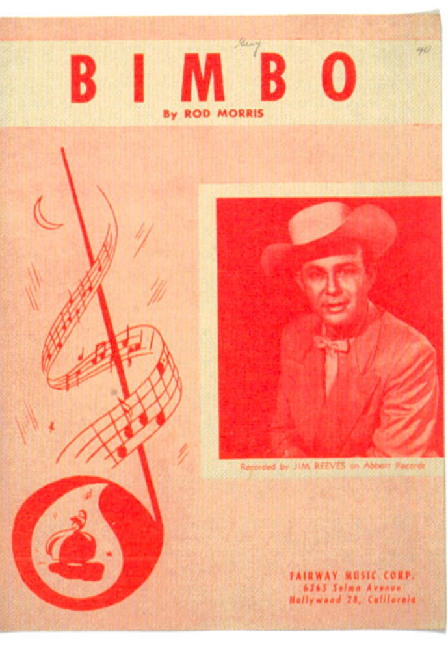
BIMBO
By ROD MORRIS
Recorded by JIM REEVES on Abbott Records
FAIRWAY MUSIC CORP.
6263 Selma Avenue
Hollywood 28, California

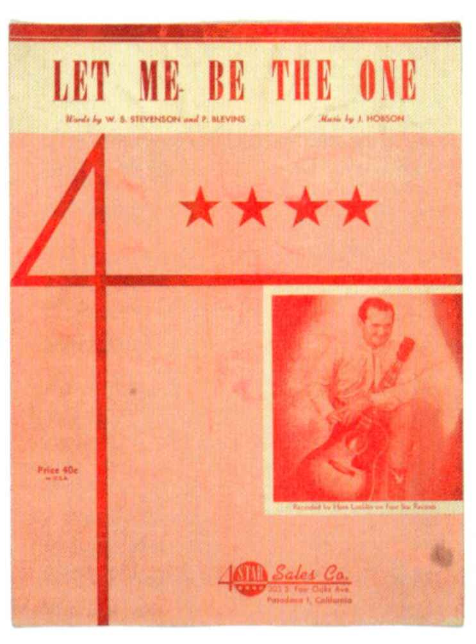
LET ME BE THE ONE
Words and Music by W. S. STEVENSON and P. BLEVINS
Music by J. HOBSON
Price 40c
Recorded by Hank Locklin on Four Star Records
Astra Sales Co.

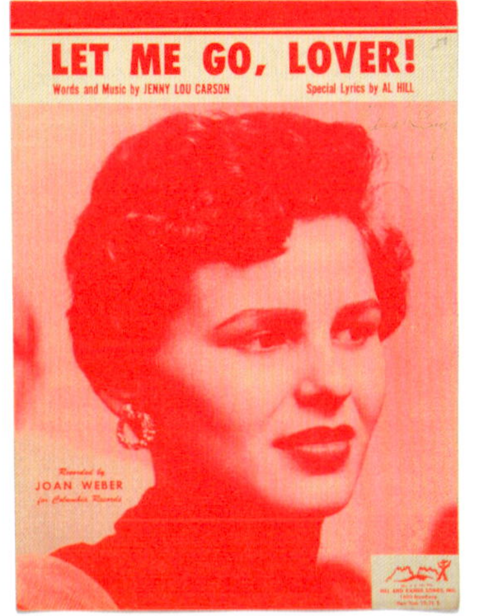
LET ME GO, LOVER!
Words and Music by JENNY LOU CARSON
Special Lyrics by AL HILL
Recorded by JOAN WEBER
on Columbia Records

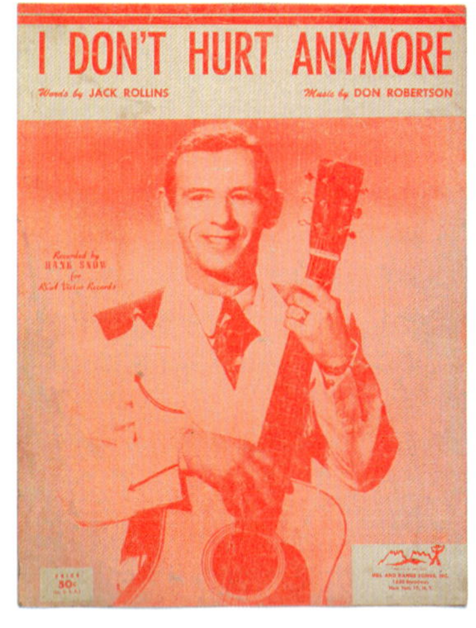
I DON'T HURT ANYMORE
Words by JACK ROLLINS
Music by DON ROBERTSON
Recorded by HANK SNOW
on RCA Victor Records

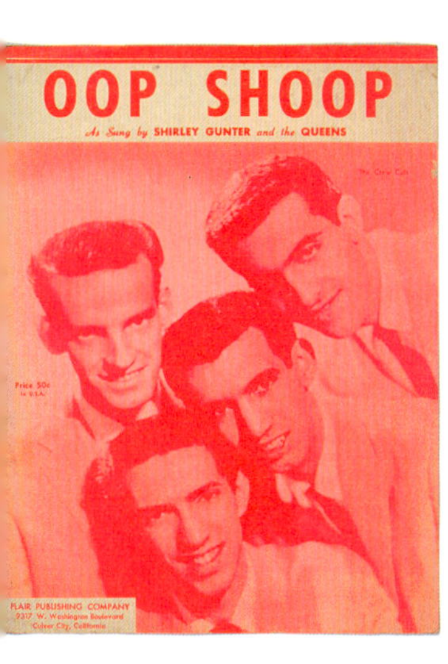
OOP SHOOP
As Sung by SHIRLEY GUNTER and the QUEENS
Price 50¢
FLAIR PUBLISHING COMPANY
Culver City, California

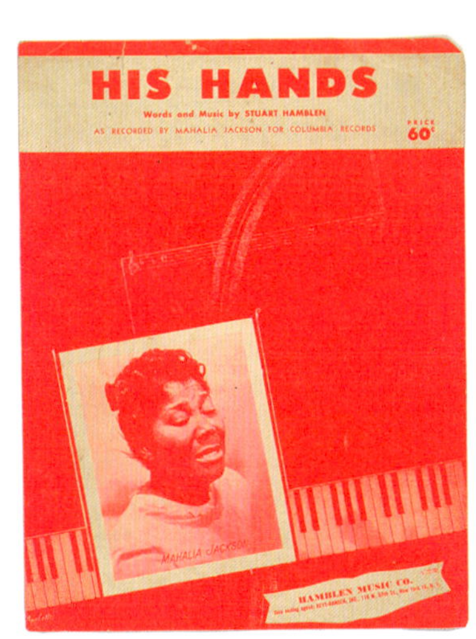
HIS HANDS
Words and Music by Stuart Hamblen
AS RECORDED BY MAHALIA JACKSON FOR COLUMBIA RECORDS
PRICE 60¢
MAHALIA JACKSON
HAMBLEN MUSIC CO.

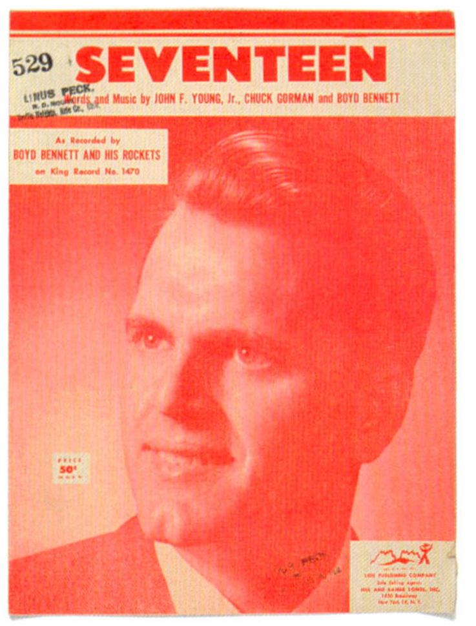
529
SEVENTEEN
Words and Music by JOHN F. YOUNG, Jr., CHUCK GORMAN and BOYD BENNETT
As Recorded by BOYD BENNETT AND HIS ROCKETS
on King Record No. 1470
Price 50¢

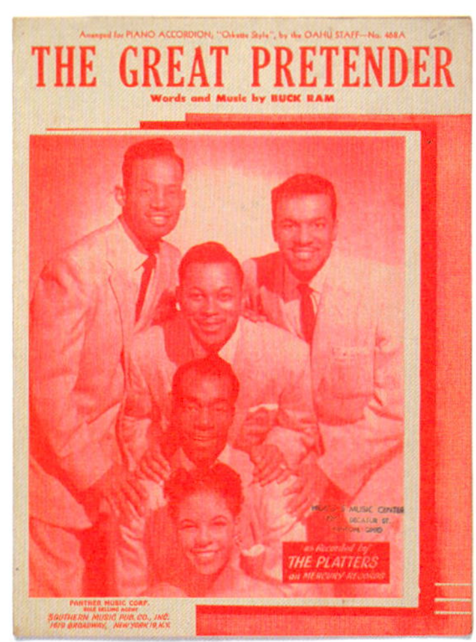
Arranged for PIANO ACCORDION, "Adesto Style", by the DAHL STAFF—No. 468A
THE GREAT PRETENDER
Words and Music by BUCK RAM
Recorded by THE PLATTERS
on Mercury Records

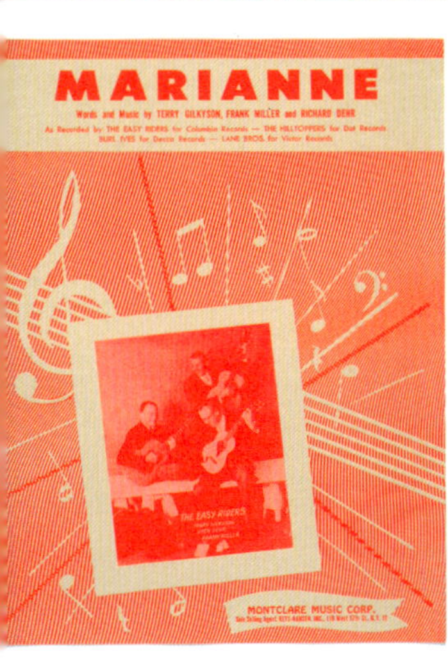
MARIANNE
Words and Music by TERRY GILKYSON, FRANK MILLER and RICHARD DEHR
MONTCLARE MUSIC CORP.

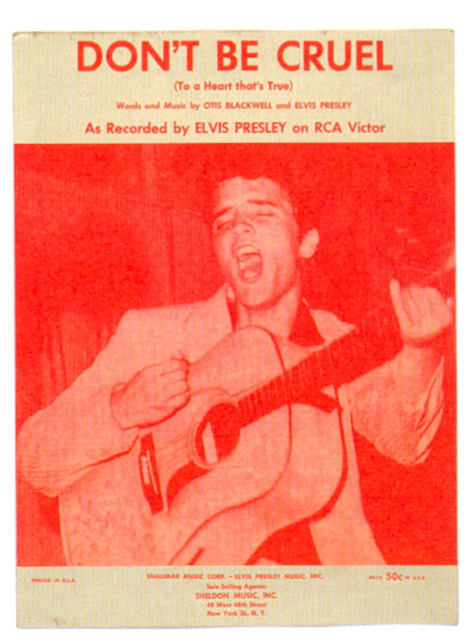
DON'T BE CRUEL
(To a Heart that's True)
Words and Music by OTIS BLACKWELL and ELVIS PRESLEY
As Recorded by ELVIS PRESLEY on RCA Victor
SHALIMAR MUSIC CORP—ELVIS PRESLEY MUSIC, INC.
SHELDON MUSIC, INC.
Price 50¢

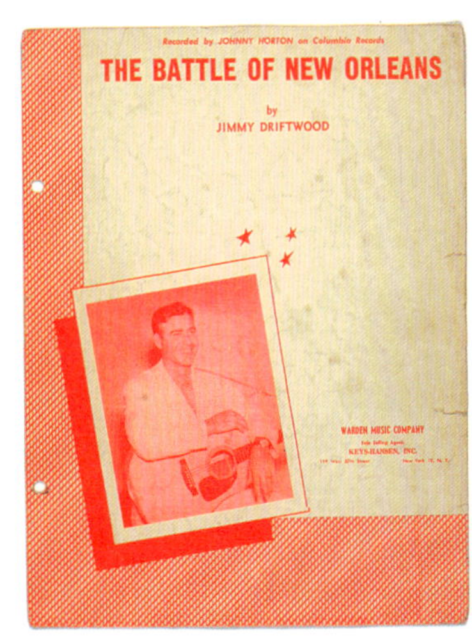
Recorded by JOHNNY HORTON on Columbia Records
THE BATTLE OF NEW ORLEANS
by JIMMY DRIFTWOOD
WARDEN MUSIC COMPANY

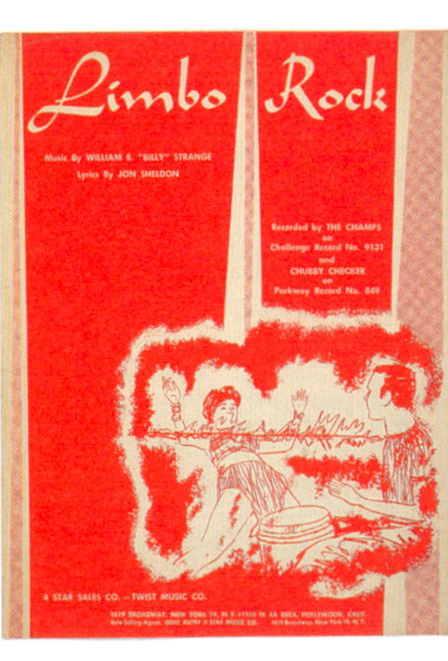
Limbo Rock
Music by WILLIAM E. "BILLY" STRANGE
Lyrics by JON SHELDON
Recorded by THE CHAMPS
on Challenge Record No. 9131
and CHUBBY CHECKER
on Parkway Record No. 849
4 STAR SALES CO. — TWIST MUSIC CO.

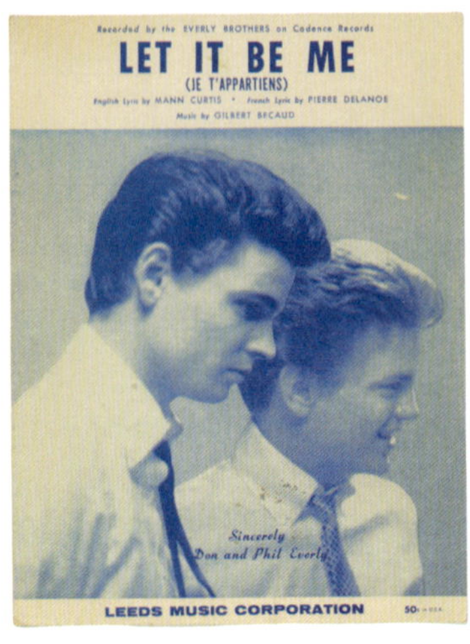

Recorded by the EVERLY BROTHERS on Cadence Records
LET IT BE ME
(JE T'APPARTIENS)
English Lyric by MANN CURTIS   French Lyric by PIERRE DELANOE
Music by GILBERT BECAUD
Sincerely
Don and Phil Everly
LEEDS MUSIC CORPORATION   50¢

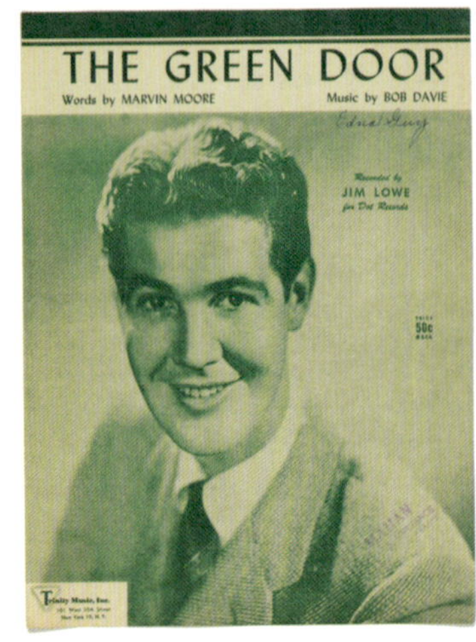

THE GREEN DOOR
Words by MARVIN MOORE   Music by BOB DAVIE
Recorded by
JIM LOWE
for Dot Records
50¢

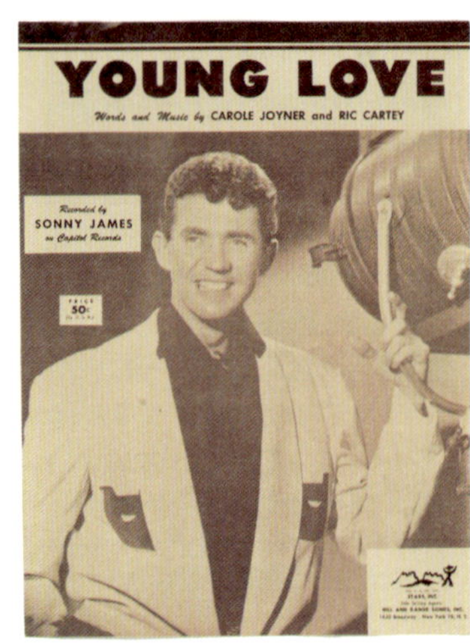

YOUNG LOVE
Words and Music by CAROLE JOYNER and RIC CARTEY
Recorded by
SONNY JAMES
on Capitol Records
50¢

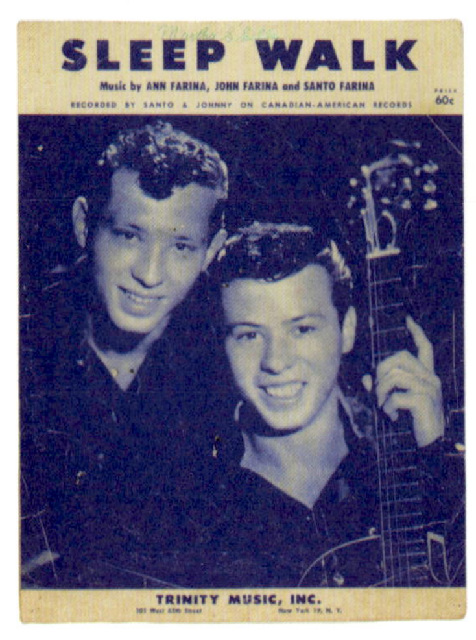

SLEEP WALK
Music by Ann Farina, John Farina and Santo Farina
RECORDED BY SANTO & JOHNNY ON CANADIAN-AMERICAN RECORDS
60¢
TRINITY MUSIC, INC.

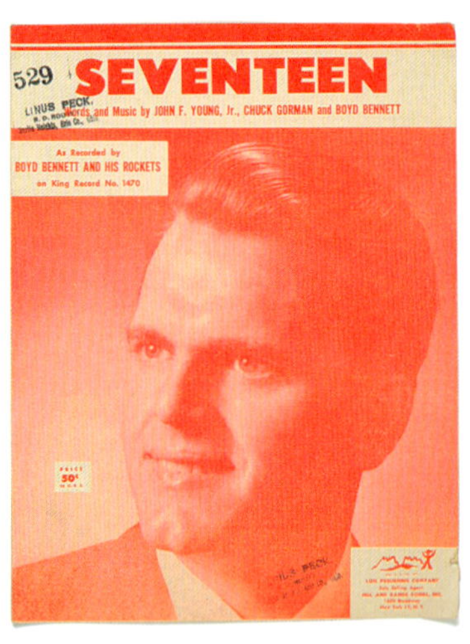

529
SEVENTEEN
Words and Music by JOHN F. YOUNG, Jr., CHUCK GORMAN and BOYD BENNETT
As Recorded by
BOYD BENNETT AND HIS ROCKETS
on King Record No. 1470
50¢

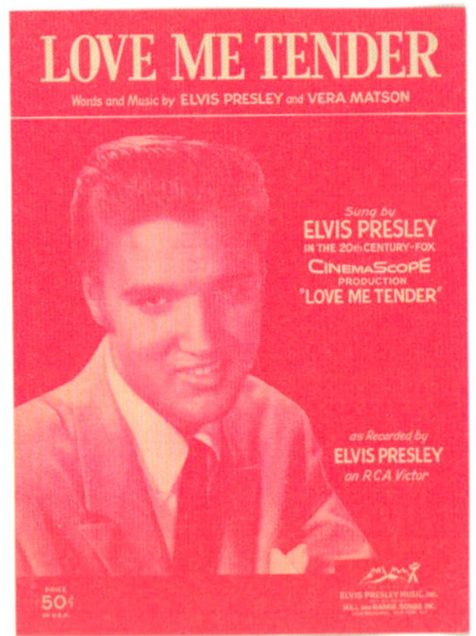

LOVE ME TENDER
Words and Music by ELVIS PRESLEY and VERA MATSON
Sung by
ELVIS PRESLEY
IN THE 20th CENTURY-FOX
CinemaScope
PRODUCTION
"LOVE ME TENDER"
as Recorded by
ELVIS PRESLEY
on RCA Victor
50¢
ELVIS PRESLEY MUSIC, INC.

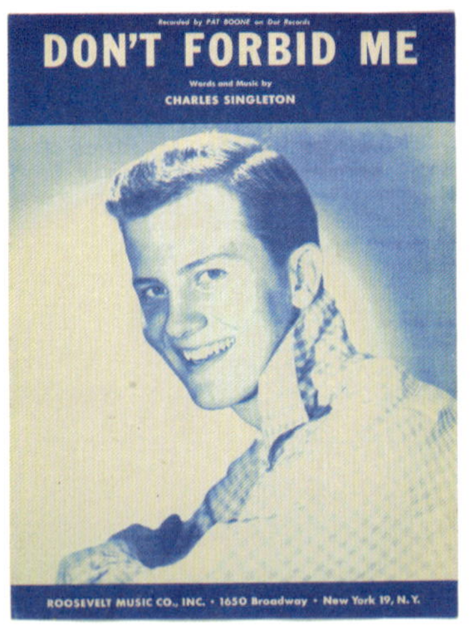

Recorded by PAT BOONE on Dot Records
DON'T FORBID ME
Words and Music by
CHARLES SINGLETON
ROOSEVELT MUSIC CO., INC. · 1650 Broadway · New York 19, N. Y.

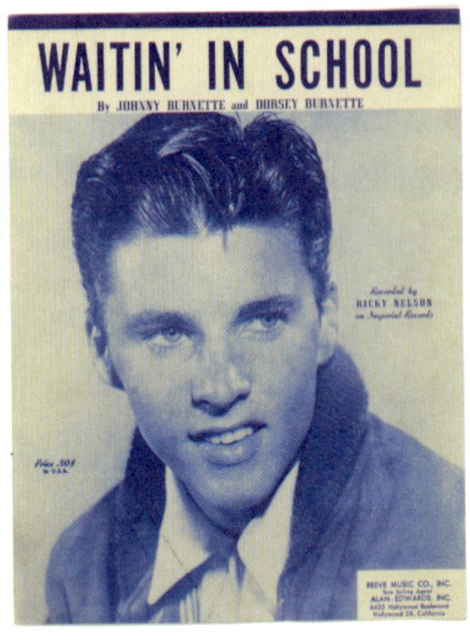

WAITIN' IN SCHOOL
By JOHNNY BURNETTE and DORSEY BURNETTE
Recorded by
RICKY NELSON
on Imperial Records
Price 50¢
REEVE MUSIC CO., INC.

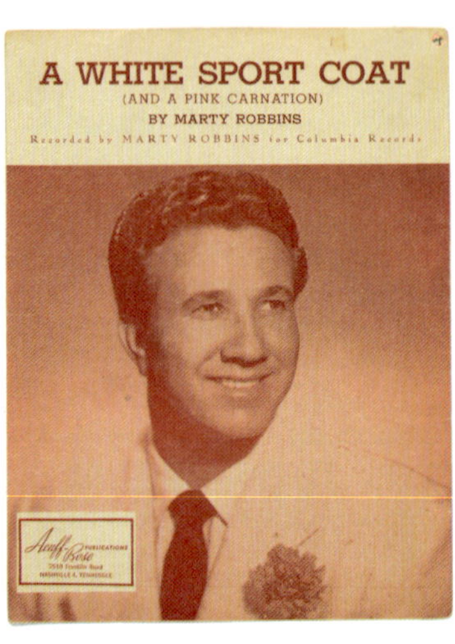

A WHITE SPORT COAT
(AND A PINK CARNATION)
BY MARTY ROBBINS
Recorded by MARTY ROBBINS for Columbia Records

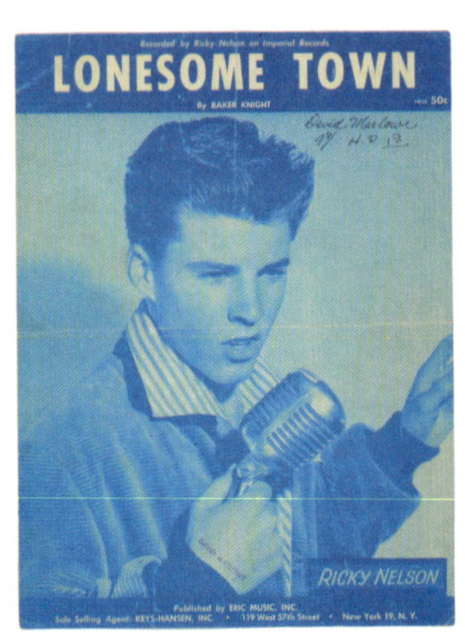

Recorded by Ricky Nelson on Imperial Records
LONESOME TOWN
By BAKER KNIGHT
RICKY NELSON
Published by ERIC MUSIC, INC.
Sole Selling Agent: KEYS-HANSEN, INC. · 119 West 57th Street · New York 19, N. Y.

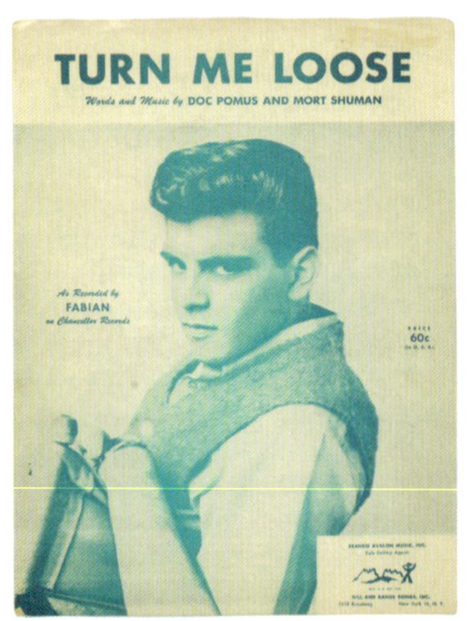

TURN ME LOOSE
Words and Music by DOC POMUS and MORT SHUMAN
As Recorded by
FABIAN
on Chancellor Records
60¢

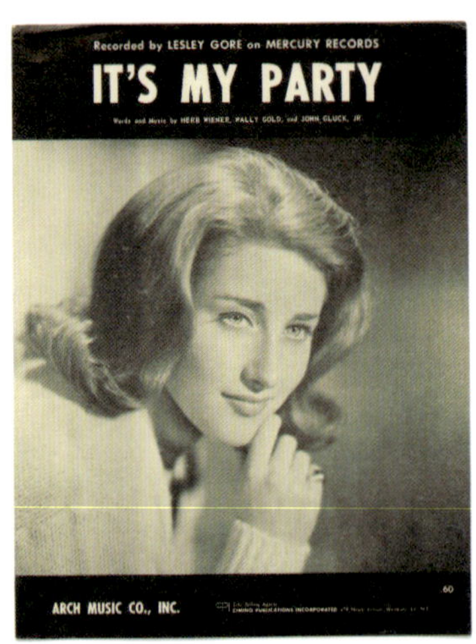

Recorded by LESLEY GORE on MERCURY RECORDS
IT'S MY PARTY
Words and Music by HERB WIENER, WALLY GOLD, and JOHN GLUCK, JR.
ARCH MUSIC CO., INC.

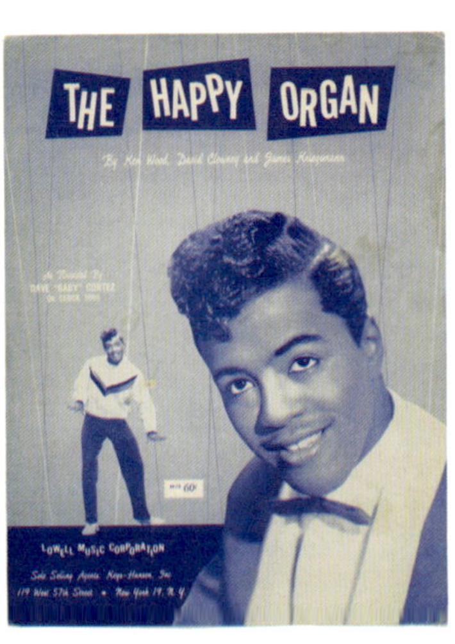

THE HAPPY ORGAN
By Ken Wood, David Clowney and James Kriegsmann
As Recorded by
DAVE "BABY" CORTEZ
on Clock Records
60¢
LOWELL MUSIC CORPORATION

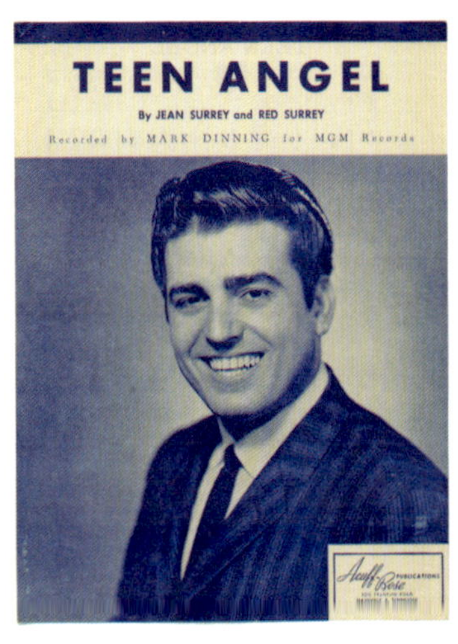

TEEN ANGEL
By JEAN SURREY and RED SURREY
Recorded by MARK DINNING for MGM Records

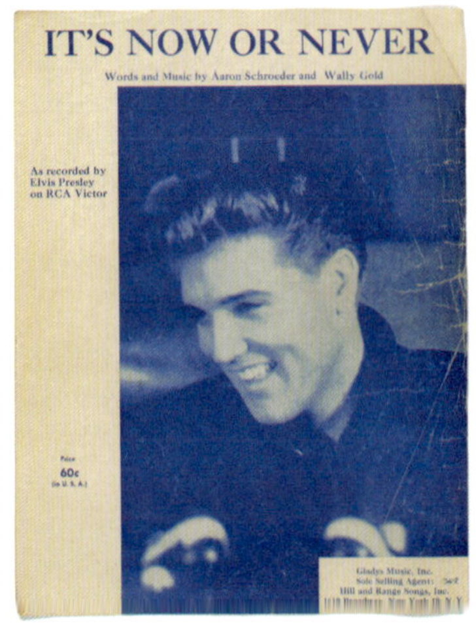

IT'S NOW OR NEVER
Words and Music by Aaron Schroeder and Wally Gold
As recorded by
Elvis Presley
on RCA Victor
60¢

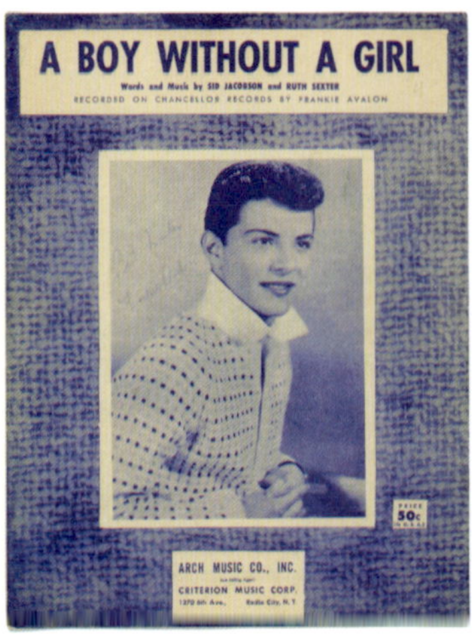

A BOY WITHOUT A GIRL
Words and Music by SID JACOBSON and RUTH SEXTER
RECORDED ON CHANCELLOR RECORDS BY FRANKIE AVALON
ARCH MUSIC CO., INC.
CRITERION MUSIC CORP.
50¢

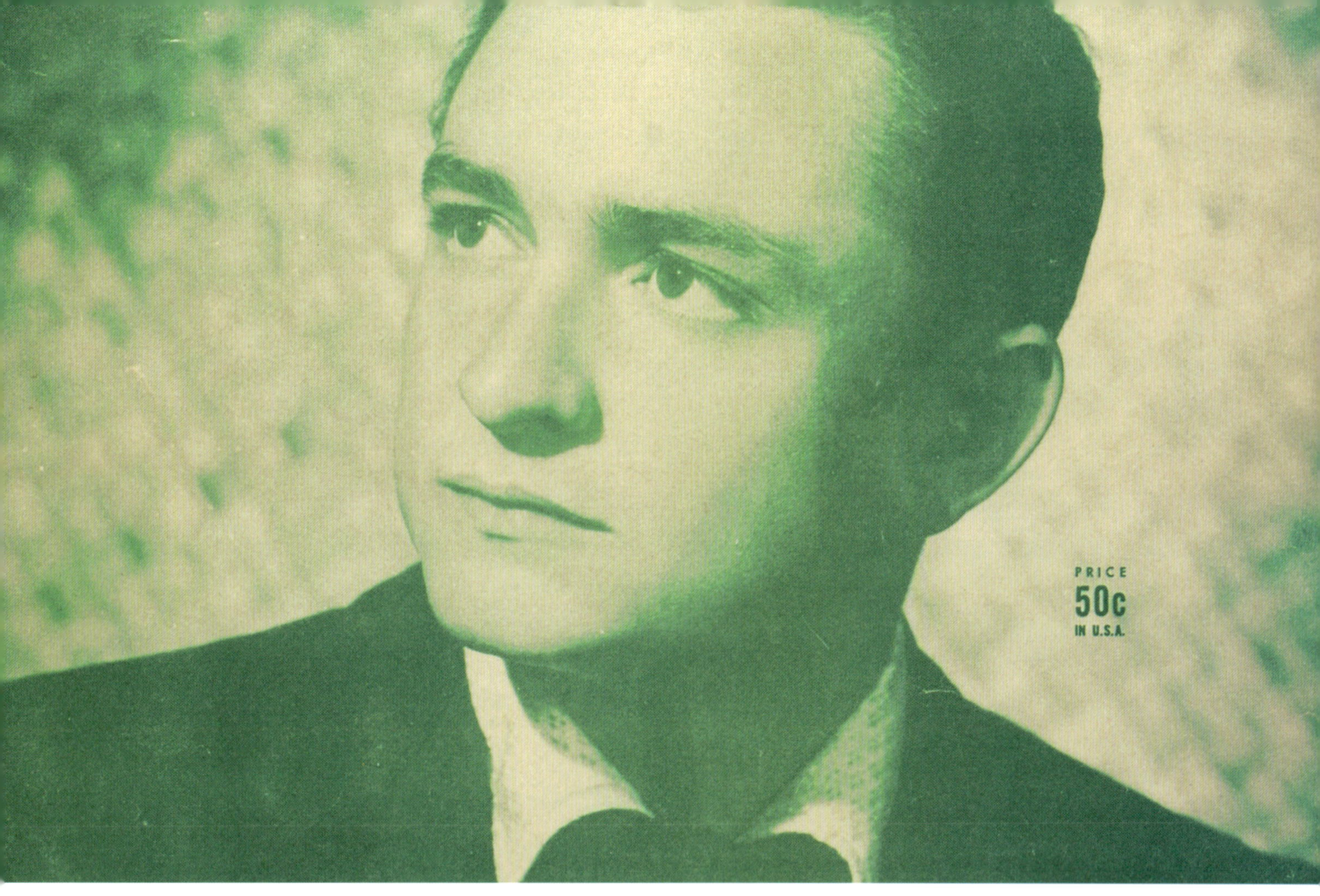

Titus Turner . . . . *A-Knocking at My Baby's Door* (Turner–Wexler–Stone), Atlantic 1227, 45, 1959
Hungry Man (Titus Turner), Atlantic 1227, 45, 1959
Wilbert Harrison . . . . *Kansas City* (Leiber–Stoller), Fury 1023, 45, 1959
Chubby Checker . . . . *Toot* (Kal Mann), Parkway 811, 45, 1960
The Twist, Parkway 811, 45, 1960
Chuck Berry . . . .*Let It Rock* (E. Anderson), Chess 1747, 45, 1960
Worried Life Blues, Chess 1754, 45, 1960
Bye Bye Johnny, Chess 1754, 45, 1960
Clyde McPhatter . . . . *Ta Ta* (Oliver–McPhatter), Mercury 71660, 45, 1960
Jimmy Jones . . . . *The Search Is Over* (Composed by Hall–Williams), Cub K9049, 45, 1960
Handy Man (Composed by Blackwell–Jones), Cub K9049, 45, 1960
Back at the Chicken Shack—Part 1, Blue Note 45-1877, 45, 1960
Back at the Chicken Shack—Part 2, Blue Note 45-1877, 45, 1960
Jorgen Ingmann . . . . *Apache* (Jerry Lordan), Atco 45-6184, 45, 1960
Echo Boogie, Atco 45-6184, 45, 1960
Mark II . . . . *Night Theme* (Wayne Cogswell–Ray Peterson), Wye 5-1001, 45, 1960
Olympics . . . . *Dodge City* (Smith–Goldsmith), Arvee 5020, 45, 1960
Dance by the Light of the Moon (Smith–Goldsmith), Arvee 5020, 45, 1960
Revels . . . . *Church Key* (Dan Darnold), Impact 1-IMX, 45, 1960
Vesuvius (Robert J. Hafner), Impact 1-IMX, 45, 1960
Roy Orbison. . . . .*Here Comes That Song Again* (Dick Flood), Monument 45-421, 45, 1960
Only the Lonely (R. Orbison–J. Melson), Monument 45-421, 45, 1960
Shirelles . . . . *Will You Still Love Me Tomorrow* (Carol King–Jerry Goffin), Scepter 1121, 45, 1960
Wanda Jackson . . . . *Let's Have a Party*, Stardust URC 4008, 45, 1960
B. B. King . . . .*Understand* (King–Josea), Kent 45x358, 45, 1961
Hold That Train (King–Josea), Kent 45x358, 45, 1961
Buster Brown . . . .*I'm Going—But I'll Be Back*, Fire 507, 45, 1961
Dick Dale. . . . . *Let's Go Trippin'*, Deltone 45-5017, 45, 1961
Del-Tone Rock, Deltone 45-5017, 45, 1961
Elliot Shaver . . . . *Yon He Go* (Elliot Shaver), Ellen 501, 45, 1961

Opposite: Sheet music 1955-1963.
Above: Detail of *I Walk the Line* (Johnny Cash), 1956.

Where Shall Wisdom Be Found ?

Words and Music by *Mel Cooley*

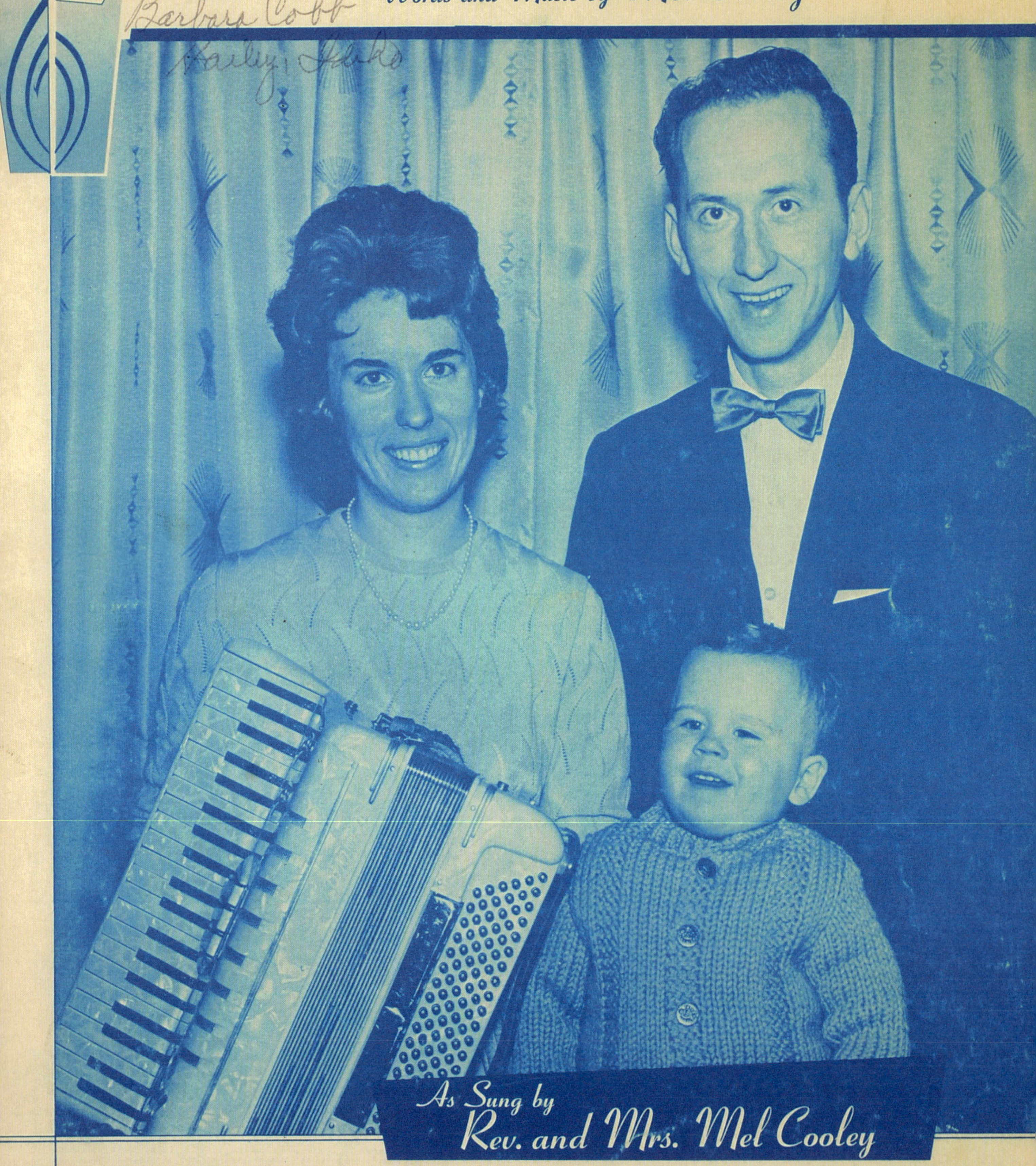

Faith Is the Key

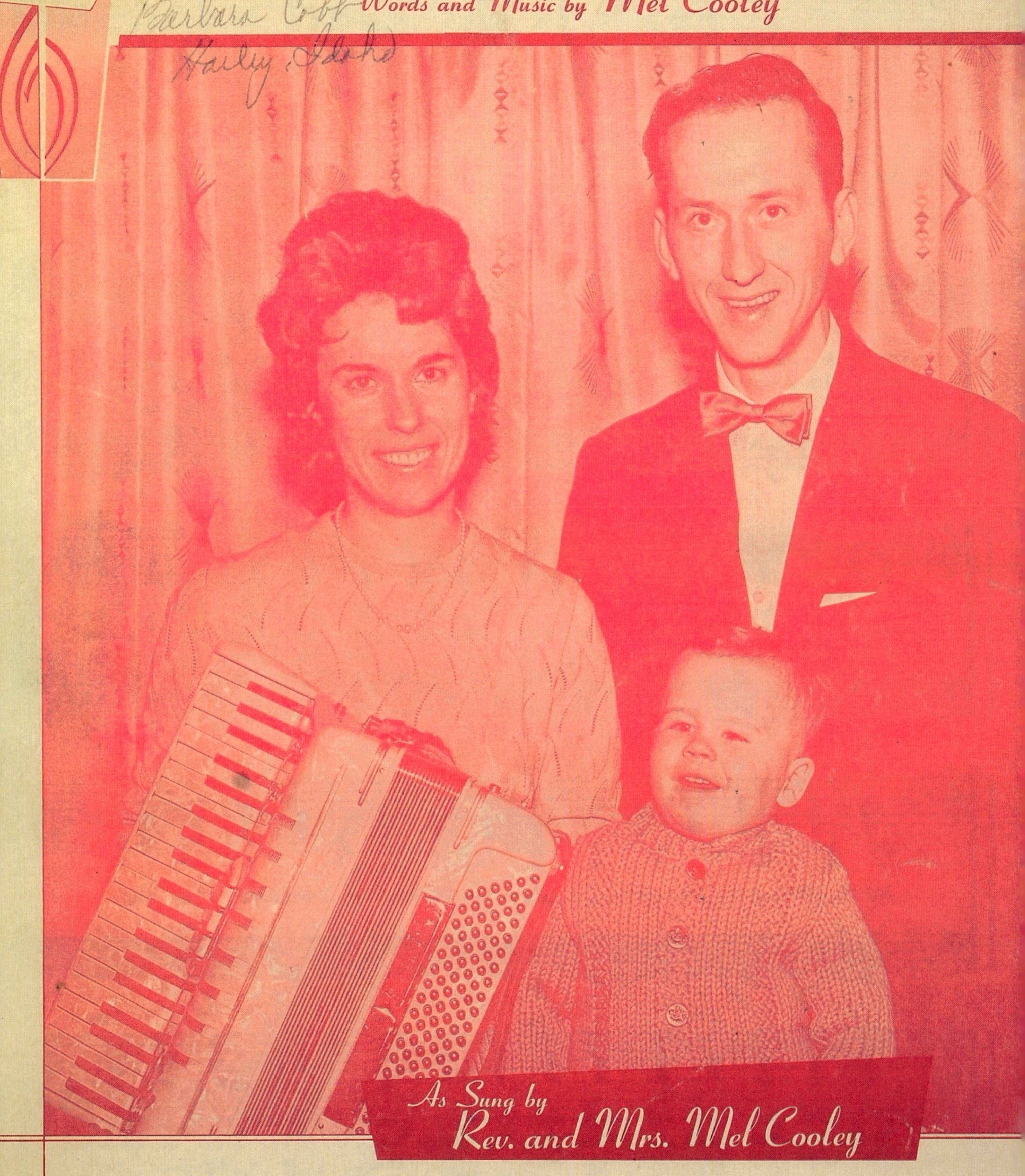

ELVIS PRESLEY SPEAKS!

25¢

Elvis Says:

"I've thought I've been in love, but mostly I've played the field. I enjoy dating more than anything. Is that wrong?"

"I like a girl who's fun to be with, who enjoys just going out and looking around."

Plus: 100 New Pictures

P D C

Elliot Shaver . . . . *Shake 'Em Up* (Elliot Shaver), Ellen 501, 45, 1961
Faron Young . . . . *Hello Walls* (Willie Nelson), Capitol 4533, 45, 1961
Flares . . . . *Foot Stomping*—Part 1 (Aaron Collins), Felsted 45-8624, 45, 1961
Jim Reeves . . . . *What Would You Do?*, RCA Victor 47-7905, 45, 1961
Little Junior Parker . . . . *Driving Wheel* (R. Sykes), Duke 335, 45, 1961
                                                Seven Days (Parker), Duke 335, 45, 1961
Paul Revere . . . . *Like, Long Hair*, Gardena G-116, 45, 1961
Ramrocks . . . . *Foot Stomping*—Part 2 (Aaron Collins), Felsted 45-8624, 45, 1961
Rose Maddox . . . . *Lonely Street* (Sowder–Belew–Stevenson), Capitol 4598, 45, 1961
Sheb Wooley . . . . *That's My Pa*, MGM K13046, 45, 1961
Wanda Jackson . . . . *Right or Wrong*, Stardust URC 4008, 45, 1961
Betty Lavett . . . . *Shut Your Mouth* (Jones), Atlantic 45-2160, 45, 1962
Esther Phillips "Little Esther" . . . . *Don't Feel Rained On* (Mike Terry–Margaret Wesson), Lenox NX-5555, 45, 1962
                                            Release Me (Miller–Williams–Yount), Lenox NX-5555, 45, 1962
Falcons . . . . *Swim*, Lu Pine 1003, 45, 1962
                                      I Found a Love (Pickett–Schofield–West), Lu Pine 1003, 45, 1962
Isley Brothers . . . . *Twist and Shout* (Phil Medley, Bert Russell), Wand 124, 45, 1962
Joe Henderson . . . . *If You See Me Cry* (Warner McPherson–Mike Terry), Todd 1072, 45, 1962
                                Snap Your Fingers (Grady Martin–Alex Zinets), Todd 1072, 45, 1962
Little Johnny Taylor . . . . *Part Time Love* (C. Hammond), Galaxy 722, 45, 1962
R. H. Harris . . . . *Pass Me Not* (Adapted by R. H. Harris), SAR 127, 45, 1962
                                    Troublin' Mind (Cleveland Ficklin), SAR 127, 45, 1962
Rays . . . . *Silhouettes* (Slay–Crewe), Cameo 117, 45, 1962
Charles Taylor . . . . *I'll Fly Away*, VeeJay VJ932, 45, 1963
                              I Will Trust in the Lord (Arranged by Charles Taylor), VeeJay VJ932, 45, 1963
Dovells . . . . *You Can't Sit Down* (Upchurch–Clark–Muldrow–Sheldon), Parkway 867, 45, 1963
Elvis Presley . . . . *(You're the) Devil in Disguise* (Giant–Baum–Kaye), RCA Victor 47-8188, 45, 1963
                      Please Don't Drag That String Around (Otis Blackwell–Winfield Scott), RCA Victor 47-8188, 45, 1963
Jackie Wilson . . . . *Baby Workout* (Jackie Wilson–Alonzo Tucker), Brunswick 55239, 45, 1963
                    I'm Going Crazy (Gotta Get You Off My Mind) (Jackie Wilson–Alonzo Tucker), Brunswick 55239, 45, 1963
Kinsmen . . . . *Louie Louie* (Richard Berry), Wand 143, 45, 1963
Little Johnny Taylor . . . . *Somewhere Down the Line*, Galaxy 722, 45, 1963
Marketts . . . . *Bella Dalena* (Saraceno–Pohlman), Warner Bros. 5391, 45, 1963
                              Out of Limits (Michael Z. Gordon), Warner Bros. 5391, 45, 1963
Bettye Swannn . . . . *What Is My Life Coming To* (Huey R. Harris), Money 108, 45, 1964
                                        Don't Wait Too Long, Money 108, 45, 1964
Carter Bros. . . . . *Do the Watusi* (Duke Coleman), Coleman SA-1925, 45, 1964
                              Consider Yourself (Duke Coleman), Coleman SA-1926, 45, 1964
Dixie Hummingbirds . . . . *Our Prayer for Peace* (Walker), Peacock 3012, 45, 1964
Drifters . . . . *Under the Boardwalk* (Resnick–Young), Atlantic 45-2237, 45, 1964
                    I Don't Want to Go On Without You (Berns–Wexler), Atlantic 45-2237, 45, 1964
Impressions . . . . *You Must Believe Me* (Curtis Mayfield), ABC Paramount 10581, 45, 1964
                          See the Real Me (Curtis Mayfield), ABC Paramount 10581, 45, 1964
Larks . . . . *Forget Me* (Don Julian), Money 106, 45, 1964
                                        The Jerk (Don Julian), Money 106, 45, 1964
Cannibal and the Headhunters . . . . *Land of 1000 Dances* (Chris Kenner), Rampart 642, 45, 1965
Dobie Gray . . . . *The "In" Crowd* (Billy Page), Charger 105, 45, 1965
Hi Way Que C's . . . . *I'll Fly Away*—Part 1 (Traditional), Peacock 3069, 45, 1965
                                I'll Fly Away—Part 2 (Traditional), Peacock 3069, 45, 1965
Jimmy Johnson . . . . *Don't Answer the Door*—Part 1, Magnum 45-719, 45, 1965
                              Don't Answer the Door—Part 2, Magnum 45-719, 45, 1965
Kingsmen . . . . *The Jolly Green Giant* (Lynn Easton), Wand 172, 45, 1965
                                Long Green (Lynn Easton), Wand 172, 45, 1965
Solomon Burke . . . . *Peepin'* (Arr. by Gene Page), Atlantic 45-2276, 45, 1965
Junior Parker . . . . *Get Away Blues* (D. Malone–A. D. Parker), Duke 406, 45, 1966
                                Man or Mouse (R. Kelton), Duke 413, 45, 1966
                        Wait for Another Day (Malone–Caple–Davis), Duke 413, 45, 1966
Little Milton . . . . *You Colored My Blues Bright* (Webber–Davis–Caston), Checker 1162, 45, 1966
Shangri-Las . . . . *I Can Never Go Home Any More* (George Morton), Red Bird RB 10-043, 45, 1966
                          Bull Dog (Jerry Leiber–Mike Stoller), Red Bird RB 10-043, 45, 1966
Troggs . . . . *From Home* (Reg. Presley), Fontana F-1548, 45, 1966

Preceding overleaf: *Where Shall Wisdom Be Found?* and *Faith is the Key*, 1966.
Opposite: *Elvis Presley Speaks*, 1956.
Following overleaf: *Living Blues* magazines 1975-1978.

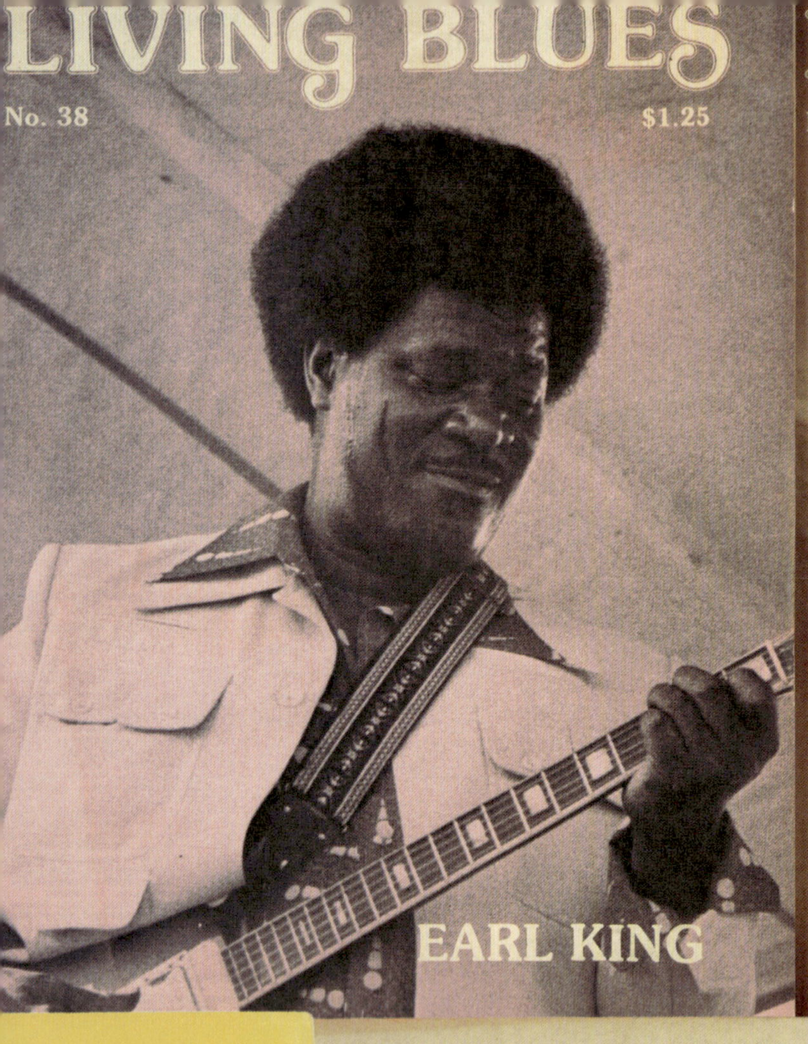
LIVING BLUES
No. 38
$1.25
EARL KING

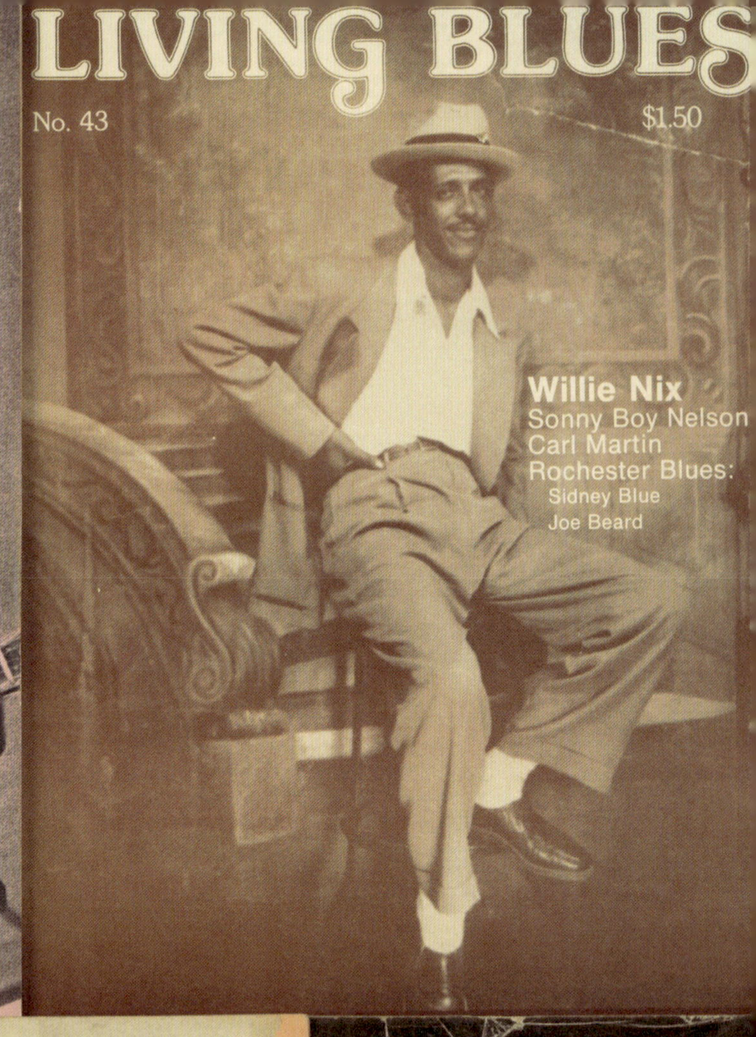
LIVING BLUES
No. 43
$1.50
Willie Nix
Sonny Boy Nelson
Carl Martin
Rochester Blues:
Sidney Blue
Joe Beard

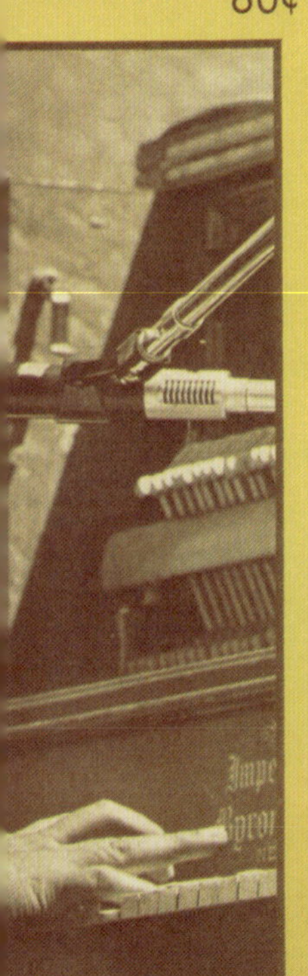
ues
60¢
Impe
Spro
NERATION OF BLUES

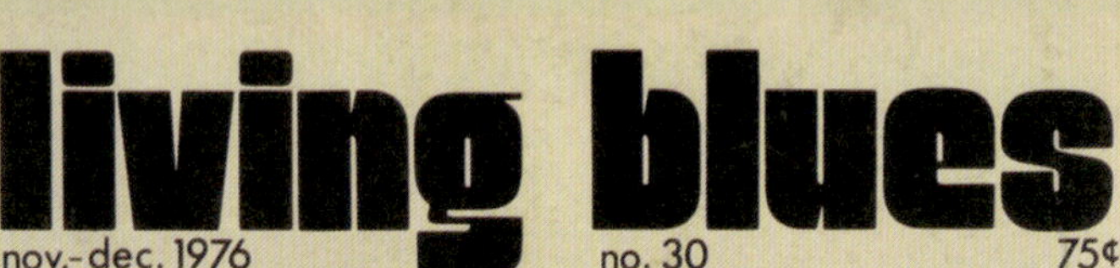

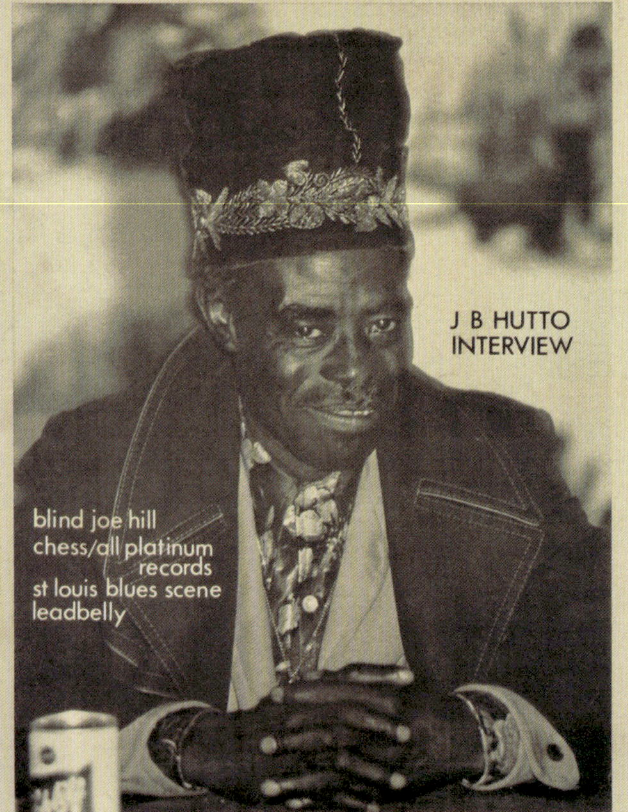
living blues
nov.-dec. 1976
no. 30
75¢
J B HUTTO
INTERVIEW
blind joe hill
chess/all platinum
records
st louis blues scene
leadbelly

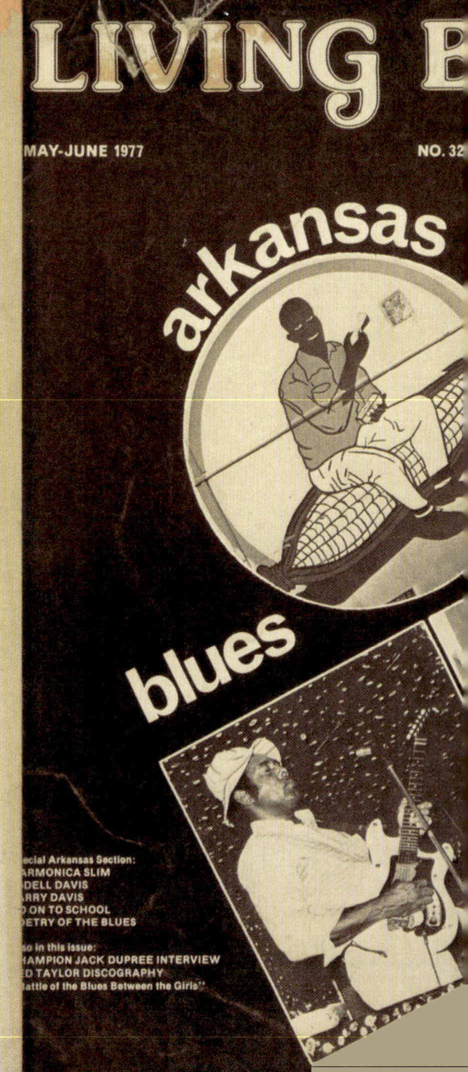
LIVING B
MAY-JUNE 1977
NO. 32
arkansas
blues
Special Arkansas Section:
HARMONICA SLIM
ARDELL DAVIS
LARRY DAVIS
GO ON TO SCHOOL
POETRY OF THE BLUES
Also in this issue:
CHAMPION JACK DUPREE INTERVIEW
ED TAYLOR DISCOGRAPHY
Battle of the Blues Between the Girls"

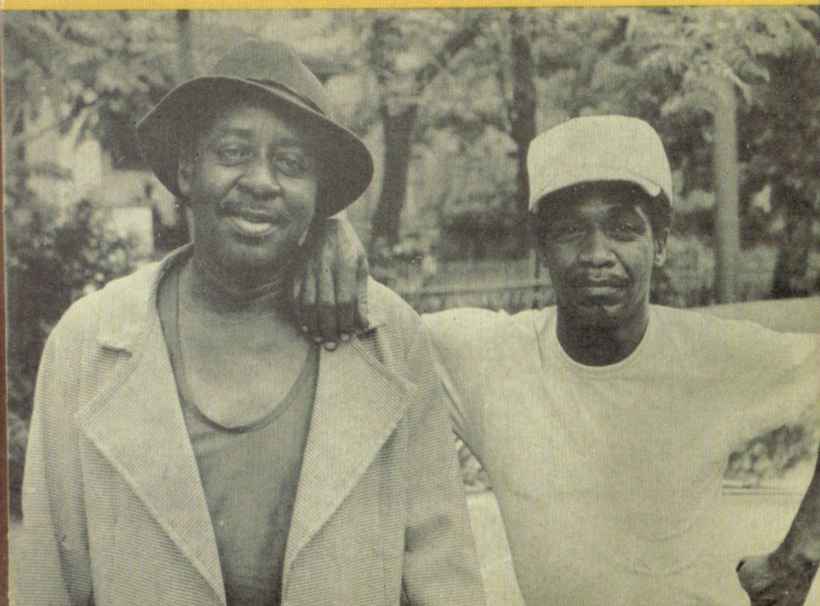
LIVING BLUES
Mar/Apr 1978
No. 37
One Dollar
The Smothers Brothers of the Blues
Also In This Issue:
Eddie Boyd
Roy Gaines
John Jackson

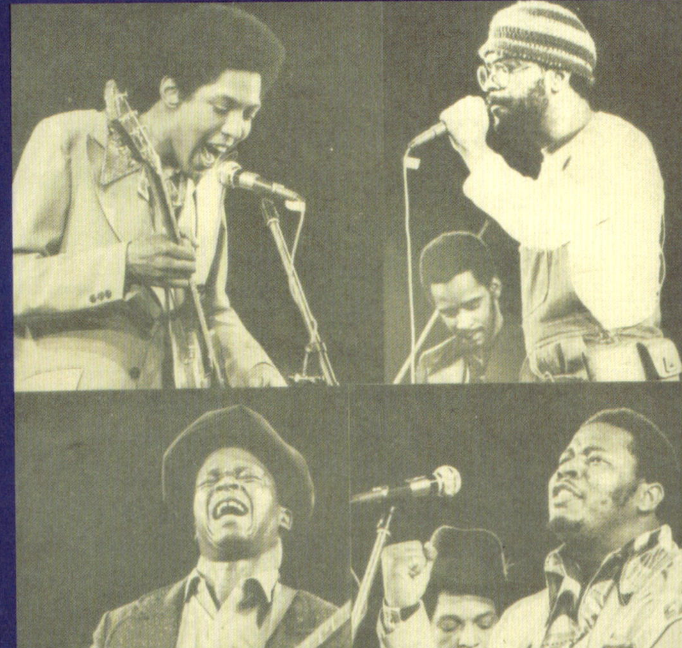
LIVING BLUES
Jan/Feb 1978
No. 36
One Dollar
The NEW GENERATION OF CHICAGO BLUES in Berlin

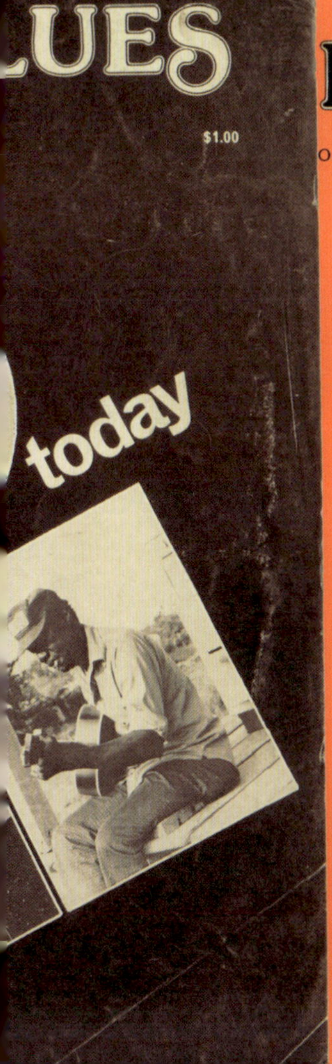
BLUES
$1.00
today

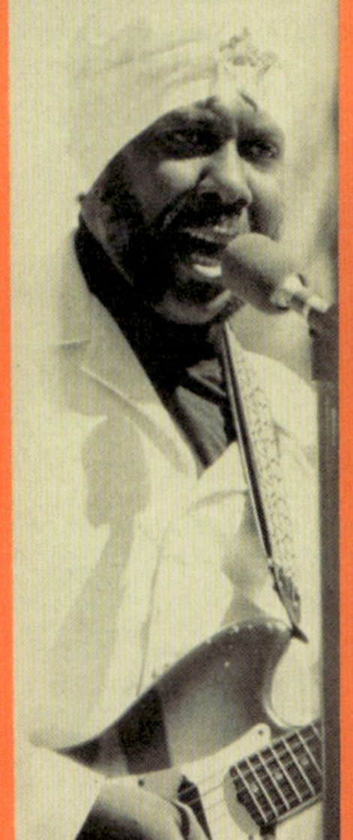
LIVING BLUES
No. 41
$1.25
SONNY RHODES
JIMMIE BELL

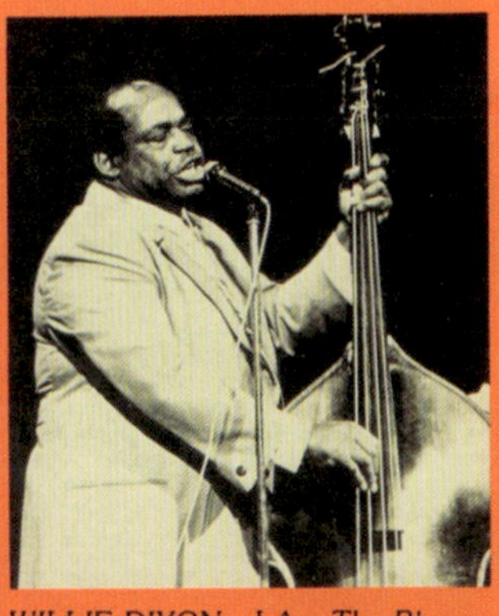
WILLIE DIXON: I Am The Blues

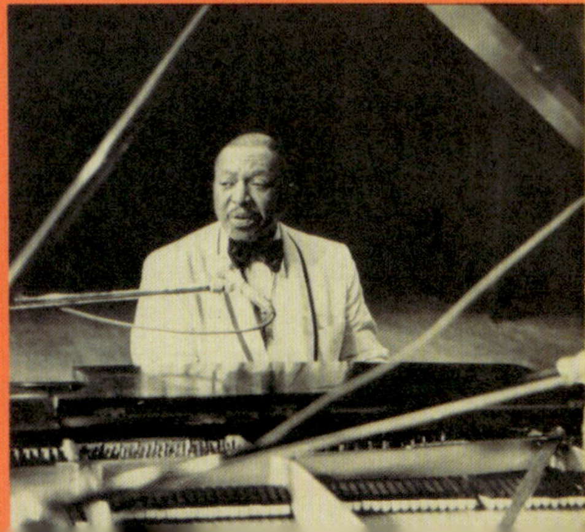

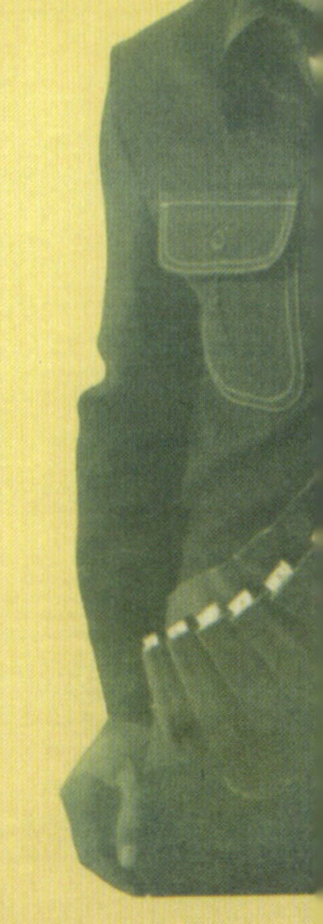
LIVING B
No. 42
Mojo Buford
Blues Club Guide
Joe Willie Wilkins
Sonny Rhodes
Sonny Rogers

Troggs . . . . *Wild Things* (Chip Taylor), Fontana F-1548, 45, 1966
Walker Bros. . . . . *After the Lights Go Out* (John Stewart), Smash S-2032, 45, 1966
The Sun Ain't Gonna Shine (Anymore) (B. Crewe–B. Gaudio), Smash S-2032, 45, 1966
Aretha Franklin . . . . *Dr. Feelgood* (Aretha White–Ted White), Atlantic 45-2403, 45, 1967
Booker T. & the M.G.'s . . . . *Hip Hug-Her* (Cropper–Dunn–Jackson–Jones), Stax S-211, 45, 1967
Summertime (Heyward–Gershwin), Stax S-211, 45, 1967
James Brown . . . . *I Can't Stand Myself* (When You Touch Me), King 45-6144, 45, 1967
There Was a Time (J. Brown–B. Hobgood), King 45-6144, 45, 1967
Troggs . . . . *Love Is All Around* (R. Presley), Fontana F-1607, 45, 1967
Albert King . . . . *You Sure Drive a Hard Bargain* (Betty Crutcher–Allen Jones), Stax S-241, 45, 1968
Cold Feet (Albert King–Al Jackson Jr.), Stax S-241, 45, 1968
Clarence Carter . . . . *Slip Away* (W. Armstrong–W. Terrell–M. Daniel), Atlantic 45-2508, 45, 1968
Little Milton . . . . *I Can't Quit You Baby* (W. Dixon–M. Campbell), Checker 1212, 45, 1968
William Bell . . . . *I Forgot to Be Your Lover* (W. Bell–B. Jones), Stax STA-0015, 45, 1968
Willie Mitchell . . . . *Beale Street Blues* (M. Hodges–W. Mitchell), HI 45-2151, 45, 1968
Soul Serenade (Ousley–Dixon), HI 45-2140, 45, 1968
Clarence Carter . . . . *Snatching It Back* (Clarence Carter–George Jackson), Atlantic 45-2605, 45, 1969
Making Love (At the Dark End of the Street) (Chips Moman–Dan Penn–Clarence Carter),
Atlantic 45-2605, 45, 1969
Ike and Tina Turner. . . . . *I Know* (Barbara George), Blue Thumb BLU 104, 45, 1969
Johnny Cash . . . . *A Boy Named Sue* (S. Silverstein), Columbia 4-44944, 45, 1969
San Quentin, Columbia 4-44944, 45, 1969
Blues Image. . . . . *Pay My Dues*, Atco 45-6746, 45, 1970
James Brown. . . . . *Get Up (I Feel Like a SEX MACHINE)*—Part 1 (J. Brown–B. Byrd–R. Lenhoff), King 45-6318, 45, 1970
Get Up (I Feel Like a SEX MACHINE)—Part 2 (J. Brown–B. Byrd–R. Lenhoff), King 45-6318, 45, 1970
Little Milton. . . . . *If Walls Could Talk* (Bobby Miller), Checker 1226, 45, 1970
Marion Williams. . . . *They Led My Lord Away* (Traditional), Recorded Anthology of American Music Inc. 224, LP, 1970
James Brown. . . . . *Hot Pants (She Got to Use What She Got to Get What She Wants)*—Part 1, People 45-2501, 45, 1971
Hot Pants (She Got to Use What She Got to Get What She Wants)—Parts 2 and 3, People 45-2501, 45, 1971
I'm a Greedy Man—Part 1, Polydor PD 14100, 45, 1971
I'm a Greedy Man—Part 2, Polydor PD 14100, 45, 1971
Little Johnny Taylor   *Everybody Knows About My Good Thing*—Part 1 (Miles Grayson–Lermon Horton), RONN 55, 45, 1971
Everybody Knows About My Good Thing—Part 2 (Miles Grayson–Lermon Horton), RONN 55, 45, 1971
Ridgecrest (N.C.) Baptist. . . . . *We're Marching to Zion* (Robert Lowry and Isaac Watts),
Recorded Anthology of American Music Inc. 224, LP, 1971
Sonny Green . . . . *If You Want Me to Keep On Loving You* (Miles Grayson–Bobby Lexing), Hill H-777, 45, 1971
Jody's on the Run (Miles Grayson–Bobby Lexing), Hill H-777, 45, 1971
Syl Johnson. . . . . *Anyone But You* (S. Johnson–R. Giuhan), HI 45-2201, 45, 1971
James Brown. . . . . . *Get on the Good Foot*—Part 1 (James Brown–Fred Wesley–Joe Mims), Polydor PD 14139, 45, 1972
Get on the Good Foot—Part 2 (James Brown–Fred Wesley–Joe Mims), Polydor PD 14139, 45, 1972
Little Milton. . . . . *I'm Living Off the Love You Give* (Homer Banks–Raymond Jackson), Stax ST-0111, 45, 1972
That's What Love Will Make You Do (Milton Campbell), Stax ST-0111, 45, 1972
John Lee Hooker . . . .*Boogie Chillun'*, Trip 167, 45, 1973
I'm in the Mood, Trip 167, 45, 1973
Johnny Taylor . . . . *Cheaper to Keep Her* (Mack Rice), Stax STA-0176, 45, 1973
I Can Read Between the Lines (Marvin Johnson–Henry Williams), Stax STA-0176, 45, 1973
Ridgecrest (N.C.) Baptist. . . . . *Jesus Is All the World to Me* (Will L. Thompson),
Recorded Anthology of American Music Inc. 224, LP, 1974
Al Green . . . . *Full of Fire* (W. Mitchell–A. Green–M. Hodges), HI 5N-2300, 45, 1975
Could I Be the One? (W. Mitchell–A. Green–A. Mitchell), HI 5N-2300, 45, 1975

COLLECTORS BOOK STORE
6763 Hollywood Blvd.
Hollywood, CA 90028

FIRST CLASS MAIL

NO TIME LEFT TO START AGAIN LPs Volumes 1–7, 2010–2012

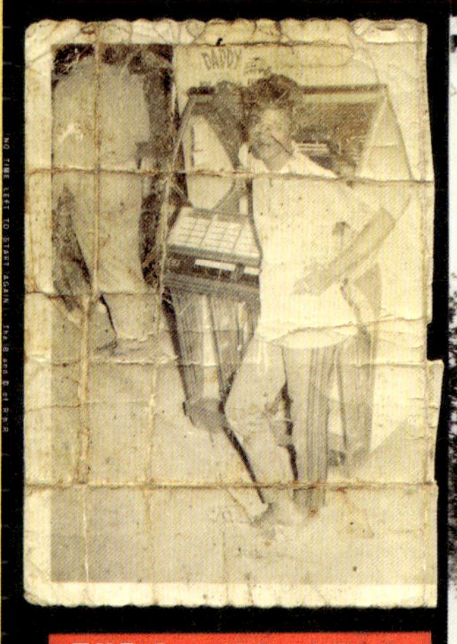
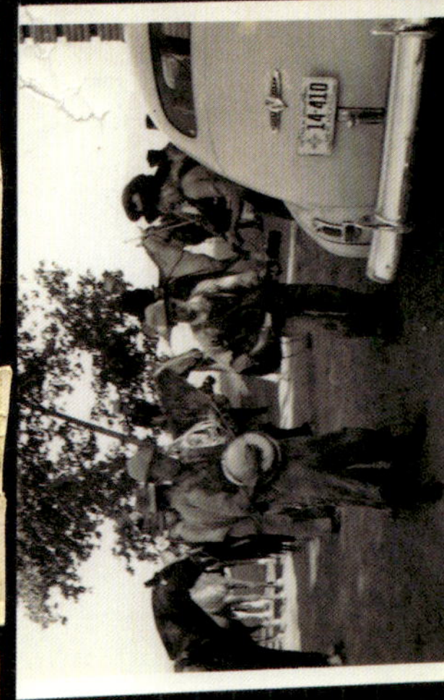

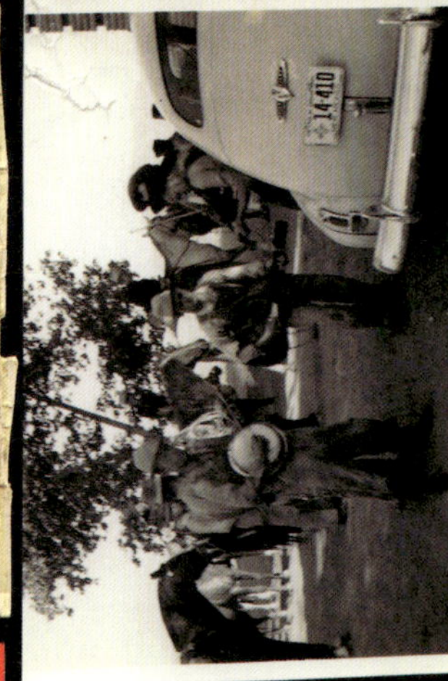

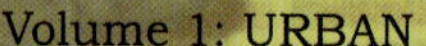
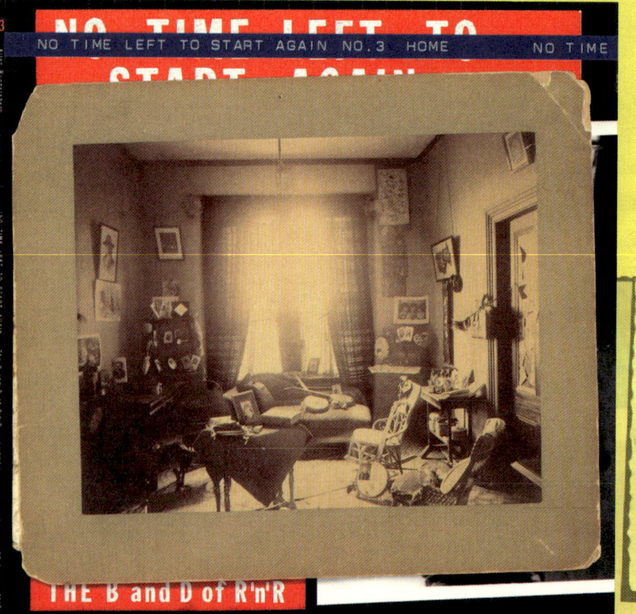

Volume 1: URBAN
A1 T-Bone Walker—*T-Bone Shuffle*
A2 Fats Domino–*La-La*
A3 Little Richard-*Send Me Some Lovin'*
A4 Ward Singers—*Oh My Lord, What a Time*
A5 Bill Black's Combo—*Smokie*—Part 1
A6 Rosetta Howard—*When I Been Drinking*
A7 Little Richard—*Ready Teddy*
A8 Elliott Shaver—*Yon He Go*

B1 Sister Rosetta Tharpe—*Strange Things Happening Every Day*
B2 Little Richard—*Hey-Hey-Hey-Hey*
B3 Lloyd Price—*Stagger Lee*
B4 The Champs—*Train to Nowhere*
B5 Shirley and Lee—*Shirley's Back*
B6 The Roberta Martin Singers—*Sinner Man, Where You Gonna Run To*
B7 Chuck Berry—*Bye Bye Johnny*
B8 Elmore James—*Sunnyland*

Volume 2: RURAL
A1 Lefty Frizzell—*Always Late*
A2 Hank Williams—*I'll Never Get Out of this World Alive*
A3 Uncle Dave Macon—*Watermelon Smilin' on the Vine*
A4 Ray Price—*Wasted Words*
A5 Vernon Dalhart—*Casey Jones*
A6 Trinity Choir—*There Is a Fountain Fill'd with Blood*
A7 "Mac" Harry McClintock—*Hallelujah! I'm a Bum*

B1 Louvin Brothers—*Where Will You Build*
B2 Rose Maddox—*These Wasted Years*
B3 Delmore Brothers—*Goin' Back to the Blue Ridge Mountains*
B4 Sid Harkreader—*The Dying Girl's Message*
B5 Hank Williams—*Never Again (Will I Knock on Your Door)*
B6 Bob Wills and His Texas Playboys—*Liberty*
B7 Webb Pierce—*That's Me without You*
B8 The Johnson Family—*Cabin in the Valley of the Pines*

Volume 3: HOME
A1 Frank Crumit—*Kingdom Coming*
A2 Riley Puckett—*You'd Be Surprised*
A3 Pie Plant Pete—*Hand Me Down My Walking Cane*
A4 Gid Tanner and His Skillet-Lickers—*Watermelon on the Vine*
A5 Uncle Dave Macon and His Fruit-Jar Drinkers—*I'se Gwine Back to Dixie*
A6 Jimmie Rodgers—*Mother Was a Lady*
A7 The Carter Family—*The Poor Orphan Child*

B1 Delmore Brothers—*Take It to the Captain*
B2 Bill Monroe and His Blue Grass Boys—*Mother's Only Sleeping*
B3 Ernest Stoneman—*The Old Hickory Cane*
B4 Smith's Sacred Singers—*Pictures from Life's Other Side*
B5 Bailes Brothers—*As Long As I Live*
B6 Charlie Poole—*White House Blues*
B7 Amelita Galli-Curci—*Home Sweet Home*

NO TIME LEFT TO START AGAIN/The B and D of R'n'R

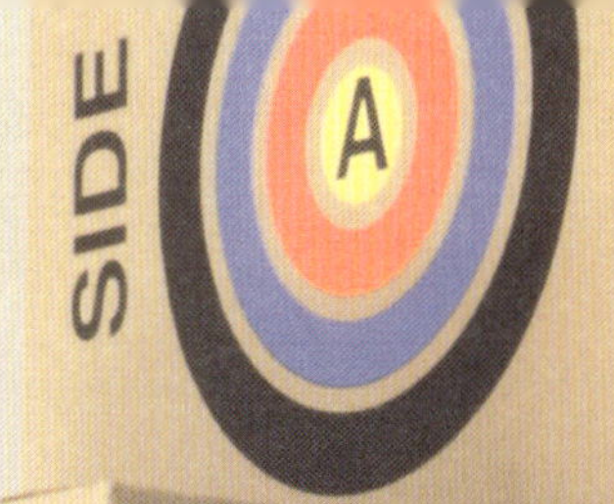

WHAT IS IT?

NO TIME LEFT TO START AGAIN is a work in five sections: Introduction, Home,
Church, Poetry and Fun. Each of these sections includes the following elements.

RECORDS

From my initial collection of around 4,000 platters, a selection of 1,500 recordings
was made. This group was chosen first and foremost for being good recordings, ones I
liked listening to, but they needed to also be of importance in the history of recorded
American popular music and to fit well into one of the five thematic sections of the
larger work as described above. From these 1,500 recordings, I compiled eight new
vinyl LPs. Volume 1 (Urban) and Volume 2 (Rural) serves as an introduction to this
series of recordings. Volumes Three through Seven are compilations of recordings
from a specific genre of music. Volume 3 (Home) is a combination of plantation, jubilee
or dixie themed songs, hillbilly records or C&W and bluegrass of some sort, and one
"heart" song: "Home Sweet Home." Volume 4 (Church) is both white and black gospel
and hymns, black spirituals, sermons and a couple of early field recordings. Volume 5
(Poetry) is a gatefold containing two LPs, one jazz and the other blues. Volume 6 (Fun)
is R&B as it becomes R'n'R. Volume 7 (Everything Else) is a little bit of everything:
after hours, pop, boogie-woogie, vocal groups, Chicago blues, New Orleans R&B, doo-
wop, calypso, novelty, ballads, etc. The front and back of the album covers, placed
end to end, form one long collage. Each cover uses images related to the theme of the
LP and all are from my collection.

WALL PANELS

The wall panels are made of pegboard, mounted on wood frames and measure 4 x 4
feet each. Each of the five sections includes eight wall panels, thirty-two running
feet of unified wall pegboards. All pegboards are silkscreened with images. The first
four in each set of eight panels are printed with a string of pennants, the sort that
hang over car lots, one word squeezed onto each different colored pennant. Together
they read like a poem. The second group of four in each set of eight are printed with
large color targets like ones used in archery practice. Each of the five sections which
make up NO TIME LEFT TO START AGAIN uses the same images but a different color
scheme, visually separating one section from the other.

PHOTOGRAPHS

The photographic history collected while collecting the recorded history translates
into a parallel visual narrative and is also divided into the same five sections. Each
section contains about 1,000 images, mostly snapshots, and covers approximately the
same time period as the recordings. The photos and other related ephemera in this
collection are used as primary source material which is copied on a high-end color
copier producing the 8½ x 11 prints that become the "pages" of the larger installation.
These copies are laminated and holes punched along the edges so that they can be
installed, using S hooks, in multiple combinations on the pegboard wall panels.

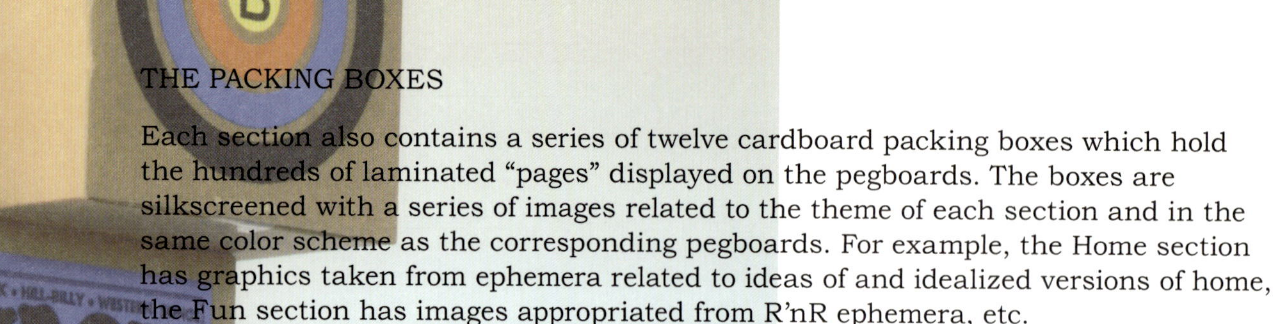

THE PACKING BOXES

Each section also contains a series of twelve cardboard packing boxes which hold the hundreds of laminated "pages" displayed on the pegboards. The boxes are silkscreened with a series of images related to the theme of each section and in the same color scheme as the corresponding pegboards. For example, the Home section has graphics taken from ephemera related to ideas of and idealized versions of home, the Fun section has images appropriated from R'nR ephemera, etc.

THE BOOK

The book is called *Collector's Paradise* and it takes the form of a collectors' catalogue or magazine. It includes a chronological list of the 1,500 records from my collection which represent a history of recorded American recorded music, a history which is also the history of rock and roll. The book includes over 600 color illustrations of related material—song books, hymnals, sheet music, teen magazines, etc.—found in the quest for the music, a visual history to parallel that told by the collection of recordings. Also included in this book are the "pages" as described above, color copies composed of the thousands of vernacular photographs collected as part this same search.

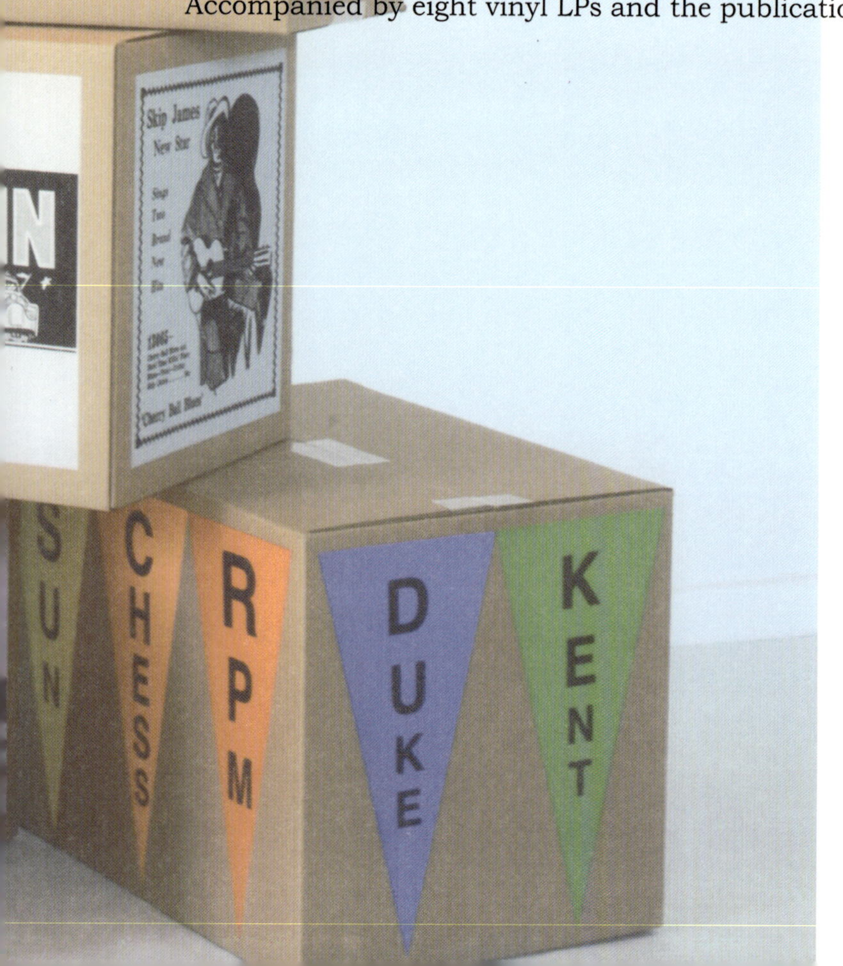

NO TIME LEFT TO START AGAIN, 2012
Installation in five sections (Introduction, Home, Church, Poetry, and Fun), each section consisting of:
8 silkscreened pegboard panels measuring 4 x 4 feet each
12 silkscreened packing boxes
approximately 3,000 laminated color 8½ x 11 inch color copies
Overall dimensions variable
Accompanied by eight vinyl LPs and the publication *Collector's Paradise*

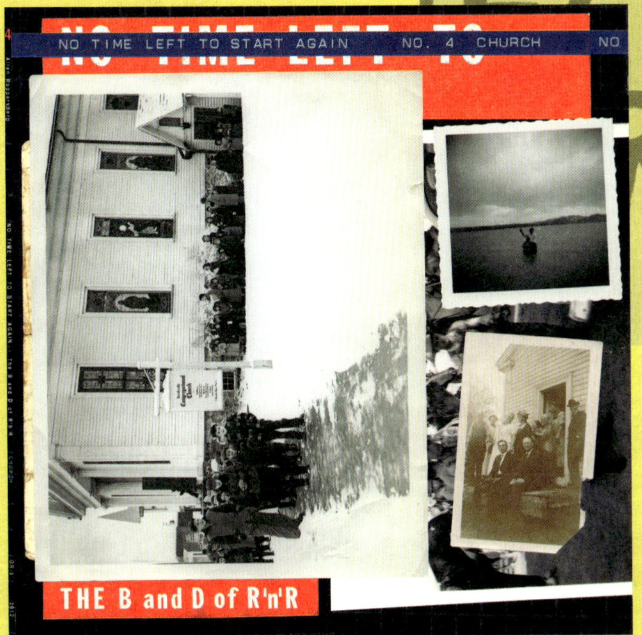

Volume 4: CHURCH

(Black)
A1 Sister Rosetta Tharpe—*Rock Me*
A2 Kelley Pace—*Holy Babe*—Part 2
A3 Jimmie Strothers—*We Are Almost Down to the Shore*
A4 The Soul Stirrers—*How Far Am I from Canaan?*
A5 Deacon Tom Foger—*Working on the Building*
A6 The Two Gospel Keys—*Can't No Grave Hold My Body Down*
A7 The Famous Blue Jay Singers—*I Feel Like My Time Ain't Long*
A8 Rev. J. M. Gates—*Death's Black Train Is Coming*

(White)
B1 Johnny Bond—*The Ninety and Nine*
B2 The Deal Family—*I'm a Rolling*
B3 Ridgecrest Baptist N.C.—*We're Marching to Zion*
B4 James and Martha Carson—*I'll Fly Away*
B5 Maddox Brothers and Rose—*He Will Set Your Fields on Fire*
B6 Lester McFarland and Robert A. Gardner—*Rock of Ages*
B7 Smith's Sacred Singers—*Life's Railway to Heaven*
B8 Bill Monroe and His Blue Grass Boys—*Mansions for Me*

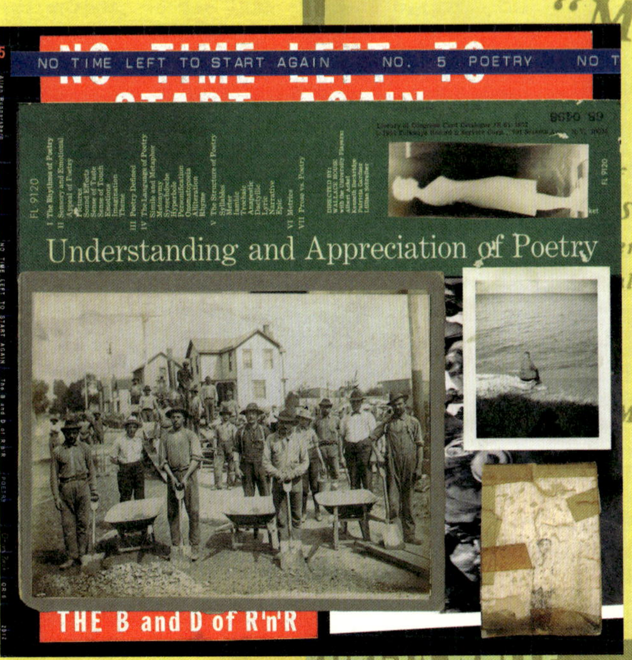

Volume 5: POETRY

(Blues)
A1 Tampa Red—*Let Me Play with Your Poodle*
A2 Leroy Carr and Scrapper Blackwell—*Mean Mistreater Mama*
A3 Lil Green—*Hello Babe*
A4 Texas Alexander—*Work Ox Blues*
A5 Lonnie Johnson—*Backwater Blues*
A6 Bessie Smith—*Cake Walking Babies*
A7 Jazz Gillum—*That's What Worries Me*
A8 Tony Hollins—*Tease Me over Blues*

B1 Memphis Minnie—*I'm So Glad*
B2 Big Bill Broonzy—*Don't You Want to Ride*
B3 Big Maceo—*Poor Kelly Blues*
B4 Georgia White—*Careless Love*
B5 Brownie McGhee—*Step It Up and Go*—No. 2
B6 Roy Brown—*Hard Luck Blues*
B7 Lightnin' Hopkins—*New Worried Life Blues*
B8 Lead Belly—*The Midnight Special*

(Jazz)
A1 Helen Humes With Bill Doggett—*Be-Baba-Luba*
A2 Cozy Cole's All Stars—*Take It on Back*
A3 Jazz at the Philharmonic All Stars—*Mordido*—Part 5
A4 Pete Johnson and Albert Ammons—*Sixth Avenue Express*
A5 King Oliver and His Dixie Syncopators—*Black Snake Blues*
A6 Count Basie—*Miss Thing*—Part 2
A7 Mary Lou Williams—*Little Joe from Chicago*
A8 Louis Armstrong—*That Rhythm Man*

B1 Meade "Lux" Lewis—*Honky Tonk Train Blues*
B2 Billie Holiday—*Born to Love*
B3 Mills Brothers and Cab Calloway—*Doin' the New Low Down*
B4 Jimmy Noone with Kid Ory's Creole Jazz Band—*High Society*
B5 Louis Armstrong & His Hot Five—*Georgia Grind*
B6 Clarence Williams & His Jazz Kings—*Zonky*
B7 Coleman Hawkins—*Bean-A-Re-Bop*
B8 Art Tatum—*Tiger Rag*

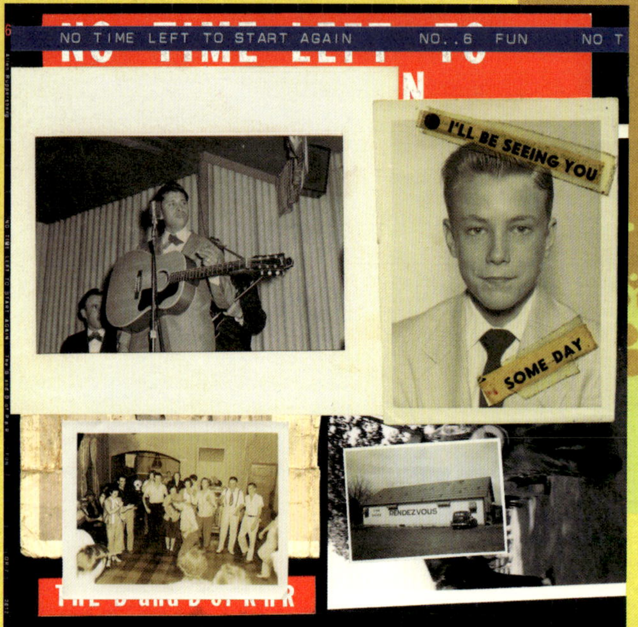

Volume 6: FUN
A1 Bo Diddley—*Bo Diddley*
A2 Fats Domino—*Mardi Gras in New Orleans*
A3 The Coasters—*Young Blood*
A4 Lloyd Price—*Lawdy Miss Clawdy*
A5 Bob Wills and His Texas Playboys—*Liza Pull Down the Shades*
A6 Joe Turner—*Honey Hush*
A7 Muddy Waters—*Diamonds at Your Feet*
A8 The Howlin' Wolf—*How Many More Years*
A9 Clyde McPhatter—*What'Cha Gonna Do*

B1 Little Walter and His Jukes—*Tell Me Mama*
B2 John Lee Hooker—*Boogie Chillen'*
B3 Jerry Lee Lewis—*Mean Woman Blues*
B4 Larry Williams—*Short Fat Fannie*
B5 Wynonie Harris—*Bloodshot Eyes*
B6 Thurston Harris and the Sharps—*Little Bitty Pretty One*
B7 Bill Monroe and His Blue Grass Boys—*Rocky Road Blues*
B8 Sonny Boy Williamson—*Don't Start Me Talkin'*
B9 Smiley Lewis—*Shame, Shame, Shame*

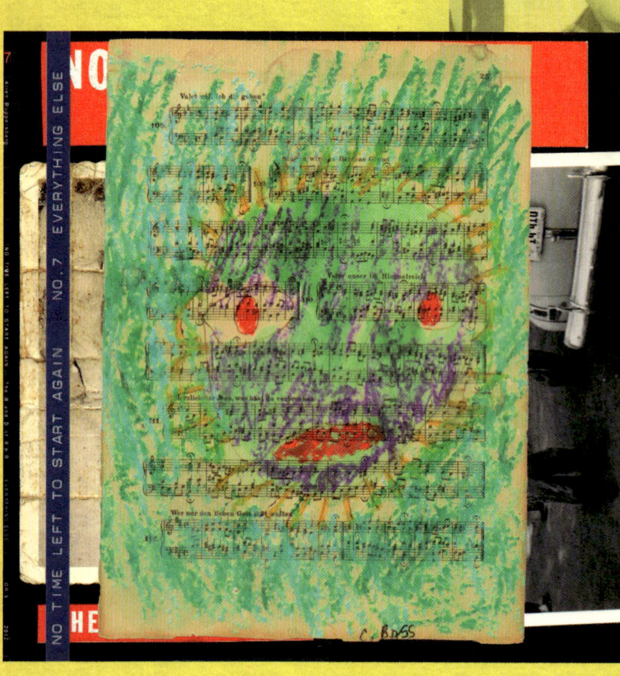

Volume 7: EVERYTHING ELSE
A1 Medallions—*Buick 59*
A2 Joe Turner and Pete Johnson—*Roll 'Em Pete*
A3 Les Paul and Mary Ford—*How High the Moon*
A4 The Clovers—*One Mint Julep*
A5 The Treniers—*Go! Go! Go!*
A6 Milton Brown and His Brownies—*Yes Sir!*
A7 King Radio—*I'll Be a Colored Hitler*
A8 Freddie Slack and Ella Mae Morse—*The House of Blue Lights*

B1 The Crows—*Gee*
B2 5 Royales—*Monkey Hips & Rice*
B3 Savannah Churchill—*Fat Meat Is Good Meat*
B4 The Chips—*Rubber Biscuit*
B5 Peter Cleighton (Doctor Clayton)—*'41 Blues*
B6 Louis Jordan and His Tympany Five—*Saturday Night Fish Fry*—Part 2
B7 Bill Haley—*Rock the Joint*
B8 Chuck Berry—*Carol*

A Collector's Paradise copyright © 2012 Allen Ruppersberg
All images from the collection of Allen Ruppersberg
Published at the time of the exhibition Allen Ruppersberg: NO TIME LEFT TO START AGAIN/ The B and D of R 'n' R,
The Art Institute of Chicago, September 21, 2012–January 6, 2013.

ISBN 978-0-9778696-5-7

Book design: Jason Burch
Editor: Christine Burgin
Photographic documentation: Augusta Wood
Front cover image: Allen Ruppersberg
Front cover production: Augusta Wood
Back cover design: Jason Burch
Book production: Laura Lindgren
Copy editor: Don Kennison
Printing: Capital Offset
Special thanks to: Kye Potter and Julia Dzwonkoski

NO TIME LEFT TO START AGAIN LPs Volumes 1–7:
Album cover images: Allen Ruppersberg
Album cover production: Augusta Wood
Albums produced by Kye Potter
Albums published by Orion Read, Los Angeles, www.orionread.com

Collector's Paradise published by Christine Burgin www.christineburgin.com